In Praise of Social Works

"This is a remarkable book that signals the coming of age of social media in higher education, a signal that could only be sent by mStoner. Co-founder and President Michael Stoner has a point of view based on his breadth of experience that drives the book, but unlike most other books in its genre, *Social Works* doesn't tell you what to do; it engages and informs the reader through the experiences of others. Leave it to Michael to crowdsource a book on social media. Brilliantly simple."
Charlie Melichar, Associate Vice President of Development and Alumni Relations Communications, Vanderbilt University

"Michael Stoner is an expert in social media communication for academic institutions. Now, he shares his many years of experience in this awesome book. *Social Works* is a useful combination of case studies and comments from some of the best social media experts in the U.S. Reading the book gives you a thousand ideas on how to develop your institution's social media strategy, and to find exciting ways to reach your audience. A fantastic good read not only for the communications and marketing departments of universities, but also for senior leadership. Social media must be part of every university's strategy – this book helps the decision makers do a better job."
Matthias Geering, Head Communications & Marketing, University of Basel, Switzerland

"*Social Works* is the perfect combination of insights leading to application. A lot of institutions have a very active social media presence, but not a lot have a solid social media strategy. In this book, Michael Stoner and the contributors lay out the steps to develope, implement and measure such a strategy. The best part is that they provide us with real case examples of colleges and universities that have been successful in using social tools to accomplish institutional goals. These case studies provide insight, information and inspiration to the rest of us as we embark on our social journey."
Tom Hayes, Ph.D., Vice President and Partner, SimpsonScarborough; Chair and Professor of Marketing, Xavier University

"Michael Stoner spotted the fit between social media and marketing of higher education way before the rest of us. *Social Works* is a luxury tour of what he knows, likes, and sees coming. Read and apply."
Meredith Jackson, Director of External Relations, Griffith University, Australia

D1530113

"A great social media campaign is equal parts inspiration and experimentation — throw in a dash of empirical evidence gained

In Praise of Social Works (cont.)

through the observance of other's achievements and failures, and you have the perfect recipe for success. *Social Works* is a social media cookbook filled with creative ideas and mouth-watering illustrations in the form of case studies from colleges and universities across the country. Readers learn from more than two dozen successful (and not so successful) stories, and benefit from the collective knowledge of 18 authors. *Social Works* will help you create and execute a social media campaign with delicious results, and is a must read for every higher education marketing professional living in the 21st century."
Lance Merker, President/CEO, OmniUpdate, Inc.

"As someone who devours edu blogs and case studies, *Social Works* is, above all, refreshing. It takes the ephemeral nature of ever-changing media landscapes and showcases concrete communicative qualities that will outlive many of the tools that created and marked success for these campaigns. The case studies in this book are nothing short of inspirational: Many of the success stories hinge upon simple ideas from outside the model of higher ed, with grand, yet flexible, plans for execution.

Each study rethinks the meaning and interpretation of the word "social," making this book a fount of creative energy necessary for anyone working with people and/or the web in conjunction with a college or university. While no two groups can implement the same campaign and achieve the same results, the examples in *Social Works* will open your mind to the possibilities within your community. The lessons learned demonstrate successes and adjustments, encouraging us to ask better questions and reflect more as we test the waters ourselves.

Regardless of where you work and with whom you are trying to engage, Social Works serves as an excellent resource."
Ma'ayan Plaut, Social Media Coordinator, Oberlin College

"Social media has fundamentally changed how we communicate with each other. Today, colleges and universities are coming up with new, creative ways to use social media faster than most of us can keep up with them. Fortunately, Michael Stoner is staying on top of the opportunities and pitfalls of higher education social media campaigns, and shares a veritable treasure trove of practical information in the new book, *Social Works: How #HigherEd Uses #SocialMedia to Raise Money, Build Awareness, Recruit Students and Get Results*. From defining a wonk in Washington, DC, to wrapping a bus in orange in Portland, Oregon, to organizing a flash mob in Port Elizabeth, South Africa, *Social Works* includes 25 fascinating case studies of successful campaigns. This is a fun, must-read book for anyone charged with launching a social media-

inspired project or convincing campus leaders to approve one."
Shannon D. Smith, Associate Director, Teaching, Learning, and Professional Development, EDUCAUSE

"The title's double entendre foreshadows the richness of *Social Works*, mStoner's must-read for higher education marketing and communications professionals. Filled with robust case studies — without the usual cookie cutter formatting — the book should become a veritable instruction manual for those launching social media campaigns, leveraging social media for public relations, incorporating social media into fundraising, and using social media to engage audiences from alumni to legislators. Fast-forward five years: I see *Social Works*, heavily tabbed and weathered, holding a favored position on many marketers' bookshelves."
Teri Lucie Thompson, CMO & Vice President Marketing & Media, Purdue University

"Michael Stoner is the oracle when it comes to higher education's use of the internet and social media .... and he proves it yet again in his new book *Social Works*. In just a few short years, social media has grown from a peripheral tool to a dominant force in today's communications and marketing. Higher education has been slow to adapt to this rapidly changing PR landscape, but Michael has effectively pulled together 25 examples of how some colleges and universities are harnessing this force for compelling and successful campaigns for everything from boosting enrollment and broadening institutional awareness, to building alumni engagement and increasing giving. Every college communicator will find useable examples to employ in their own communication, marketing, promotion, alumni, and donor engagement campaigns. *Social Works* — a collection of case studies from campuses around the world — bridges the gap between the rhetoric of potential to being a truly valuable chronicle of the successful uses of social media in integrated communications campaigns. A must-read for every higher education PR leader, alumni director, fundraiser, and marketer alike."
Michael L. Warden, APR, Vice President, Institute Communications, Georgia Institute of Technology

"I had goosebumps as I read *Social Works*, because I realized our industry now has the counsel, data and examples necessary to build support for the use of social media campaigns for our campuses. Michael Stoner pairs the sage advice for which he is known with detailed case studies from higher education's strongest practitioners. Together, they provide the foundation for social media campaigns, and the specific examples and best practices for achieving success."
Teresa Valerio Parrot, Principal, TVP Communications

Social Works

Social Works

How #HigherEd Uses #SocialMedia to Raise Money, Build Awareness, Recruit Students, and Get Results

Michael Stoner, Editor

EDUniverse Media

EDUniverse Media
St. Louis, MO

Project Manager: Kylie Stanley Larson
Copy Editor: Robin Netherton
Designer: Michelle Pais
Cover Design: Kevin Rieg

The cover text is Quatro Slab; the interior text is Sentinel Book (body), Whitney (headers and captions), and Ziggurat (pulled quote/highlight).

Published by EDUniverse Media, St. Louis, Missouri. EDUniverse Media is a division of mStoner, Inc.

Notice
Knowledge and best practices around social media are constantly changing. Practitioners and researchers must rely on their own experience and judgment in evaluating the case studies presented in this book. The tactics and strategies described herein may not be suitable for your situation or your institution. You should consult with a professional where appropriate. Neither the publisher nor individual authors shall be liable for any loss of profit or any other commercial damages, including but not limited to special, incidental, consequential, or other damages.

Library of Congress Cataloging-in-Publication Data

ISBN (pbk): 978-0-9888788-0-8
ISBN (ebk): 978-0-9888788-1-5

Printed in the U.S.A. by Thomson-Shore, Inc.

Contents

Preface

Nearly every college and university in America (and, I'd bet, most in Europe, Africa, and Asia) uses social media in alumni relations, student recruitment, institutional marketing, brand-building, awareness-raising, or advocacy. Or for all of them.

And many of these institutions are combining social channels like Facebook, Twitter, or YouTube with other online and offline channels to create a campaign of some kind. In fact, respondents to a survey we fielded with the Council for Advancement and Support of Education (CASE) and Slover Linett Strategies in early 2012 indicated that institutions used social media in 50 percent of campaigns focused on initiatives like brand-building, alumni engagement, and student recruitment. Some institutions are beginning to incorporate social media into fundraising campaigns.

This happened relatively fast. In 2009, when colleges and universities began to get serious about social media, I started to hear about institutions that had built campaigns around a Facebook presence, blog, YouTube site, or other social channel. In the spring of 2009, I began looking for campaigns that I could include in a presentation for the CASE Summit, an international meeting of senior fundraisers, alumni officers, marketers, and external relations staff at schools, colleges, and universities. At the time, I defined a campaign as "a focused effort to achieve goals using a variety of channels appropriate to the results sought." (This distinction was important, because at that time there were no examples of highly effective, social media–driven fundraising campaigns.)

I found a number of good examples and later wrote case studies about them for the mStoner blog. Two stand out as early examples of interesting, humorous, and successful early attempts to create social media–based campaigns:

» Nazareth College's Flight of the Flyers campaign, aimed at boosting attendance at the alumni reunion on campus, which relied on Google Maps, a Flickr gallery—and stuffed mascots mailed around the country from one graduate to another.
» Emory University's Blue Pig campaign, which used Facebook, newspaper ads, and even a table on campus—plus a blue-colored piggy bank—to encourage class giving.

Over the next few years, I continued to track the development of campaigns like these. In 2010, I wrote case studies of Oregon State University's Powered By Orange branding campaign, which relied heavily on social media, and profiled the mascot search conducted by the College of William & Mary. Both were imaginative—and successful.

Fast-forward to 2012. It's pretty clear that staff at many institutions are now aware of how valuable social media can be in a campaign and, furthermore, are comfortable enough to begin to develop some innovative and effective strategies for rolling social channels into campaigns focused on achieving many different kinds of outcomes. And, what's more, some institutions have successfully used social media in campaigns focused on boosting class giving or annual fund contributions. So while I'm not aware of any large-scale fundraising campaigns that employ social media, I won't be surprised to hear about college or university development offices that are seriously exploring social media–powered fundraising initiatives aimed at securing larger gifts.

There are still plenty of questions about how and when to use social media. I hear questions like these from people on Twitter and in the conference presentations and workshops I do:

> » We're rolling out a new brand. What's the best way to incorporate social channels into our communications and marketing?
> » We're struggling with our class gift program. How can we use social media to infuse some energy into what we're doing?
> » We need to build support from our community for some controversial initiatives. Can social media play a role?
> » We want to enhance the profile of some of our faculty experts, and we're considering how we might use social media to do this. But we're stuck at what to do.
> » We've got some great videos of our students. Can we create a viral video from them?
> » We're thinking about our crisis communications plan. What's the role of social media in a crisis?

But there's no doubt that, as awareness of the value and importance of social media in various kinds of campaigns has expanded—and comfort and sophistication about using social media have increased—so has the need for models. Knowing what's worked for other colleges or universities is very helpful to staff tasked with creating a campaign or to those who think that their institution might be ready to mobilize friends, fans, and followers to take on a challenge of some kind. And knowing about successful campaigns that other institutions have conducted is the best way I know to convince a cautious or reluctant senior leader to give the go-ahead for a social media–inspired campaign.

And that's what inspired this book.

Those blog posts about the Blue Pig, the Flight of the Flyers, Powered by Orange, and the William & Mary mascot search—all written in 2009 and 2010—are still some of the most-accessed items on the mStoner website. As I thought about this, I realized that there is enduring value in these case studies and set out to discover additional examples that can inform and inspire friends and colleagues at colleges and universities across the world.

Unfortunately, not much exists. If you're good with Google, you can find blog posts (some of them ours), Mashable articles, and other sources that provide some examples of ways in which institutions have combined social and other channels in successful campaigns.

We aim to expand that knowledge base with *Social Works*.

In the first portion of this book we examine some of the basic precepts of social media that underlie all successful campaigns. Then we look at research that suggests practices common to institutions successful with social media. We move on to explore ways in which an institution can develop a successful campaign, drawing on examples from the case studies in this book.

Following that we share 25 case studies of successful campaigns. We've worked hard to identify interesting, inspiring, and ground-breaking campaigns and to develop detailed case studies that illustrate the thinking that went into creating and executing them. In all, 18 authors contributed case studies to *Social Works*—and some played a key role in designing or executing the campaigns they wrote about.

Everyone's goal for their case study for *Social Works* was to share insights into how the campaigns were created, shaped, and conducted—and what institutions learned from them. We asked writers to think about the following questions while conducting their research and interviews and writing their case studies:

» What challenge or problem was this initiative trying to solve? Who was the institution trying to influence?
» How was this initiative conceived? What kind of planning occurred?
» What role did social media play? What other channels were used?
» How was the campaign deployed?
» What kind of results did the initiative achieve?
» What lessons were learned? What worked and what didn't?

One of the key takeaways from these case studies is that institutions that use social media successfully don't focus on social media because it is cool, nor do they use social channels solely in their campaigns. While social channels are important or even key components of these initiatives, they are augmented by other media and other channels. That's a primary reason these initiatives were successful.

Acknowledgements

A lot of people worked very hard to make this book happen. Here are some who particularly deserve recognition for their contributions:

» Cheryl Slover-Linett and Bill Hayward from Slover Linett Strategies; Rae Goldsmith, vice president for communications at CASE; and Judith Kroll, senior director of research at CASE, with whom we've partnered for the past three years on a survey of social media in advancement. These surveys benchmark the use of social media in institutional advancement, but more importantly, offered many insights that informed this book.

» Joanne Catlett, former director of award programs at CASE, and Heyward Smith, who now holds that position, for enabling me to chair CASE Circle of Excellence Awards judging panels for social media and websites.

» Jesse McDougall and Shay Totten, who served as early inspirations and convinced us that the tools exist that enabled us to publish *Social Works* ourselves.

» Julie Schorfheide, CASE's director of books publishing, who cautioned us about the perils of doing it ourselves (and whose advice we clearly flouted).

» Copy Editor Robin Netherton, who worked mightily to ensure that we authors conformed to AP style, moderated by our house idiosyncracies (it's "website"—dammit!—not "Web site!") and that the final print and ebooks are as free of errors as humanly possible. If you find errors, they most assuredly aren't due to Robin's careful work.

» Michelle Pais, a smart, hard-working designer who designed the ebook and print editions of *Social Works*.

» Kevin Rieg, who designed the cover for *Social Works*. In the spirit of this book, he used Pinterest to organize the sources that he drew on for inspiration.

» My colleagues at mStoner, who provide inspiration, insights, and support in so many ways, every day.

» Rob Cima and Voltaire Miran, the co-founders of mStoner, who have learned over the years we've worked together to roll their eyes when I come up with a crazy idea like this one—and then help to figure out ways to make it happen.

Social Works would not have been possible without the

contributions from the people who wrote the most important parts of the book: the case studies. So a huge THANK YOU to each and every one of them: Andrew Careaga, Georgy Cohen, Jennifer Connally, Susan Evans, Terry Flannery, Ellen Foley, Joel Goodman, Dana Howard, Erika Knudson, Kylie Stanley Larson, Nicole O'Connell, Rebecca Salerno, Melissa Soberanes, Donna Talarico, Justin Ware, Mallory Wood, and Fran Zablocki. What a terrific, inspiring group you all are!

Social Works would never have been published without Kylie Stanley Larson, who served as project manager. Kylie made multiple contributions to this book, researching options for creating the various formats in which we're publishing, wrangling content from me and the other contributors, keeping us on track, sweating the details of editing and proofing, keeping multiple versions of content straight. I learned pretty quickly that I didn't have to worry about anything as long as Kylie was on the case.

Today, none of us has to work in a vacuum. Those of us in higher ed are particularly blessed by a community of smart, plugged-in, opinionated people who are ready, willing, and able to share their knowledge and insights in conference presentations, conversations, interviews, blog posts, videos, and tweets. Social tools make it possible to ask questions and have them answered quickly, to seek leads and find them within a few minutes, and to reach out for help and receive it quickly. I'm very grateful for the many people I connect with and for the insights they share and the many ways they enhance my learning:

> » The folks who've worked with me on CASE judging panels for the past five years as we've explored social media.
> » The bloggers in higher ed and elsewhere from whom I've learned.
> » My Twitter followers, many of whom can be counted on to respond to a plea for help, and to Karine Joly, who encouraged me to jump into Twitter in the first place.
> » And the many others who've helped me learn about this intriguing, maddening new mode of communication. **SW**

THE
Successful
Social
Campaign

I first became interested in how institutions used social media as part of larger, focused initiatives—campaigns—in 2009. A few pioneers had built campaigns around social media, but most institutions were struggling with adopting social channels as components of their marketing and engagement strategies. And since social media weren't established, much less well managed, on most campuses, there weren't many campaigns of this sort under way.

This wasn't surprising to me. Though it seems hard to remember a time without Facebook or Twitter, they're fairly recent additions to the marketing and engagement toolkit—and not just in higher ed. Though .edu is often slow to adopt new channels or tactics, some social channels were well-entrenched by 2009. Blogging, for example, was fairly common. Many institutions were using Facebook. So there was a lot of experimenting going on with different social channels based on Web 2.0 precepts.[1]

In 2010 we began collaborating with the Council for Advancement and Support of Education (CASE) and Slover Linett Strategies to find out how institutions approached their use of social media. For the white paper we developed from the 2010 CASE/mStoner/Slover Linett Survey of Social Media in Advancement,[2] we researched and wrote case studies of The College of William & Mary's mascot search and Oregon State University's Powered By Orange campaign. In fact, because these early campaigns contain lessons that are relevant today, we've updated both of those case studies for this book.

Still, it wasn't until 2012, in the third annual survey, that we asked specifically whether (and how) institutions used social media in campaigns, defining a campaign as "a focused effort to achieve goals using a variety of channels appropriate to the results sought." We adopted this definition in recognition of the fact that, at present, many campaigns involving social media have objectives other than raising money. Of course, some are focused on fundraising, too.

Fully 50 percent of our respondents told us that their institutions were using social media as part of campaigns, though fewer than 25 percent used it in every campaign. The goals of these campaigns varied—a lot. Here are some of the open-ended responses from the 2012 survey, which provide a sense of some of the purposes for campaigns deployed by many different kinds of institutions:

---

(1) If you're curious about the relationship of Web 2.0 and social media, or want to learn more about some of their basic principles, read our brief review in the Appendix.
(2) Cheryl Slover-Linett and Michael Stoner, "Succeeding with Social Media: Lessons from the First Survey of Social Media in Advancement," white paper, August 2010. Available here: mstnr.me/SMA2010

» "Event promotion and attendance."
» "A $100 challenge match for alumni."
» "We promote the career resources offered to alumni and other career initiatives such as networking nights and webinars across all of our social media platforms."
» "All of our annual giving appeals included some social media component, whether it was posts on Facebook, to Facebook advertising, to encouraging Twitter use for peer-to-peer solicitations."
» "We used social media in a newly designed undergraduate admissions piece."
» "In 2011 we used social media (Twitter, Facebook) to highlight our annual April Fool's Day prank, which featured a revision of the homepage and related content."
» "Increased participation and giving—alumni giving went from 19 percent to 26 percent."
» "One goal was increased requests for information on our website; . . .we used Facebook and our often-changing website to garner interest by using fresh, relevant content. We went from approximately 80 requests for info per month to approximately 200 per month."
» "Online contest to raise awareness of research and programs. Received more entries than expected."
» "We wanted to raise awareness of and encourage participation in the celebration of our 150th birthday by having people attend in-person events, and for those who couldn't do that, having them participate virtually. It was a big success."

The campaigns profiled in *Social Works* represent a wide variety of approaches. Some had fixed starting and ending points. Others are ongoing. Some focused on one major constituent group, like prospective students or alumni. Some had clearly defined goals established in the beginning that didn't change much as the campaign progressed; in others, goals changed, developing and solidifying as the campaign unfolded. Some campaigns were based on fairly detailed plans from the start. Others followed a principle of "launch and learn," meaning that those responsible for the campaign paid close attention to what their audiences responded to and adjusted their tactics accordingly.

These case studies can offer important lessons for other institutions that need to launch a campaign of some kind. And though they are all different, as a group they show there are some basic approaches that form a strong foundation for every campaign. We'll explore some of these shortly.

Table 1. Frequency of use of specific goals for social media in advancement, 2012

GOALS OF SOCIAL MEDIA	2012	
	"not at all" or "not much"	"quite a bit" or "extensively"
Engage alumni	6%	83%
Create, sustain, and improve brand image	75%	77%
Increase awareness/ advocacy/rankings	18%	60%
Engage current students	20%	55%
Build internal community	22%	51%
Engage current faculty and staff	25%	43%
Engage admitted students	36%	46%
Engage prospective students	36%	43%
Engage the local community	30%	38%
Recruit students	43%	38%
Engage parents of current students	38%	35%
Engage the media	45%	26%
Conduct research on audiences (alumni, students, etc.)	43%	25%
Raise private funds	46%	26%
Crisis and issues management	56%	22%
Recruit faculty and staff	72%	7%

Source: 2012 CASE/mStoner/Slover Linett Survey of Social Media and Advancement

Table 2. Percentage of respondents reporting use of specific social media channels for any audience in institutional advancement, 2010–12

SOCIAL MEDIA CHANNEL	2010	2011	2012
Facebook (create/manage communities within Facebook)	94%	96%	96%
Twitter	67%	75%	80%
YouTube	59%	65%	73%
LinkedIn (create/manage communities within LinkedIn)	61%	65%	68%
Blogs	36%	43%	55%
Flickr or other photo-sharing sites[1]	33%	40%	51%
An institutional website that is an aggregator of social network sites	58%	41%	43%
Social communities provided by vendors through proprietary software (such as Harris Connect, iModules, etc.)	33%	36%	33%
A community created in-house by your unit (create/manage communities)[2]	5%	12%	27%
Geosocial services (such as Foursquare or SCVNGR)[3]	n/a	n/a	17%

Source: 2012 CASE/mStoner/Slover Linett Survey of Social Media and Advancement

(1) In 2010 and 2011, we asked about Flickr only; we changed the wording of the question to "Flickr or other photo-sharing sites" in 2012.

(2) In 2010, Ning was still widely used to create in-house communities, so we asked about it specifically.

(3) New in 2012.

.EDUs and Social Media Success

At the time we developed the 2010 CASE/mStoner/Slover Linett Survey of Social Media in Advancement, there was plenty of research about how people used social media in their personal lives and many studies that looked at how businesses were using social media to market to and engage with consumers. But we could find none that looked at how colleges and universities were using social media for this kind of outreach. We've conducted our survey twice since then. Three year's worth of data have helped us look at changes in the use of social media over time. But, more pertinent to our purposes here, the survey findings also help us understand what the 22 percent of respondents who consider their social media activities to be "very successful" do to deliver that success.

It's clear that colleges and universities are using social media to achieve a broad range of goals, as shown in Table 1. And to do so, they're using a range of social media, as shown in Table 2.

Of course, there are other important channels that aren't listed here, and new ones emerge all the time. Right now, there's a lot of interest in Pinterest and Instagram. Though there are universities that are experimenting with Pinterest and sharing their experiences, positive and negative, through blog posts and articles, it's too early to tell whether these experiments will really pay off. It's also a little early in the hype-cycle for Instagram, but that channel could be even more significant than Pinterest because Instagram enables people to share images from their mobile phones, allowing a perfect bridge between mobile and social communication.[3]

Most importantly, though, institutions are starting to see results from their initiatives, moving past the numbers of "likes," "retweets," and other social shares to more significant outcomes. Some institutions are more rigorous in their assessments, gauging success based on surveys and measurable outcomes such as attendance at events or applications for enrollment. That's not to say there isn't more work to do in assessing the real results of social media activities—but there has been progress.

In our most recent survey, conducted in early 2012, we looked at the responses of those institutions that reported being "very successful" to see what attributes they might share. Here's what we found:

> » Staff at successful institutions believe that social media will help
> them achieve their goals. Based on that belief, they are willing

---

(3) It's important to note that we encourage experimentation: Indeed, it's really important. But we also believe that those experiments should occur after an institution's website is well-designed and well-managed, and the important social channels (YouTube, Facebook, Twitter, LinkedIn) are attended to. These tools are fundamental to any institution's marketing and social strategy and should be supported fully first, before emerging and unproven tools or channels are adopted.

to take actions—and risks—that will increase their chances of success. Belief also enables them to commit resources (most notably staff time) to planning and executing activities on various social channels.

» Units (such as offices or departments) that are successful manage their own social media activities with a fair amount of independence, without being forced to take direction from other individuals or offices at their institution. This allows them to be responsive and engage their audiences directly and as necessary.

» Successful units and institutions use multiple metrics to measure their success. In other words, "likes" and "shares" may drive toward another action—such as attendance at an event— and aren't just ends in themselves. This is especially important in developing a campaign with social components, since an increasing number of campaigns focus on real-world outcomes.

» While successful units have independence, they are usually part of an institution where social media is appreciated and engagement through social channels has broad support. This appreciation and support can take the form of resources, but other key components are training, policy, and the awareness and the backing of CEOs, deans, provosts, and other senior leaders.

» Successful institutions have policies in place addressing social media activities. At present, these policies primarily focus on content, branding, and privacy. But in higher education, as in business, development of a policy covering social media signals an awareness of how important social channels are for communicating and nurturing relationships with constituents.

» Not surprisingly, successful institutions have more staff members focusing on social media. This doesn't necessarily mean full-time employees focusing on social media exclusively, though it can; it often means that many staff members have some responsibility for social media as part of their jobs.

» Institutions that are successful with social media understand that planning is crucial. And, because they realize how important planning is, they want to do more of it.

» On average, communications and marketing staff tend to think their social media efforts are more successful, while development staff think theirs are less successful. This makes sense: The outcome that defines success for a development officer is dollars raised. And everyone acknowledges that it's very hard to raise money through social channels right now.

» Because successful institutions are experienced at developing and managing the important social channels, they've mastered Facebook and they're active on Twitter. Now, they're trying other things: They have the experience and the flexibility (and vision) to beta-test new channels such as Pinterest, Google+, SCVNGR,

Successful institutions regularly incorporate social media into broader campaigns, using not only social channels but also a variety of other online channels as well as offline media.

and other newer networks.

» They know how to market their social media activities using multiple channels.

Finally, and most important, successful institutions regularly incorporate social media into broader campaigns, using not only social channels but also a variety of other online channels as well as offline media. In fact, in the 2012 survey, institutions reported that they used social channels in fully 50 percent of campaigns—with that term encompassing not just campaigns dedicated to fundraising, but a range of broad initiatives focused on achieving a specific goal.

In the white paper we wrote about the results of the 2012 survey,[4] we noted:

> By using social media in multi-channel campaigns, institutions are finding that this integrated approach—with proper planning and goals in place—has increased results and benefits that continue far beyond the campaign. Not only can development and communications staff reach a broader audience, but they can now reach them through the most engaging and appropriate channel. And, with social media in the mix, institutions have an opportunity to build on the friend-to-friend encouragement that social media provides, further expanding their reach and impact. Social media is also a more effective way to reach young alumni, who many institutions note are the most difficult audience to contact and engage.

What goes into developing a campaign? The answer isn't difficult: Good campaigns begin with a plan. Most great ones begin with a detailed plan.

Planning a Campaign

Not every campaign needs a detailed plan, but every campaign needs a plan, and the more complicated the campaign is, the more detailed the plan should be. It's not just that writing a plan is an important exercise in and of itself, but that developing a plan forces you to think through the many aspects of a campaign. Trust me: Even in the best circumstances, there will be a lot that you won't anticipate. That's why it's important to think through as many of the fundamentals as you can before you actually start to do anything.

It helps to start off with a creative idea for a campaign or one that

(4) Cheryl Slover-Linnet and Michael Stoner, "#SocialMedia and Advancement: Insights from Three Years of Data," white paper, Aug. 27, 2012. Available here: mstnr.me/CAS-ESMA2012

can be expressed in an amusing way, at least for some audiences and in some channels. But humor can be dicey: You need to know your audience and understand how open they can be to an offbeat idea or approach. Clearly, MIT and Cornell University alumni proved very willing to engage in a competition involving fantasy alumni and take it (semi-)seriously. And Nazareth College alumni are engaged in a game involving stuffed birds. But not every audience will react well to approaches like these. You need to know what your particular audiences will accept before you get started.

Here are the essential components of a plan:

>> goals/objectives
>> audience(s)
>> channels, tools, and assets
>> staff/participants
>> marketing/promotion
>> timeline
>> budget
>> benchmarks/measurement.

Let's examine each of these in turn.

Goals/objectives. No campaign should start without some clear goals in mind. What exactly do you need to accomplish through your campaign? What outcomes are important to your institution? You must be clear about this from the start because it should influence the other decisions you make.

This isn't the place for a lengthy discussion on goal-setting: There are plenty of frameworks you can use to set your goals. We particularly like the SMART framework:[5] SMART goals are specific, measurable, attainable, relevant, and timely. And some universities have preferred frameworks for goal-setting, tying goals to a division's strategic plan or to the institution's strategic plan. Whether or not your institution operates this way, the fact is that it's important to set goals. Plus, the more specific the goals are, the better. It will be easier to determine whether or not you met them (or exceeded them!).

The University of Nottingham's Election 2010 campaign began with specific objectives that included quantitative measurements like "involving at least four new politics academics in media activity by the end of the campaign" and "supporting student recruitment and increasing applications by at least 5 percent." These goals were tied to the university's strategic plan.

But not every campaign starts with measurable objectives in mind. Some really successful initiatives, like William & Mary's

---

(5) Link: en.wikipedia.org/wiki/SMART_criteria

mascot search, began with higher-level goals of improving engagement rather than seeking a certain number of mascot suggestions, blog comments, or Facebook likes.

It's easier to set goals for a focused campaign of a shorter duration. Take the Battle of the Blues challenge between Elizabethtown College and Messiah College: It played out over the course of four months. Its goal was to boost the number of donors at each institution and thereby increase alumni participation and giving. Neither institution set a specific target number for the increase, but they could have.

In contrast, Oregon State University began its Powered By Orange campaign with a goal of reaching out to stakeholders in Portland, the state's largest city and most important media market. The "fictional alumni" contest between MIT and Cornell began as an effort by Cornell's alumni association to gain more Facebook followers than MIT's alumni association, which escalated into a competition fueled by the alumni bodies of both institutions. In these cases, the objective of the campaign was "engagement," and the planners did not set specific numerical goals.

Sometimes an institution has to be opportunistic. Take Murray State University, which found itself in a highly competitive basketball season with a national championship within reach. The university jumped in with both feet, capitalizing on a video by a student rap group and using social media to achieve an incredible amount of engagement and attention that is often out of reach for a small, regional institution.

While goal setting is essential, so is being realistic about what you can accomplish. You have to be focused and deliberate in order to be successful in social media, but you also have to pay attention and adjust what you're doing if it isn't working.

Audience(s). Is there a specific audience—or audiences—you need to influence to accomplish your goals? Just as it's important to be clear about what you're trying to accomplish, it's vital that you know who you're trying to reach.

Your perception of who your audience is for the campaign influences the other choices you're going to make. For example, what channels will you use in your campaign? Using Foursquare or SCVNGR is not a wise choice if your goal is to encourage alumni to give, unless it's tied in some way to a reunion or other event where a group will be on campus checking in. Developing a campaign for prospective students based on Pinterest is likewise a time-wasting proposition right now except in some very special cases.

For a broader campaign—one such as OSU's Powered By Orange or American University's American WONK—you may need to segment your audience, taking one approach with alumni, another with current students, and a third with faculty and staff.

Knowing what audience you want to reach will help you determine what kind of approach you'll develop for the campaign and help you make decisions about such issues as the role of humor. Having a creative idea and a light, humorous touch may well be a masterstroke, just the kind of energy that your campaign needs. Or not. What resonates with one audience—such as alumni—might not work with another. For instance, staff at Murray State University were concerned that some alumni might not appreciate the student-created rap video that played a role in their campaign.

And, it (almost) goes without saying that what works at one institution might not work at another. For example, as noted above, alumni of Cornell and MIT appreciated the offbeat approach of the fictional alumni campaign. At another institution such an approach may simply fall flat. Or worse, it may not seem to be authentic or have any grounding in institutional reality. It's important to remember that the focus in social media circles on "authenticity" isn't simply cant. It's an important value. When people sense authenticity in communications, they believe they can trust the institution they are engaging with. But they're quick to sniff out something that is inauthentic or unreal. And being real is an important value in an era where determined researchers can use the internet to ferret out just about any fact they want to learn. So, make sure your concept and approach fit with the personality (dare one say "brand"?) of your institution, and if you have any doubts, ask members of your target audience what they think.

Channels, tools, and assets. Though the case studies in this book are focused around the use of social media in campaigns, most of the campaigns use many other channels besides social ones. In fact, I might argue that the most interesting and engaging campaigns are those that operate in both the online and offline worlds, using multiple channels. It's the "everything is connected to everything else" principle that I've written about before, where an ecosystem of images and messages reinforce one another, whatever the channel.[6]

One consequence of planning a multi-channel campaign is that you'll need to plan to develop content to feed your different channels. A content strategy is essential, and the more complicated a campaign is, and the more channels it contains, the more detailed it should be.

If you're launching a campaign in which you hope to crowd-source content, you still need to prepare a substantial amount of content and hold it in reserve in case the crowd needs prompting for its contributions. Even highly motivated and engaged

---

(6) "mStoner's First Law of Branding," blog post, Nov. 4, 2010. Available here: mstnr.me/RsGTlv

participants on a social channel don't necessarily contribute much beyond likes and shares.[7] This is exactly what the University of Wisconsin-Madison did for its #UWRightNow initiative: The campaign planners made sure that their colleagues on campus were prepared to contribute news stories and videos to the campaign as they simultaneously reached out to alumni and other stakeholders to share their own content.

The simple fact is that the more you want to accomplish, the more comprehensive your reach needs to be and the more channels you should consider using. Perhaps the best example I can cite here is Powered By Orange. The staff at OSU worked hard to establish and populate some key social channels right after PBO was launched. When they were ready to roll out the first public phase of the campaign, which focused on Portland, these social channels had content and fans and followers aplenty, and PBO's online presence was robust. OSU staff augmented PBO's online presence with bus wraps, advertising in Portland's light rail system and elsewhere, tables in heavily trafficked public squares in the city, and OSU-branded swag such as t-shirts.

One reason that this was important to PBO—and is important to your institution, too—is that you can't count on the people you're trying to influence to be tuned in to your message on a specific social channel. So even if the bulk of your campaign activities occur on one channel, such as Facebook, you must market your campaign as broadly as possible using appropriate means: website banners, blog entries, tweets, emails, advertisements, postcards, direct mail. Breaking through the thousands of messages your audiences receive every day, from every channel, is never easy; it's really hard to gain their attention and muster their participation unless your marketing is pervasive and persistent.

And different channels have different strengths. Many social channels are a great way to hit people now, in a moment of consumption, when they'll see something smart or interesting and do something: like it or share it. This immediacy is incredibly powerful.

But the other side of it is that tweets or Facebook posts are very transitory—here this minute, gone the next. They're quickly buried in a flood of new tweets or posts that overwhelm a newsfeed. In contrast, print has a much longer tail, and blog posts are searchable (and findable) years after they appear online. Print can have a

---

(7) This is just one of the important messages in *Here Comes Everybody*, Clay Shirky's excellent book about social media. In Chapter 5, "Personal Motivation Meets Collaborative Production," he discusses endeavors such as Wikipedia and Flickr groups. Both rely on crowdsourcing content, and in both, the bulk of contributions are made by a very few individuals. This makes crowdsourcing efforts particularly difficult and unpredictable. Clay Shirky, *Here Comes Everybody: The Power of Organizing Without Organizations* (Penguin Books, 2008), 109–42.

significant pass-along effect (this is one reason why teens still like viewbooks—they can share them easily), and blog posts or other web content can also be shareable, provided that you make it possible. This gives content that you are developing specifically for your campaign significant staying power, at least in some channels.

Remember, too, that channels reinforce one another: William & Mary's Ampersandbox package for prospective students combined print with a website that had social components. Those who received the print piece could follow urls in the piece to the website; people who visited the website could explore it and contribute to it, making the whole package mutually reinforcing.

Staff/participants. One reason you need to be clear about the channels that you'll use for the campaign is that you need to determine who among your colleagues will be involved. And what will they do? Do you need help developing a website or adding a new section to an existing site? Will you need a graphic designer to create a series of postcards for marketing your campaign? Will you need to produce a video? Will you need someone to write content for the campaign and contribute as it unfolds?

It's fairly obvious that you'll need to bring people on board who will help you generate content or execute what you want to do. Remember, though, that you may also need other, less direct support.

Consider the approach that OSU took to Powered By Orange. The staff involved in planning the campaign realized that they needed widespread support, so their vice president made presentations and scheduled meetings with stakeholders across campus to gain their buy-in for PBO. Similarly, the news staff at the University of Nottingham knew that they needed to gain the support of several key faculty members first, before their academic colleagues would sign on to the Election 2010 initiative.

So: What other kinds of support will you need to help your campaign succeed? One respondent to the CASE/mStoner/Slover Linett Survey of Social Media in Advancement remarked, "Get champions among your alumni," indicating the importance of going beyond "likes" to actual advocacy from key stakeholders. And 61 percent of respondents in 2012 indicated that they "agreed" or "strongly agreed" that "a champion is essential to the successful implementation of social media in our institution."

Remember, too, that a social campaign will succeed if and only if it is shared by your friends, fans, and followers. In addition to marketing it to them, you may need to gain support from at least some of your friends, fans, and followers before the campaign actually occurs, reaching out to them via email or even by personal phone calls to gain their support. As my colleague Susan Evans, now a senior strategist at mStoner, points out, these channels have become even more powerful because they are typically used less frequently now.

Another question to ask is whether anyone who will be instrumental in your campaign needs training of any kind. This might involve being taught how to post on a WordPress blog, how to crop and size a photo, or how to interact with the media. Will you need to set up formal training for these people? Will they require online help, networking, or webinars? How can you keep them engaged and motivated during the campaign, which is a real challenge for longer initiatives?

In any case, you'll need to know this before you begin. The more you think ahead about your needs, the more successful you'll be in executing them.

While our research indicates that the level of comfort with and experience in using social media is more widespread among college and university staff now than it was in 2010, it's worthwhile pointing out that institutions that are more successful with social media do a better job of training staff in using it. Also, many campaigns need the involvement of many staff members in order to succeed. Some are likely to be less familiar with some of the tools they'll be using. Make sure that any participants who are likely to require training get it before your campaign commences.

Finally, remember that you'll need to plan for (and budget for) people to manage your campaign from launch through conclusion. And when you reach the point where a campaign is "over," in the best case, you'll end up with an energized and engaged group of friends, fans, and followers. What happens then? What's your plan for follow-on engagement? I don't believe that you want to be in perpetual campaign mode, but plan on continuing to engage your audience once the campaign ends or risk losing their attention.

Marketing/promotion. In general, the more you market your campaign, the more successful it will be. That's why it's very important to determine who you're trying to influence and the best ways to reach them.

Let's consider a specific example. In its Election 2010 campaign, the University of Nottingham targeted reporters, bloggers, and other members of the news media at top national and international outlets. They compiled a list of sources from their own files and from the contacts of faculty members involved in the campaign. They then reached out to these individuals through a variety of channels, including the phone. In this way, they were able to market the insights about the election that faculty members were sharing on the campaign blog, Twitter, and YouTube.

Table 3 provides a look at the broad range of channels that institutions used to market and promote their campaigns, according to the 2012 CASE/mStoner/Slover Linett Survey of Social Media in Advancement.

Remember when you think about promotion to ask engaged

Table 3. Percentage of respondents reporting use of specific tools to promote campaigns, 2012

TOOL	%
ONLINE CHANNELS	
Website	91%
Email	88%
Social media	79%
Blogging	23%
Search engine optimization or search engine marketing	21%
PRINT MEDIA	
Internal publications	67%
Direct print mail	52%
External publications (not your institution's publications)	21%
ADVERTISING AND PROMOTION	
Outreach and marketing at events	91%
Radio	88%
TV	79%
Other	23%

Source: 2012 CASE/mStoner/Slover Linett Survey of Social Media and Advancement

audience members to help you in marketing your campaign. Reach out to those who will support the campaign because of their previous engagement or interest in its focus; consider who else might be interested in promoting it. Market to them first, seeking their support as you roll out the initiative more broadly.

And in the context of an integrated campaign, channels may be essentially equal in their power to draw attention and focus on your messages and objectives. Sharing on social channels may power the campaign, but an email may inspire a key volunteer to take action as other channels work together to raise awareness. Every channel is both a recipient and provider of momentum and promotion for each other channel; all your boats rise on the same tide.

Timeline. For your initial plan, you'll have to lay out a timeline for your campaign. When will it start? When will it conclude? Will it have different phases? What will you need to do to promote these phases, and to whom? How will activities like a website launch be coordinated with other campaign activities? Will you need lead time to print and mail a postcard? Or to place an ad in your alumni magazine?

Budget. In the early years of the social media hype, I was very frustrated by conference presenters who asserted that using social media was great because it was "free." My response was something like: "Yes, it's free, like a 'free' puppy."

It's true that there is little or no fee involved to use some of the most significant social channels. At their most basic levels, Facebook, Twitter, YouTube, and Vimeo are free to anyone, at least for the moment. A few social channels like LinkedIn do offer tiered services.

But if you want to take advantage of some more-advanced features of services, you'll often pay more. If you want to advertise on Facebook, which can be an effective way to promote a campaign, you'll pay for the privilege. If you want to make sure that more fans see your posts in their newsfeeds, you'll pay for that privilege, too. And some monitoring services, such as Radian 6, can be very expensive.

Of course, the cost of staff time to use these services is not "free." Your institution pays for salaries and benefits for those individuals. Furthermore, staff members who are spending time on social media are not spending that time doing something else. Institutions that wish to invest in social media will require staff to engage in these channels on the institution's behalf. That time should count—make sure the results are worth it.

In particular, social channels require content—blog posts, images, videos. Someone has to create this content, by writing, shooting photos, and capturing and editing videos. You won't be able to rely on the crowd to generate content for your initiative unless it's a large crowd. If you want to succeed, staff members will need to be involved as writers, photographers, or videographers. And staff members will need to serve as community moderators, reviewing the contributions of your audience and spurring engagement on campaign channels. Online and offline promotion (think Facebook ads, for example) will also incur costs—none of it "free."

A responsible budget takes these—and other—aspects of a campaign into account and comes up with a realistic assessment of its true costs, in staff time and in dollars allocated for essential elements of the campaign.

Benchmarks/measurement. In planning a campaign, it's essential that you think about how you're going to measure your results. And good measurement usually begins with benchmarking. You really can't measure progress if you don't know where you start. Here's where clarity in what you want to accomplish helps you focus on what's important, as long as you have the baseline data that allow you to show progress.

It's one thing to create a campaign to grow your Facebook fans or boost the likes on your Facebook page. Honestly, that seems like a fairly trivial goal—and it's certainly easy to measure using Facebook's tools. But this can be very important as the foundation for another campaign. For example, there's no doubt that having robust, well-managed Facebook and Twitter channels allowed Missouri University of Science and Technology to use these channels to deal with a campus crisis. You may need to take this initial step to build a more engaged audience in preparation for an initiative like announcing a new president or garnering support for a campus building plan.

In exploring success in social media via the CASE/mStoner/ Slover Linett Survey of Social Media in Advancement, institutions that used social media reported that these channels have been most successful in helping them to increase engagement with their target audiences (57 percent said that's true). And they also find that social channels are helping to increase awareness of their institution among external audiences now that campaigns are focusing on this engagement as a specific outcome (14 percent said that's true). [8]

In looking at the challenges higher education faces, I can say that driving real outcomes of one kind or another is one of our big challenges going forward. So focusing on meaningful goals—and achieving outcomes that matter in the real world, not just on Facebook or Twitter—will be the real measure of campaign success. That's why the achievements of institutions like Elizabethtown College, Madison College, Messiah College, and the University of Nottingham are exciting and important: They show that campaigns

---

(8) Slover-Linnet and Stoner, "#SocialMedia and Advancement: Insights from Three Years of Data."

with significant social components can boost enrollment, broaden institutional awareness, and increase giving among important donor segments.

There's something else to keep in mind: Often social campaigns generate earned media. That was certainly true for many of the campaigns in this book. William & Mary's mascot search was picked up by ESPN and *The Chronicle of Higher Education*, among many other major news outlets, and culminated in a segment on "The Daily Show" (whose host, Jon Stewart, is a William & Mary alumnus). Murray State's initiative reached well beyond campus because of exposure on ESPN and other sports channels. Nelson Mandela Metropolitan University's flash mob was widely covered by the media in South Africa.

This reach is important in several respects: Not only does it increase awareness of the institution itself, but these mentions can generate credibility on campus, leading to broader recognition of the value of a specific campaign or social media in general and more support by leadership.

Of course, it's difficult to measure the achievement of some campaigns. The main reason is that in campaigns with broader goals, such as Powered By Orange, which focuses on raising awareness of OSU among many key audiences, results are complicated and expensive to measure. Before PBO was launched, OSU had completed a significant amount of research and had good data on what people thought about the university. In order to measure the success of PBO, OSU would have to do a similar study to measure whether attitudes had shifted and how much of any shift was attributable to PBO.

In these cases, it's appropriate to use measures like website accesses from a targeted location, blog visits on the day of launch, and other measures of traffic, which are an indication that the targeted audience is responding to the campaign. But be clear that these are more simple indications of success, not true tests of whether a campaign has really succeeded.

Table 4 gives an indication of how advancement is measuring social media success, based on the CASE/mStoner/Slover Linett Survey of Social Media in Advancement . In general, we're still counting ("friends," "likes," "shares"), though more institutions are looking for engagement in other channels in addition to online channels. Boosting participation in events seems to be working for some of the units that responded to this survey, for example.

Executing Your Campaign

In some ways, planning is much harder than executing. Executing is fun and engaging. There's excitement around the launch of something—so much so that the tendency for many people is to

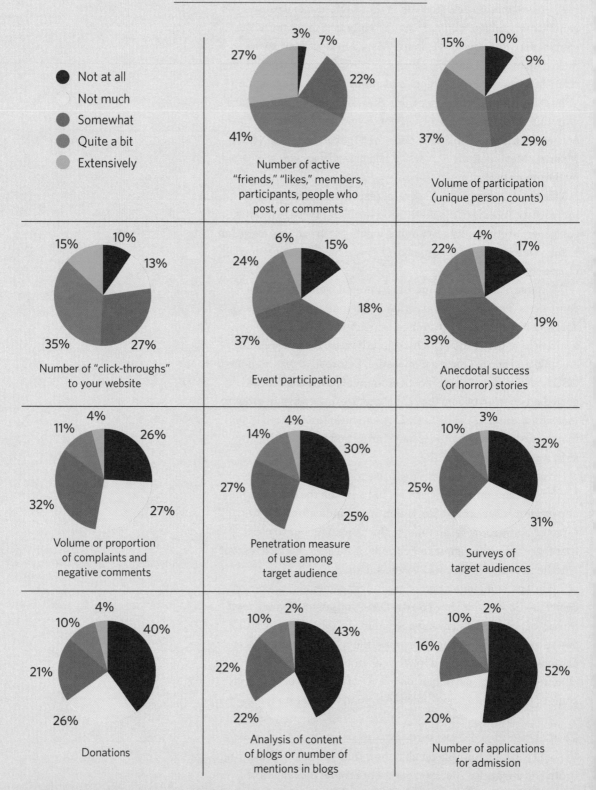

Figure 4. Frequency of use of specific measurements of success with social media, 2012

Legend:
- Not at all
- Not much
- Somewhat
- Quite a bit
- Extensively

Number of active "friends," "likes," members, participants, people who post, or comments
- 3%
- 7%
- 22%
- 41%
- 27%

Volume of participation (unique person counts)
- 10%
- 9%
- 29%
- 37%
- 15%

Number of "click-throughs" to your website
- 10%
- 13%
- 27%
- 35%
- 15%

Event participation
- 15%
- 18%
- 37%
- 24%
- 6%

Anecdotal success (or horror) stories
- 17%
- 19%
- 39%
- 22%
- 4%

Volume or proportion of complaints and negative comments
- 26%
- 27%
- 32%
- 11%
- 4%

Penetration measure of use among target audience
- 30%
- 25%
- 27%
- 14%
- 4%

Surveys of target audiences
- 32%
- 31%
- 25%
- 10%
- 3%

Donations
- 40%
- 26%
- 21%
- 10%
- 4%

Analysis of content of blogs or number of mentions in blogs
- 43%
- 22%
- 22%
- 10%
- 2%

Number of applications for admission
- 52%
- 20%
- 16%
- 10%
- 2%

Source: 2012 CASE/mStoner/Slover Linett Survey of Social Media and Advancement

jump in and do something, now, without thinking through the how and the why first. And while that may be fine for a short-term initiative, even a simple campaign like Webster University's Summer Ticket Giveaway involved planning its multiple steps in advance of its launch. The more you think through your campaign in advance, the fewer surprises you'll have as it unfolds day to day and week to week.

Planning also helps to ensure consistency in communication across channels. And remember that on the social channels in your campaign, keeping up your end of the conversation is essential to getting engagement and sustaining interest throughout the course of the campaign.

Launch and learn. As a campaign progresses through its various phases—whether they are short and simple or long and complicated—you'll need to check on progress and make adjustments in your tactics and perhaps in your overall strategy. This is important when you're in a position to respond to fast-changing external conditions—as was Murray State University in their We Are Racers campaign focused around an NCAA basketball championship season.

Powered By Orange is the longest-running campaign featured in this book. I'd written about it three times before and attended several presentations by OSU staff who were involved in the campaign. When I wrote the case study for *Social Works*, I was struck at how many different phases PBO went through and how the staff needed to respond differently at different times. They were able to do this because they took a "launch and learn" approach to the campaign. They kept monitoring the progress they were making and tweaked what they were doing based on what they learned, making decisions based on how their audience was responding to various initiatives within the campaign.

Be aware of campaign fatigue. When a campaign involves a lot of excitement—as was the case during Murray State's ongoing basketball season, when the team was winning and enthusiasm was high—it's easy to stay engaged day-to-day. But attention lags when a campaign goes on for a long time. It's easy to get bored creatively, as Melody Oldfield, OSU's director of marketing, said happened with PBO. She pointed out how important it is to stay focused and make sure there are appropriate creative challenges ahead.

Keep champions engaged. During implementation is where engaged friends, fans, and followers become incredibly significant. They become your online ambassadors, extending your voice and reach into their own networks. You'll need to keep them engaged and active through the life of the campaign. Part of the planning for Florida State's Great Give campaign was preparing a lot of content— sample tweets and Facebook posts—that could be shared with their ambassadors via emails that encouraged them to take action.

Provide campaign updates. You'll want to develop ways to share updates with your partners and your champions while a campaign is under way. Set up a schedule to report on accomplishments and metrics. This is especially important with longer campaigns because it's more difficult to keep people focused on these initiatives.

Offer ongoing training. Some ongoing campaigns depend on recruiting new participants regularly. For example, each year, Saint Michael's College must recruit some new student bloggers. New participants need to be trained.

Think about how to wrap up the campaign. Do you throw a party for your on-campus partners and your online ambassadors? Do you send t-shirts to volunteers? In any case, you'll want to thank them for their efforts and the contributions they've made to the institution.

Primarily, though, how you proceed depends a lot on the type of campaign you're running, the channels you're using, and your objectives. The 25 case studies in *Social Works* illustrate how different campaigns proceeded—and how they used social media to help achieve success. **sw**

Case Studies

Powered By Orange: A Comprehensive Social Media Campaign at Oregon State University

By Michael Stoner, mStoner | @mstonerblog

Michael Stoner is the president and a co-founder of mStoner, Inc. In more than 30 years as a communicator and consultant, he has provided strategic advice on institution-wide web strategies, led countless web development projects in higher education, and earned an international reputation as an authority on integrating marketing, communications, and technology.

O regon State University created its Powered By Orange (PBO) marketing campaign to replace an advertising campaign with a limited reach. Launched initially across a variety of social channels, PBO grew into a branding campaign widely embraced on and off campus. Further, PBO expanded from its social core into a multi-channel effort.

In developing PBO's initial messaging and visuals, OSU staff used insights from a lengthy research process, grounding the initiative in institutional reality. The team relied on strong messaging, a sense of humor, a willingness to give up control of imagery and messaging, and an attitude of "launch and learn"— essentially, watching how its audiences responded to PBO—to grow the campaign. PBO was the first university branding initiative launched on social networks and remains a model of how to prepare for and launch a similar initiative.

A Firm Foundation

In 2008, OSU launched an integrated marketing communications strategy and plan[1] linked to the university's strategic plan. The preparation of the marketing plan gave OSU staff plenty of information and articulated clear guidelines. Approximately 2,000 stakeholders shared their perceptions of OSU through focus groups, conversations, and surveys.

According to this research, OSU faced a number of challenges and opportunities, including replacing a "modest, old-fashioned image as Oregon's land grant university" with one that reflected some of the dynamic, cutting-edge research on campus. Many people didn't know that OSU scientists, researchers, and

---

(1) Available at mstnr.me/OregonSt1

agronomists were creating solutions to contemporary problems that were relevant to cities as well as rural areas. Accordingly, one of the plan's three objectives was to position OSU "as a national and global contributor of knowledge, innovation, and talent; national and international audiences will recognize the unique value and contributions the university makes, particularly in the areas of earth systems science, health and wellness, and economic growth and social progress."

OSU's plan introduced a brand summary—"Better living for all"—and the following brand statement:

> Oregon State University turns ideals into reality with a unique approach characterized by collaboration and strategic focus, making a positive difference on quality of life and the natural world in Oregon and beyond. As an international research university, OSU attracts exceptional students and faculty who are taking an interdisciplinary approach toward solving some of the world's most pressing problems. We apply our land grant heritage in contemporary ways by leading innovation and scholarship in the areas of earth systems science, health and wellness, and economic and social progress.

The marketing plan also suggested these brand benefits: "greener," "healthier," "safer," "kinder," "more sustainable," "more prosperous," "more innovative."

At the time it was completed, the marketing plan didn't have messaging, graphic, or creative assets associated with it. This campaign, conducted in the state's largest media market, focused on stimulating awareness of OSU among influencers in the media and parents of prospective students. The original plan had been to broadcast a TV commercial, supported by additional ad buys.

Drawing upon the insights from the research and from the brand platform, a group of staff from University Marketing and Web Communications developed a plan and a creative approach for a different kind of campaign, based on a website and social media channels, which they dubbed Powered By Orange. This telegraphed an important message for OSU: that the university's research and people powered much of what happened regionally.

One of PBO's main goals was to use engagement in the various social channels as a means of shifting awareness of OSU stakeholders toward a new way of thinking about the university. The goal was to showcase how the people of OSU—faculty, staff, students, alumni, and friends—were making a positive impact on the environment and community.

On-campus stakeholders who previewed PBO responded

National and international audiences will recognize the unique value and contributions the university makes, particularly in the areas of earth systems science, health and wellness, and economic growth and social progress.

positively. According to Luanne Lawrence, who, as then–vice president for advancement at OSU, served as a key champion for the campaign, "The feedback was consistently supportive of the Powered By Orange concept. So, we developed the campaign a bit more and tested it at a few alumni events and in focus groups and discussions with faculty, staff, and students. Each conversation improved the concept and grew it."

At the same time, staff members used what they learned—and the growing number of advocates gained through the various social channels where PBO launched—to seed social networks in preparation for a broader launch, involving more channels, in Portland.

Channels and Components

The initial "hub" for the Powered By Orange campaign was a website,[2] developed on WordPress by OSU's web team in collaboration with university marketing. According to David Baker, director of web communications, planning and execution of the site and social networking components "took a couple of months from first concept to site launch. We were able to move quickly because we had the research."

The PBO site invited people who were "powered by orange" to share their stories. Who's "powered by orange"? Here's the answer from the PBO website: "It's you—the network of alumni, students, faculty, staff, friends, and fans connected to Oregon State University. It's the positive impact you make every day in Portland and beyond—on the economy, the environment, and the community. Use this website to tell your story and connect with the other practical idealists who are Powered By Orange."

OSU's research emphasized the necessity of connecting with younger alumni, who are essential to future giving, and reinforced that this audience in particular wanted reassurance that OSU was making an impact on the world. "It was a no-brainer to reach out to young alumni through channels that they were familiar with," Baker said. That meant a significant number of social components.

One key focal point of the site was a Google Map that allowed people who are "powered by orange" to place markers for their locations. In June 2009, I interviewed Baker for a blog post about PBO and he told me, "Lots of people are adding themselves to the map because they are connected to OSU and OSU has played a part in making them who they are. They're showing that they are part of their community—and not just through their profession. In fact, this reinforces how community-oriented OSU students are."

Content from a blog[3] was prominently featured on the site. Blog content was syndicated to a LinkedIn group, and when the PBO

---

(2) Link: poweredbyorange.com
(3) Available at mstnr.me/OregonSt2

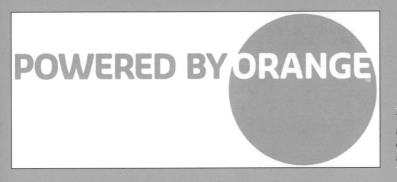

The PBO campaign embraced a wide range of social media channels in an effort to reach a large and diverse audience.

campaign rolled out in Portland on Sept. 21, 2009, it was also syndicated on OSU's Portland Metro[4] website and featured on top-level pages of the OSU site.

Content for the PBO blog was written especially for it, but its editors also shared or repurposed content from elsewhere on campus if it pertained to OSU's research and impact in alternative energy development, disease prevention and management, sustainable food systems, climate change, or other areas where OSU was active.

OSU also focused heavily on developing video content for PBO. Initially, a graduate assistant with video experience created the videos. The PBO team also experimented with other ways of capturing video—providing OSU students with Flip cameras, setting up a booth in the student center and doing intercept interviews with students there, and roaming around campus asking students what "powered by orange" meant to them. Currently, the Powered By Orange YouTube channel[5] contains 127 videos.

Of course, there was a Facebook page.[6] Originally titled "Powered By Orange—10,000 Beavers," its name was changed after it garnered more than 10,000 fans. There was also an extensive Flickr Gallery,[7] which is still being updated. There, fans could post photos of Benny, the OSU mascot, "visiting" various places on campus and around the world. First, they could download an image of Benny from the PBO site[8]—along with a doorhanger, PBO website tags, and wallpaper for a computer screen or smartphone. Finally, OSU set up a separate Twitter feed for the campaign: @poweredbyorange.

As this work proceeded, OSU was quietly promoting all these social channels among friends, fans, and supporters. Right before the campaign launched publicly, Baker said, "we hadn't done much

(4) Link: oregonstate.edu/portland
(5) Available at mstnr.me/OregonSt4
(6) Link: facebook.com/poweredbyorange
(7) Available at mstnr.me/OregonSt6
(8) Available at mstnr.me/OregonSt7

The PBO site allows visitors to connect with the university and community in ways that make sense to each individual.

promotion to speak of—no print buys, no advertising, no PR. But we already had more than 10,000 page views on the PBO site and more than 1,600 members in our Facebook group. PBO resonated well with the alumni who'd discovered it, both young and old."

First Portland, Then Beyond

The Powered By Orange campaign launched publicly in Portland as planned on Sept. 21, 2009, with press events there and in Corvallis. University marketing went all out, wrapping cars on Portland's light rail with PBO graphics and posting signs in cars and buses around the city. University staff members also planned and participated in outreach events in some of the major public squares in Portland. They also placed print ads, developed a swag bag for the launch, made signs that alumni or others with strong OSU affiliations could put in the windows of their businesses, and printed a variety of t-shirts.

September 21 was a big day on the PBO website: The site racked up more accesses than any previous day. More important, 22 percent of the traffic that day was from Portland, and there was a 6 percent overall increase in traffic to the OSU domain from the Portland area that day. Meanwhile, the Facebook group had racked up 3,137 members, and LinkedIn 2,800 members.

The acceptance of PBO on social media and the response to the launch in Portland convinced the OSU team that PBO had legs. Social channels and video provided plenty of examples of cutting-edge OSU research and demonstrated its impact; this message could be reinforced through a variety of stories told in text, video, and images. And the voices sharing those examples were unique— and therefore powerful. They provided something invaluable that, heretofore, branding and messaging campaigns at other universities largely lacked: authenticity.

"Our audiences were prepared to believe that OSU was a small-town school with agricultural roots," Baker said. "In reality, we were doing amazing things that they were not aware of, but they wouldn't have believed glossy ads or videos. By using voices of alumni, we were able to showcase what OSU is doing with great authenticity. And that authenticity is very important to our audience."

Of course, the acceptance of PBO externally didn't mean that people on campus knew much about it. The task of internal champion largely fell to Lawrence, who knew that she had to be proactive in unveiling PBO to OSU constituencies. She said, "I decided to try to take PBO out on a road show to gauge its ability to create excitement, shared vision, anecdotes, and dreams of how to implement it. We also wanted feedback on how to make it better." This meant building awareness by talking with and giving presentations to campus staff and leaders. PBO even became part of the orientation sessions for new students, who received water bottles and window clings with the PBO message.

"The response exceeded my expectations," Lawrence said. "PBO became something for people here to hold on to. Faculty, staff, and students began defining what the campaign meant in their own way. Our goal was to not control this campaign, but to let others run with it. I wanted Beavers of all walks of life to define what it means to be 'powered by orange'—to define their contributions as Beavers to their professions and communities, and to use our main color, orange, to express themselves artistically, to make it their own."

This approach—not monitoring PBO use or locking down its imagery—may be one of the most important elements of PBO's success. It empowered people to adopt PBO and gave them some amount of creative freedom to make it their own. By inspiring adoption, the act of giving up control helped the campaign to go viral. Of course, this was still largely theoretical in 2009, when the staff took the campaign beyond its social media core. But in the real world, too, PBO imagery and the approach of the staff behind it proved to provide the appeal that the campaign needed to expand.

At this point, there hadn't been much pushback on the PBO campaign, Baker reported. What little has occurred, Lawrence noted, came from communications professionals who were uncomfortable with the notion that OSU had launched a campaign and didn't intend to control it. "I run up against some who subscribe to older models— pushing out press releases, paying for ads, controlling events, et

> **By using voices of alumni, we were able to showcase what OSU is doing with great authenticity. And that authenticity is very important to our audience.**

cetera. While we still had these tactics in our mix, we were risking as much as we could to empower larger communities," she said.

Success Breeds Recognition

By spring 2010, PBO was well entrenched on campus and had been recognized by industry heavy-hitters such as Mashable.com, which rarely covered activities like this in higher education, and the Council for Advancement and Support of Education (CASE), which awarded PBO a Grand Gold Award in its Circle of Excellence competition. While this validation was important to PBO, there was plenty of other evidence that the campaign was working well.

Baker noted that keeping PBO flexible was an important element in helping it spread: "We've been flexible enough to allow users to define the campaign for themselves. It's powerful because PBO gives them a language to talk about OSU." That ability to adapt—plus the increasing number of authentic expressions of the campaign across numerous social channels—contributed to PBO's power. Even the students liked it, Baker said.

Indeed, he added, this was one of the surprises of PBO. "Other departments and units at OSU became interested in adapting it for their purposes," he said. "That made us change our thinking and our direction to enable people to use the campaign to be their own advocates. We're trying to be flexible in giving up control. That resonates with people who are used to having control over their communication, rather than having it dictated to them."

On campus, this meant that university divisions, extension offices, colleges, and other units could talk about PBO in their specific contexts, expanding its scope beyond that originally envisioned by its creators. "This wasn't planned for, but it became very useful. Powered By Orange became a buzz word that reached a lot of different audiences," Baker said.

For example, OSU's Alumni Association organized a "Haunted by Orange" homecoming event.[9] Health and Human Services put together a Powered By Orange 5-kilometer run. The athletics department rolled out an "I am Orange" campaign. Faculty even created a "Furloughed by Orange" logo to protest staffing cuts.

And, as further evidence of the fact that the PBO meme had spread, Baker noted, "We even saw it in the media, showing up in titles of articles or as a play on words. It was used without us soliciting the media to use it!"

As the campaign matured, the staff redesigned the Powered By Orange website and kept adapting PBO messaging over time. Early messages revolved around ways in which OSU research has made an impact on everyday lives, particularly around food, water,

---

(9) Available at mstnr.me/OregonSt8

Originally envisioned as a limited marketing campaign, PBO grew into a widespread branding campaign, popular both on and off campus.

modern engineering, sustainable energy needs, and climate. In 2010, messaging shifted toward emphasizing OSU's impact on the economy, primarily through a focus on alumni-run businesses and graduates entering the work force.

To do this, the OSU team initiated the Orange Spotlight.[10] The feature invited nominations for businesses that are "powered by orange." As the web page explained, such businesses are "owned by an Oregon State alum, have lots of OSU alums working there, or are just friends of OSU. They also drive innovation, support economic growth, [and] serve in the community." Each month, a winning business was selected for the Orange Spotlight, which included a feature story on OSU's website, promotion on its social networks, and inclusion in a campaign to push OSU fans to featured businesses. People who nominated businesses were entered in a drawing for OSU football season tickets.

The result? "We got hundreds of nominations for businesses with some kind of OSU connection," Baker said. The benefits could be real for businesses chosen to be profiled. For example, an Orange Spotlight feature on Lamborn Family Vineyards in the Napa Valley, whose owners are graduates of OSU and who use sustainable growing techniques, resulted in great publicity for the vineyard when Wine.com picked up the story. Meanwhile, the Orange Spotlight nominations enabled OSU to gain detailed information on hundreds of businesses with an OSU connection.

Enduring Accomplishments

By 2012, while the spotlight no longer shines so brightly on the Powered By Orange phrase itself, the messaging and imagery

---

(10) Available at mstnr.me/OregonSt9

I AM THE PULSE OF OREGON STATE.

I AM ORANGE.

OS FOOTBALL

BEAVER OS AUTHENTICS

BE ORANGE. OFFICIAL 2009 FOOTBALL TEE ON SALE NOW.
EXCLUSIVELY OFFERED BY BEAVER AUTHENTICS. CLICK HERE TO ORDER.

Click here to continue to OSUBeavers.com   Permanently skip this page

PBO was successful, in part, because the campaign allowed others to adapt its message.

behind the campaign undergirds many ongoing communications and marketing activities at OSU. This is a good time to assess what OSU accomplished with PBO.

For one, PBO demonstrated to the OSU marketing and advancement team, their colleagues across campus, and many others in higher education that social media can and should play a key role in an institutional marketing campaign. The high-profile success of Powered By Orange—not to mention media attention and awards—drew attention to the innovative use of social media and the fact that Facebook, Twitter, and the social channels could work with plenty of other channels and media, from print ads to bus signs. The extent to which a mixture of channels supported and extended Powered By Orange is still distinctive. And though the approach is less risky now than it was in 2009, many colleges and universities today would still not go as far as OSU did in its initial planning and launch of PBO.

Second, PBO was innovative in the freedom it gave to others on campus to adapt its imagery and messaging, slyly co-opting them into the campaign while they did so. This proved to be an effective demonstration that if you create an authentic campaign with compelling messaging and are willing to let it go, others will adapt it and (largely) honor its original intent. Here's another place where the OSU staff took a big risk—one that paid off. Of course, the way you let it go makes all the difference. PBO wasn't just released into the wilds of the OSU campus by email with a couple of embedded links. Lawrence and others spent plenty of time selling PBO's concept and rationale, and they used third-party endorsements of their initial efforts to build support for further development of the campaign.

Third, PBO demonstrated that a long-term campaign can continue to grow and adapt as conditions and channels change. In fact, to be successful, any long-term campaign must evolve. This only happens when staff are listening to friends, fans, and followers and paying close attention to their behavior. Then, they must be willing to shift tactics quickly, based on what they've learned, and they must be prepared to respond quickly when social platforms change.

Fourth, much of PBO's longevity was possible because it was solidly ground in institutional reality. The staff chose particular elements of this reality to package, with appropriate messaging, as "powered by orange." But they chose themes and messages that were important to many of their stakeholders, both on and off campus. They emphasized research that was well established at the university. Their messaging was aspirational, but not so aspirational that it didn't ring true. Because it was so closely linked to institutional reality, it could be supported by authentic stories.

Moving Past Orange

Today, while the staff is no longer as energized by PBO itself, they appreciate the enduring value of the many assets they created as part of the campaign. Now they're assessing their progress and trying to figure out how to evolve further. "We view PBO as a really successful campaign, and since we've been doing it for three years, we don't want to put it aside entirely," said Melody Oldfield, director of marketing. "We're still using the color orange to represent OSU, and that really works for us, especially since we focus on a single color instead of a pair of colors—we're not powered by orange and black, for example. Every week or so, we have a conversation in which we ask about something, 'How would this fit with PBO?' So I don't think we'll ever be 'done' with it," she said.

She anticipates that the PBO website, which has been the focus for collection of a large amount of content, will evolve into more of a magazine-style site so that OSU can leverage these stories and continue to demonstrate how people associated with the university are making a difference. "The goal is to be able to continue to have it work for us, so we can be flexible with our marketing and storytelling," said Oldfield.

A key aspect of the PBO campaign from the start was the notion of "launch and learn." Looking back over the three years of the campaign, it's clear to Oldfield and Baker that the university learned a lot from launching PBO. While "powered by orange" may have been a tagline initially, it evolved into an organizing principle for OSU's marketing efforts. That's one enduring contribution of the campaign.

Moreover, the organization of PBO and its rollout provided a template that staff can replicate in other instances. One example Oldfield cited was the opening of a second OSU campus in Bend—OSU is the first university in Oregon to create a second

> **Every week or so, we have a conversation in which we ask about something, "How would this fit with PBO?" So I don't think we'll ever be "done" with it.**

location, and the PBO campaign provided an effective model for communicating about the opening, both in Bend and more broadly among the university's constituents.

Another early lesson was that OSU staff would have to be proactive in generating some of the content they needed to feed their social channels. Video was an early challenge. The void was partially filled when communicators on campus generated videos that could be used by PBO. "For example, a staff member in international studies recorded about 15 videos of students sharing what PBO means to them—and speaking their native language. This was part of a recruiting program to bring international students to OSU," Baker said. The PBO team could then repurpose those videos for the campaign.

The PBO team also compensated for the initial lack of user-generated video in other, creative ways. "We hosted an event to get students to share their definition of PBO. We attracted about 100 students and, as a result, created ambassadors to talk about OSU. Now we do this wherever we go," Baker said.

A further lesson from a long-running campaign like Powered By Orange is that it can be easy to get bored creatively. Oldfield advises, "Figure out a way to avoid campaign fatigue, if you can. Trying to keep it fresh for us was hard. Around the middle of our second year, we began asking, 'If we don't use the phrase Powered By Orange, how do we keep momentum going?' So we were actively looking for messaging and ways to keep PBO fresh visually."

Finally, the campaign's success depended on strong leadership, in several respects. First, support from a visionary leader—vice president Luanne Lawrence—helped get PBO off the ground and empowered OSU staff to stretch in ways that were perceived as very risky at the time. "This is not a high-comfort area for some in higher ed," Lawrence observed in 2009. "If I weren't a vice president with such a passion for making this campaign viral and in using a mix of traditional with very nontraditional media, I'm not sure this PBO campaign would have seen the light of day."

Lawrence made developing on-campus support for PBO a priority and by all accounts was a tireless advocate for it. By the time she left the university in 2010 (she is now vice president for communications at the University of South Carolina), the campaign was well entrenched and successful, making it difficult for a successor to tinker with it or reshape it—had new leadership wanted to do so.

Second, Baker said, he realized how important it was to incorporate campaign messaging into leadership communications—newsletters, emails, speeches, and other communications from the president, the provost, and other senior leaders. "Integrating these messages into leadership communications from the start would have helped immensely," he said. "I believe that people would have embraced it even more fully than they did." **sw**

Using Social Media to Shape, Socialize, Launch, and Monitor Brand: American University

By Teresa Flannery | @higheredwonk

Teresa (Terry) Flannery has worked in higher education marketing roles for two decades. She is American University's first vice president for communication. There she established a full communications and marketing organization and program, beginning with market research to inform the brand strategy.

When American University chose a bold concept for a campaign to illustrate its brand, we faced a dilemma. Our internal team had developed a concept that addressed the brand strategy requirements very effectively. However, creative testing revealed that the concept's greatest strengths also represented its greatest risks. In order to manage a successful launch, it was clear that we would first need to "socialize" the concept through a variety of channels, especially social media.

Getting Our Wonk On

Located in the nation's capital, chartered by Congress and founded in 1893 to meet President George Washington's ideal of a national university to build the public service, American had long been known in the Mid-Atlantic region and in certain academic circles for its historic and distinguished programs in public affairs and international service. Market research demonstrated, however, that most audiences did not effectively distinguish between American and competitors in Washington, and outside of our home market, many did not recognize American University or know its academic strengths. We needed a simple, distinctive concept that would not only build on current brand associations, but also develop recognition for the extraordinary student experience at American, the quality of the faculty, and expertise in other areas like law, communications, arts, and business. Moreover, that concept needed to help us position new strategic initiatives, like the development of programs in public health and neurosciences.

The idea for the WONK campaign came from a source close to home. Our team was inspired by an illustration that Nate Beeler, an AU alumnus and award-winning editorial and political cartoonist, created for the cover of our university magazine during the 2008 presidential election season. Beeler roughly sketched the skyline of Washington's monuments in the background, and in the foreground, depicted a group of bald eagles (AU's mascot), perched on a wire, that on closer inspection appeared to be bespectacled men in grey suits, chirping in unison, "Wonk, wonk, wonk!"

WONK fit the requirements for American's brand strategy like a glove. Our concept needed to grab attention, and this short, curious, strange-sounding word surely did that. Our campaign would need to reinforce the brand position, which focused on active citizenship, learning from leaders, and Washington as a powerful laboratory for learning. In Washington, wonks had long been known inside the Beltway as intelligent and well-connected influencers who used their knowledge to influence policy and politics, so the idea had the ability to call to mind our known brand associations. And since "wonk" is "know" spelled backward, the word had recently come into vogue to reflect passionate experts of all sorts—not just policy wonks—so it had the potential to help us pivot from historic academic strengths to more recent areas of expertise. In short, the WONK concept perfectly matched all our criteria.

At the same time, however, it introduced several risks. First, the word "wonk" was virtually unknown to traditional-age undergraduates and many outside of Washington. In focus groups, when shown the word alone, prospective students had no recognition. Asked for any associations, they said, "It sounds funny" and "Willy Wonka," but they were at a loss to define it. When shown a definition, however, of an intellectually curious person who uses deep knowledge to effect meaningful change on issues he or she cares about, they warmed up. And in a pattern that repeated itself with focus groups of all audiences, when they realized that "wonk" was "know" spelled backward, and a wonk was someone who knows something backward and forward, they smiled and leaned forward, recognizing the cleverness in the simple word. And finally, a word that focused on a passion for knowledge was roundly appreciated as a good fit for an academic institution.

Second, for older audiences, the word had dated and negative associations that lagged well behind current usage. Some people thought of wonks as socially awkward nerds who narrowly focused on policy and handed off their knowledge to others who would actually do something with it. For our active, engaged citizens, and on a campus routinely recognized by *Princeton Review* as the most politically active in the nation, those associations wouldn't do. When we showed focus groups examples of current usage, as well as illustrations of poised and confident wonks who were actively using their expertise in many areas, not just policy, again, the concept worked like a charm.

> **Since "wonk" is "know" spelled backward, the word had recently come into vogue to reflect passionate experts of all sorts—not just policy wonks—so it had the potential to help us pivot from historic academic strengths to more recent areas of expertise.**

A 2008 cover for *American Magazine*, illustrated by alumnus Nate Beeler, inspired the WONK campaign.

Making matters more challenging, we knew that the first thing someone was likely to do if they didn't recognize the word was to Google it. But online references such as Wikipedia and Urban Dictionary showed only dated associations, not the usage that we saw in the media hundreds of times every day, reflecting positive references to smart people who use their knowledge and passion to do real good.

And finally, for those who either knew the term or looked it up, it seemed to be deeply rooted in policy, just like AU. We didn't want to limit our brand to its historic associations. But when we showed focus groups sample ads that demonstrated wonks of all sorts, the smiles broke out again and we actually saw people adopting the term. They began to ask, "What kind of wonk am I?"

So we had a powerful distinctive concept that made people stop, consider, and identify with it, and it held the capacity to tell the story AU needed to tell—but only if we could successfully define it in modern terms that showed smart, cool people using all sorts of expertise to actively engage with and change the world.

Paving the Way for Launch

After the creative testing, the brand team, the university's marketing advisory council, and our leadership all recognized

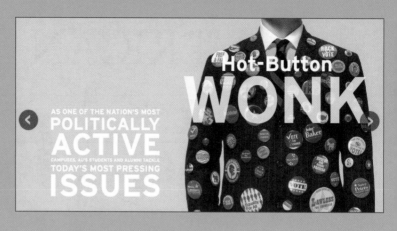

Adopting WONK as a branding strategy was a risk; initial focus groups revealed a general unfamiliarity with the word and its positive attributes.

that we were not ready to launch our brand strategy. Instead, we knew we had to first familiarize our community with the term, demonstrate how the WONK campaign would do the job we needed it to do, and lay the groundwork for those who searched for the term through digital and social tools.

From the beginning, AU's brand team included members of the marketing and communications staff representing all the important areas of strategy, creative development, and execution. Designers, writers, editors, a videographer, a copywriter, a web strategist, and a social media coordinator were all part of the team, and all had responsibility for bringing their areas of expertise to the team's work. Now the team needed to develop tools that would lay the groundwork for launch, and it was clear that students and social media were going to be key elements over the next few months.

AU's brand team met weekly (on what we called Wonk Wednesdays) and turned its attention from creative development to educating various audiences about wonks prior to launch. We had evidence from the creative testing about where each audience— students, alumni, faculty and staff, parents, others in higher ed—was likely to be, based on demographics like age, geographic region, and familiarity with American University and Washington.

For some audiences, more traditional channels were appropriate. Faculty and staff were very important. We wanted them to understand how the campaign reflected the brand they lived every day, so sharing elements of the campaign and the rationale were key. They were easy to reach and in close proximity, so we invited them in small groups to luncheons and teas, where they could learn about the campaign and rationale for WONK, see the relationship of "know" to "wonk," view evidence of the term's versatile and positive use in mainstream media, and share their feedback and ideas for refinement before launch.

For these audiences, our education tools were slide presentations, supported by video and web content on a website named American

Wonks[1] that, at that point, had no visible relationship to AU. The website's purpose was to provide a definition, examples of wonks in the news, and original content that demonstrated the relationship of "know" and "wonk" as well as the variety of wonks, well beyond policy and politics. Every luncheon and tea ended with the distribution of bookmarks—lenticulars that shifted from KNOW to WONK, provided the definition of wonks (intellectually curious, engaged citizens who use their knowledge to create change), and listed the website url. By the time we had finished with these gatherings, we had identified almost 50 brand ambassadors—faculty and staff who were excited about the campaign and were willing to participate by demonstrating what kinds of wonks they were— on the web, in class, and elsewhere. (We followed up with these individuals to take their photos and write wonk profiles, presented as "People in the KNOW," when the brand launch began.) We also heard from those who were not fans—helpful as well, because it helped us prepare for the inevitable criticism that surfaces when an organization introduces a new identity or positioning strategy, often because it reduces a complex institution to a few simple ideas.

Enlisting Social Media Natives

When it came to presenting the campaign to younger audiences, we realized we needed more digital natives than we currently had on the brand team. We put out a call for students to join two student brand teams, one for undergraduates and one for graduate students. We hired them for a summer internship for the weeks between summer and fall terms (with a small, one-time stipend of $500 each and an expectation that they would give us at least 10 hours per week). We immersed the students in the market research, the brand strategy, the campaign rationale, the creative testing results, and the challenge: How would we pave the way for the WONK campaign to be successful?

The student teams were enthusiastic and excited. They were required to develop proposals of their ideas for consideration by the brand team, and we chose several for implementation.

Then we set the students loose. They researched the sources and means to influence definitions of "wonk" in dictionaries and reference sites. They submitted content to provide evidence of current use in the media. When these sites proved difficult to influence, they quickly decided that they needed to define the term themselves.

One of their early projects involved "man on the street" interviews in Washington. Donning black shirts printed with WONK in white type, they took videocameras and definitions

---

(1) Link: americanwonks.com

of the word to tourists, students, shoppers—anyone who would agree to be on camera. "What's a wonk?" they would ask. Absent other information, their interview subjects would demonstrate, in humorous detail, how little the term was known. Then the student interviewers would share the definition and show that "wonk" was "know" spelled backward, and the subjects would jump in with examples of wonks and ideas about what kind of wonk they were or would like to be.

The interviews were lightly edited with music and a few effects, and then posted on the American Wonks website. The team established a Facebook page and began to tweet and share links to the interviews. The videos became part of our presentations to various audiences—current student leaders, faculty and staff, alumni—about the upcoming campaign.

Another example of the students' social work was a stop-motion video. Challenged to show the relationship between "wonk" and "know," and to show that "wonk" applied to experts in all areas, not just policy, they scripted and produced the video,[2] which was then posted to Youtube, Facebook, and Twitter in support of the pre-launch efforts.

A final example of the student teams' work was the creation of a "wonk box." They built their own version of a soap box—a small wooden box that served as a podium, emblazoned with WONK. They took this across campus and around the city to engage in impromptu speeches on issues about which they were passionate and hoped to create meaningful change. These, too, were filmed and shared through social channels, still without explicitly identifying the American Wonks website as associated with American University.

Preparing to Launch

For each of the digital and social channels, we monitored activity to track growth and response. We also tracked the use of the term "wonk" in mainstream media across the world, as well as doing web searches for "wonk." Interestingly, the frequency of the use of the term began to increase, most dramatically just at launch. Again, we aggregated this evidence and incorporated it into presentations of the campaign.

The pre-launch phase, which lasted four months, reinforced our confidence in the power of the concept to serve as a successful branding tool. In the process, we learned which approaches most effectively created a desire to learn more about the idea and adopt it, and we embraced refinements to the creative work of the campaign. We also amassed a significant amount of original content, created by our own students, faculty, and staff, that would

Each design of shirt used a different color of material (recycled, of course), and most included an original illustration of a particular type of wonk, courtesy of Nate Beeler, the original source of our inspiration.

(2) Available at mstnr.me/AmUniv2

The AU student team created a stop-motion video as part of the pre-launch phase of the American Wonk campaign.

help us widely introduce the campaign through our own brand ambassadors in the fall of 2010.

Next, we established a new American Wonks website. This time, we clearly branded the site with AU's identity and incorporated the campaign's creative developments, with a strong leading purpose of the site to define the term and introduce the campaign. We prepared the primary AU social channels (Facebook, Twitter, YouTube, Vimeo, and more) to simultaneously introduce WONK and link to the site. Brand ambassadors stood ready to respond in their own words to reactions of all sorts when the campaign launched.

If It Works for Rock Concerts...

Incorporating input from the students, we developed 20 variations of a wonk t-shirt. On the sleeve, each shared an equation that represented our graphic shorthand for the definition of the term: Smart + Passionate + Engaged + Focused = WONK. Each design of shirt used a different color of material (recycled, of course), and most included an original illustration of a particular type of wonk, courtesy of Nate Beeler, the original source of our inspiration.

We sought to take advantage of the usual rhythm of the new semester. During welcome week, hundreds of new students participating in our Freshman Service Experience were given "Service WONK" shirts to wear to their service sites. We shot footage of them getting on Metro trains headed out to sites all over the city. New international students were introduced to the campaign and were given "Global WONK" shirts. Residence hall staff and move-in volunteers received "Welcome WONK" shirts. After each of these presentations, we monitored the traffic on our social channels, the AU website, and the specially created campaign site.

On the first day of classes, a barbeque on the Quad for the entire community served as the site for the community launch. We announced the event and a t-shirt giveaway on Facebook and

The term "wonk" was understood in the D.C. area, but the WONK campaign sought to expand the word's reach and relevance to those outside the immediate area.

Twitter, as well as in an interview given to the student newspaper detailing the campaign's goals and objectives. Then we set up a booth under a tent and hung up all the different t-shirts in a display rather like a concert concession booth. The staff and student brand team answered questions and gave away shirts and bookmarks. One end of the tent had shirts imprinted with "_____ WONK" and fabric markers that allowed students to identify what kind of wonk they were. (Residence hall floors and Greek letter organizations were the most prominent choices.)

We produced 5,400 t-shirts and anticipated giving some of them away over the course of the three-hour event. Instead, we ran out of shirts. As we ran out of specific designs, our social media coordinator tweeted and posted which were the first to go—Green WONK, Peace WONK, and Political WONK. As others ran out, he kept posting, creating a live demonstration of the most popular types of wonks on the AU campus.

We were gratified that student interest demonstrated an understanding of the term and the desire to affiliate. In the days that followed, we were even more gratified to see students and others wearing their shirts on campus and off. A faculty member in the school of communication told of seeing a graduate student she did not know in the grocery store. They were both wearing "Communication WONK" shirts and swapped a high-five as they passed in the aisle.

The Social Media Response

We anticipated that there would be some strong reactions, positive and negative, to the campaign. Any time an organization decides to actively manage the way it represents itself, stakeholders rush to chime in. At this point, the role of social media was to help us monitor and respond to concerns and criticism, and to reinforce support. On most of our social channels, as well as in independent blogs and in comments in mainstream media, we took our share of lumps on a host of predictable issues. However, our student brand teams and faculty and staff ambassadors were more than willing to share their point of view, often in early counterpoint to criticism or negative feedback. Their views, shared willingly and enthusiastically, helped us keep the public conversation balanced.

Moreover, every example of adoption—a student using a WONK campaign photo as her Facebook profile photo, or an alumnus tweeting a picture of his new WONK license plate—provided opportunities for the ambassadors to share and reinforce the new brand position through social media.

In addition to monitoring response to the early campaign reactions, the team used social media as a tool to increase affiliation and adoption. At each phase of the campaign, we included a way to engage with it. Challenges with faculty and alumni ("match wits against our wonks") were promoted through social channels and drove users to the campaign website. The users could then share their scores on Facebook. We ran a weekly contest that asked students, "What kind of wonk are you?" Students earned a chance to win an iPad if they took a picture of themselves with their favorite type of wonk and posted it through Twitter or Facebook. And when our students presented President Bill Clinton with AU's first Wonk of the Year award, before a packed arena, those in the audience pushed AU and Bill Clinton to a trending topic on Twitter. Student government leaders identified this as the turning point in student attitudes toward the campaign. Social engagement through posts, shares, and tweets increased 175 percent during this phase of the campaign.

Outcomes

We're now two years into the WONK campaign. Our use of social media was crucial in educating, launching, and encouraging adoption of the term "wonk" as a means to convey American University's distinctive brand. Facebook and Twitter channels, both the university's and those directly related to the campaign, continue to play important roles as a part of our overall web presence, providing ways for us to engage with our audiences and increase traffic to the campaign site. In the first phase of advertising for the campaign, web traffic (visitors) increased 58 percent on the AU home page and more than doubled on our

Every example of adoption—a student using a WONK campaign photo as her Facebook profile photo, or an alumnus tweeting a picture of his new WONK license plate—provided opportunities for the ambassadors to share and reinforce the new brand position through social media.

admissions vertical. That trend was consistent with increased prospects (17 percent) and a record number of applications for freshman admission (representing a 10 percent gain in one year).

American University now comes up fifth or sixth in searches of the term "wonk," whereas we didn't register at all before the campaign. Dictionary sites still come up first and second, however, and we have had no luck persuading those sites to reflect the current use of the term. We will persist, and we think we will eventually succeed.

This year, *US News & World Report* ranked American University higher than ever before, a six-point swing in one year—a result of the improvement in our academic reputation. When we put out the news on Facebook, it drew more "likes" than any other university post we've made on that page.

Lessons Learned

If there is one thing that's changed in marketing in the past decade, it's that any change in your brand or identity must incorporate social media in the very early planning, or you won't be ready to manage and leverage the reaction. Think of social channels as the town square, where important announcements and public debates will happen, whether you are there or not. Better to be there, learning and influencing, than to let it happen without you.

A surprise for us was how useful these social channels were to us *before* launch. Our students taught us that this form of communication is a powerful educational tool that can lay the groundwork for important institutional initiatives, as well as a terrific means of content generation that authentically radiates the brand. **sw**

How a Flash Mob Helped Build Awareness for Nelson Mandela Metropolitan University

By Kylie Stanley Larson | @kylieslarson

Kylie Stanley Larson is a project manager at mStoner, where she serves as a primary point of contact for clients working with her consulting team. She has a broad background in higher education including policy research, fundraising, and college admissions counseling.

Flash mobs are a recognizable fad in America and the United Kingdom; however, they are rarely done in South Africa. In 2011, Nelson Mandela Metropolitan University (NMMU) made waves as the first South African university to organize one, earning thousands of YouTube video views of the event and a Silver Award in the CASE Circle of Excellence Awards in 2012—placing the university along with MIT, Cornell, and other widely recognized institutional brands. More importantly, however, NMMU was able to use the flash mob to achieve measurable results in student recruitment and brand recognition when the video was marketed through social and traditional media.

NMMU sits in Port Elizabeth, on the southern coast of South Africa about 750 kilometers (466 miles) east of Cape Town. A relatively new entity, NMMU was born out of the 2005 merger of three historical institutions in the area: PE Technikon (PE), the Port Elizabeth campus of Vista University (Vista PE), and the University of Port Elizabeth (UPE). UPE, which opened in 1964, was South Africa's first dual-language residential university, with courses conducted in both English and Afrikaans.

Today, NMMU includes six campuses, employs nearly 4,000 individuals, and enrolls 27,000 undergraduate and graduate students in a broad range of educational programs. On Twitter, NMMU brands itself as "a new-generation university, distinguished by its wide range of study options and commitment to serving society." Its website outlines a vision "to be a dynamic African university, recognised for its leadership in generating cutting-edge knowledge for a sustainable future."

Shortly after receiving the CASE award, Director of Marketing and Corporate Relations Pieter Swart commented in a news interview,

NMMU @NMMU4U   23 Jul
Watch Kayla's dream come true at bit.ly/P15kh5. Remember
#NMMU applications close on 1 August.
▶ View media   ↩ Reply   ⇄ Retweet   ★ Favorite

NMMU tailored its campaign for each social media channel, including Twitter. (top)

Dressed to blend in with other shoppers, the 50 NMMU choir members filled the mall's food court as they broke into song. (bottom)

"We are thrilled with the news of this award as it positions us as a global player—a university that can hold its own internationally."

The Organized Mob

The NMMU Marketing and Corporate Relations Office consists of 30 staff members with varying roles and levels of responsibility. Two individuals, though, have accepted much of the charge for social media operations: Debbie Derry, senior communications manager, and Beverley Erickson, online community manager. "Social media is so demanding if you're going to do it properly, because of the immediacy," Derry explained. "It's not static, not like a website—it's constant engagement. That takes so much time."

The university supports official channels on Facebook, Twitter, and YouTube. With over 2,600 followers on Twitter, 6,300 likes on Facebook, and 15,500 video views on YouTube, its footprint grows each day. Updates include both information for internal audiences (such as those posted after a city water pipe broke on campus) and external brand-building posts (such as "Did You Know" tweets posted by @NMMU4U). The social media channels also encourage community participation—for example, a Facebook drive urging students to enter a "What does NMMU mean to you?" competition.

Conscious of social media trends, Derry and Erickson originally conceived of conducting a flash mob at NMMU after seeing a video of a Hallelujah Chorus flash mob staged in a shopping mall and another in London's Victoria Station. They had complete confidence in their university choir's ability to participate in a caper of that size. NMMU receives international attention for its choir, and the group has performed worldwide, in locations as diverse as Beijing, Chicago, Austria, and Italy. Yet, as Derry noted, they "needed an excuse" for a flash mob event, because well-organized flash mobs are expensive, and the NMMU budget is "very limited."

Derry and Erickson posed the flash mob idea to the university's design agency, Boomtown Strategic Brand Agency, which then pitched it as a way to increase admission applications to NMMU in advance of the August 1 deadline. It wasn't until June 2011 that the corporate relations team received the go-ahead (and essential financing) for the undertaking. By that point, they faced two significant challenges: First, they had only a couple of weeks to plan and execute the flash mob, and second, NMMU exam week fell in the middle of their timeline.

Unwilling to let the opportunity pass, the marketing and corporate relations team approached the student-led choir with the project. The 50-member choir took the challenges in stride and immediately began preparing a set list, adhering to the admission campaign theme of "You" and considering songs from a range of genres. They also conceived of a small-group practice schedule that allowed participants time together but acknowledged the reality of exam week. The first rehearsal with the entire group did not take place until June 24, the eve of the performance. Yet any effects of the rushed timeline and scheduling challenges are not even noticeable in recordings of the event.

At 11:30 a.m. on Saturday, June 25, 2011, the members of the NMMU choir strategically placed themselves throughout the food court of Greenacres Shopping Centre in Port Elizabeth. Surprised shoppers first heard a booming baritone, disguised as a maintenance worker high up on a ladder; soon the whole choir was in action. The show lasted five and a half minutes, and the video is compelling in its entirety. The songs ranged from "Shosholoza," an African folk song, to "Fireworks," a pop song by American artist Katy Perry. Images from the event show spectators initially befuddled, but soon enamored with the routine; at the end of the set, shoppers are softly singing and unconsciously dancing along with the choir's rendition of "You're the One That I Want" from the 1978 film *Grease*.

Professionally recorded and filmed by Rooftop Productions, the video of the flash mob[1] was posted on YouTube 10 days later. The video was viewed, liked, and shared by thousands across the world. As of October 2012, the video had more than 145,000 views, nearly 1,000 likes, and 230 comments. "The real campaign was to get students to apply before the first of August, but from [a general] brand-building perspective, it was fantastic," Erickson said.

Media stories after the event heralded NMMU for being both the first university in South Africa to successfully stage a flash mob and

> **The show lasted five and a half minutes, and the video is compelling in its entirety. The songs ranged from "Shosholoza," an African folk song, to "Fireworks," a pop song by American artist Katy Perry.**

(1) Available at mstnr.me/NMMU1

for being the first group to stage a flash mob in Port Elizabeth. One commenter on YouTube exclaimed, "We need more and more of this!!! I LOVE South Africa!" Another noted, "What a delight to see amongst the often negative reports on South Africa. A wonderful example of South Africa at the best of times! South African and proud of it."

"The thing that struck us most was the incredible sense of patriotism," Derry said. "That's one thing that we've always noticed Americans are very good at—Americans are so patriotic. South Africans are not nearly up to that level. Seeing the connection that people felt watching this flash mob—the diversity, the vibrancy, the singing, the connection to the university. Those who knew the university felt very close to it after watching. Those who didn't know the university, we could get an idea by reading the comments that they, too, felt an affinity and they saw something that they really liked."

Erickson highlighted the top two quotes on YouTube as evidence of the extraordinary sense of patriotism:

> » "I love feeling homesick for a place I've never been to."
>   — qpsumusic
> » "Proud to be South African." — 88skydiver

The flash mob video not only was a social media success but also produced concrete results. That year NMMU saw a 27 percent increase in applications, from 23,756 applications in 2010 to 30,141 applications in 2011. While noting that the increase can be attributed to a number of factors, Erickson said, "We have no doubt that the flash mob contributed to that." A year after the initial production, Erickson and Derry received word of the CASE award. Said Erickson, "It was the first time we've entered anything internationally, and to be up against those names like MIT and Johns Hopkins ..."

Building on Dreams

The Marketing and Corporate Relations team did not rest on their laurels following the flash mob success. The group quickly began work on the next social media adventure: Dream Starter.[2] The launching pad for Dream Starter is its website, where the campaign beckons to idealistic and energetic students considering NMMU:

> Is yours the one that began on your maths book cover page?
> Or perhaps age and hope inspired you to picture
> a world absent of pain?
> But you could be the brave who challenges the grain,

---

(2) Link: dream-starter.co.za

The Dream Starter campaign builds on social media lessons with high-impact YouTube videos at its heart.

Who pursues excellence instead of gain ...
Or maybe let's say you're just a lover of
the way things are made,
The way night intricately turns to day
Or the way that same book you scribbled in, can provide
a lifetime of change.
Whatever your dream is,
Start it at NMMU.

The campaign extends beyond the website presentation into both print and social media; the highlights of the campaign are the corresponding YouTube videos. NMMU asked visiting students to post their dreams to an on-campus wall using provided notecards. Prospective students were then surprised at home by NMMU supporters who helped them to take the first step toward achieving their goals. All of these high moments were captured on video and posted to YouTube as part of the Dream Starter video series.

In one of the episodes[3] we see teenager Kayla Draai called at home by South African TV personality Michael Mol, who personally invites her to come to the studio and explore her dream of "acting or presenting, anything to do in media." Kayla's video is, arguably, even more powerful than the previous cycle's flash mob display.

The NMMU Marketing and Corporate Relations staff members also carry the Dream Starter message throughout their work on Twitter and Facebook. Just before applications closed in 2012 @NMMU4U tweeted, "Watch Kayla's dream come true at http://bit.ly/P15kh5. Remember #NMMU applications close on 1

(3) Available at mstnr.me/NMMU2

August." Derry and Erickson noted that each channel is unique and the message is tailored to be appropriate for the audience.

"We'd love to do more, but it's about capacity," said Erickson. Ideally, the team would like to hire someone for a full-time social media position. While they do enlist the help of student interns, and they've managed to cobble together impressive material in addition to juggling other communications work, they believe a full-time person could bring continuity, institutional knowledge, and additional quality. "You can be less formal on Facebook and Twitter, but we won't compromise on quality. We are an institution of higher learning, and we never want to lose sight of that," Derry said.

Thus far the monetary investment in social media has been minimal, and the results impressive—judging from the audience interactions and growing number of followers. "We're doing the best we can, and we feel we're reaping the benefits: We've had rewards, and we've had awards," said Erickson.

So, what's next? A lip dub! Inspired once again by YouTube, the team would like to create a video similar to the Grand Rapids "American Pie" feature.[4] But, as Derry noted, "It's a big job. We need the money."

The Takeaways

Based on their experience in creating memorable social media campaigns, Derry and Erickson advise other communications professionals to keep a few principles in mind:

Inspiration abounds. The NMMU Marketing and Corporate Relations staff members are active participants in the social media world. They get the best ideas for their institution by carefully watching and listening to material produced in other places around the globe. As noted earlier, the Hallelujah Chorus flash mob inspired them to pull off a flash mob of their own, and they're already thinking of ways to replicate the Grand Rapids lip dub. They take pride in adopting such cultural phenomena and making them distinctly South African—and therefore relevant to the NMMU context.

Social media takes time. Each channel requires careful planning, monitoring, and responding—in a way that is unique and appropriate to the channel. Erickson and Derry both repeatedly noted the strain this places on a team with many other job responsibilities. Social media is always on, and it would be within reason to assign a full-time individual to the task.

Social media messaging must be appropriate to the channel. The communication norm and expectations on YouTube are significantly different than those on Twitter, for example. Yet far too many institutions blast out the same message to each of

> **Social media takes time. Each channel requires careful planning, monitoring, and responding—in a way that is unique and appropriate to the channel.**

(4) Available at mstnr.me/NMMU3

their social media accounts. NMMU's staff members learned to communicate the same idea in many different ways as they switch between channels, and this helped to launch the messages to a much wider audience.

Campaigns should have both short-term and long-term goals. The first goal of the flash mob caper was to increase applications to NMMU in advance of the August 1 deadline. However, the corporate relations team was fully aware that this investment was also meant to influence the larger perception of the university and would ideally build awareness and inform opinions for years.

Social media should be an amplified truth. It seems as if every few months there is a new social media channel. The challenge as institutions join each new venue is to remain true to their core mission, even when they're communicating in a substantially new way. Institutional accounts need to keep the messaging in line with university core values, even as the form of the message shifts.   **SW**

Building Public Support for Campus Expansion in Wisconsin's Referendum 2010: Madison Area Technical College

By Ellen Foley | @Ellen_M_Foley

Ellen Foley is a veteran journalist, president of Foley Media Group, and senior communications strategist at Rippe Keane Marketing in Madison, Wis. She led the successful Madison Area Technical College $134-million referendum in 2010.

With the hiring in late 2004 of a college president who had led successful referendums in Iowa, Madison Area Technical College began to put into action its strategic vision of "transforming lives, one at a time." Its 1970s-era buildings would become the foundation for a 21st-century campus to open in 2013.

How would the college pay for the needed changes during a recession that walloped the nation and Wisconsin? With the strong leadership of Jon Bales, then-chairman of the district's board of trustees, in 2008 the college began to quietly consider the risky strategy of a referendum. The clever use of integrated media channels, hitchhiking messaging on the election campaigns for hotly contested races, and a very tight campaign timeline to avoid undue opposition helped the referendum pass with almost 60 percent of the vote, to the surprise of everyone, including the college president, Bettsey Barhorst.[1]

"Looking at 'conventional' wisdom, the referendum should not have passed," said Linda Brei, a community leader who ran the community advocacy campaign. "On the other hand, when you have so little time, you only think about the task. We all had either enthusiasm or know-how or both. We had a good plan and simply executed it."

In the summer of 2010, the timing seemed impossible. The economy had been faltering in Wisconsin and the nation for more than 18 months. An anti-tax mood was emerging. The college weighed its options carefully. Eventually the district board decided to ask voters for $134 million in tax increases with only eight weeks before Election Day. The campaign would need strong tactics to

---

(1) Available at mstnr.me/MadTech1

convince recession-weary taxpayers to essentially give themselves
an added property tax to build the new campus.

In the face of anti-tax sentiment that ushered in a conservative
governor who would soon begin to reduce state spending on
education, Madison Area Technical College, which prefers to be
called Madison College, used extensive communication strategies
that engaged the media and business community. It also reached
out to student populations and the Twitter generation in ways
previously unknown at the college.

To the voting public, the move to go to referendum may have
looked like a last-minute decision. However, the board's action
followed a successful campaign by the Madison College Foundation
to elicit donations from almost 70 percent of college faculty and
staff, more than three times the typical participation rate at other
community colleges. The foundation had created an internal
person-to-person network, a website, a newsletter, and other
communication tools for outreach. The lessons learned in that
campaign would prove useful when faculty, staff, and consultants
began working in late spring 2010 to develop consensus about
whether a referendum was needed and what kind of message could
support its success.

This careful, thorough, consensus-oriented approach reached out
to all corners of the college and became the key management tool that
allowed the referendum leaders to move fast and employ innovative
communications techniques, particularly in the social space. This
was the hallmark of the campaign and led to a national award.

I was the executive leader of this campaign. When President
Barhorst assigned me to begin researching the possibilities in 2009,
none of us had a good sense of what we were in for. Initially, support
for the referendum among internal leaders was wobbly. However,
the president's enthusiasm combined with the district board's
support would in the end push the effort forward.

Smart Community

Madison College serves approximately 750,000 residents in 12
counties on nine sites. About 40,000 students attend classes at the
college. Its largest campus was built near the Madison airport in
the late 1980s and had no major upgrades in 30 years.

The college experienced a 22 percent enrollment increase
between 2005 and 2010. Facilities were overcrowded, and waiting
lists, particularly in nursing and other health care programs,
were common. Other programs slated for growth were protective
services and advanced manufacturing.

In the summer of 2010, teams of faculty and staff pulled together
a plan for garnering referendum support with the knowledge that
the district board needed to approve the action. The college had

used the word "smart" in other campaigns, most recently for the foundation effort, which was called "Smart Future." The organizers dubbed a potential referendum campaign "Smart Community," and an advocacy group that began organizing separately from the college began to call itself "InvestSmart." An internal promotional campaign, led by the college's marketing department, dubbed "Get Smart," had a lot of fun using the vintage television show's themes.

One word here about the rules of a referendum for Wisconsin's technical college system. The college, as a taxpayer-supported entity, could only *educate* voters about the possible benefits of a tax increase. Employees could not *advocate*. The job of advocacy belonged to the separate community-based organization, which operated with non-taxpayer money. Keeping these efforts separate was a mandate. It was challenging, however, because the goals of the two groups were similar.

With white papers and elevator speeches in hand, the organizers developed communications plans and brainstormed materials. The college ramped up an internal campaign to gather support from its 40,000 students and 1,200 faculty and staff, who were seen as ambassadors who could carry pro-college messages to their neighbors and families.

The central call to action, gleaned from research, was the need for job training. Copies of the elevator speech were stuffed into folders that were brought to the more than 100 community meetings. The folders included FAQs and other college facts. To our surprise, participants clamored to take the folders home with them. The elevator speech read:

> This November, voters will find the Madison College Smart Community plan on their ballot. It's a $133,770,000 plan for new facilities, renovations, and upgrades to meet the increasing demand of local residents who need affordable education and job training.
>
> Madison College is considering this now because student enrollment and waiting lists are at all-time highs, while interest rates and construction costs are at all-time lows.
>
> This expansion will provide an opportunity for more students to learn in high-tech classrooms that will prepare them for the increasingly complex jobs that keep our community running.
>
> The property tax impact on a home valued at $245,000 will be $33.10 per year, or $2.74 a month.

The document went on to emphasize enhancements in three

It's time to secure that promise for the next 100 years.

Zebradog, a design firm in Madison, WI, helped communicate a vision for the college's future.

popular and oversubscribed programs: health care, protective services, and advanced manufacturing, also known as high-tech manufacturing using robotics.

As the message was taking form, leaders outlined a communications and marketing strategy that integrated traditional and innovative new media approaches. The plan included direct mail; radio ads; a small television buy; an emotional video;[2] newspaper endorsements; and 132 face-to-face presentations, including meetings with our faculty, staff, and students. The college mailed informational postcards to more than 14,000 faculty and staff at the University of Wisconsin-Madison. Leaders organized appearances by Madison College staff and faculty at community centers, service clubs, media outlets, and county boards. Communications leaders also embraced a novel social media campaign that engaged not only Madison College students, but also the 50,000 students at nearby UW-Madison.

Launch and Learn

Leaders, including myself, saw the social media plan as state of the art, and media observers agreed. From a later vantage point, the plan may feel dated, given that hundreds of new tools, particularly those that can measure social media, have emerged in the few years since then. Pinterest, now a popular social space for young women, was not yet a twinkle in anyone's eye. While many divisions at the college had started their own Facebook pages, a central college Facebook page was not created until Sept. 7, 2010, the day before the district board approved the referendum effort.

Yet the college's achievements with social media were outstanding. With little more than a few weeks of planning and only eight weeks to implement, the college's social media team

(2) Available at mstnr.me/MadTech2

created an email campaign, a crowdsourcing project, a blog about alumni accomplishments, an "electronic lawn sign" campaign, and a Facebook page that attracted more than 88,000 visitors. Our metrics later indicated that in these eight weeks, we had reached more than one million friends, citizens, and neighbors.

The college, as a taxpayer-supported institution, needed to be careful not to overspend on the educational part of the campaign. We saw social media as a low-cost messaging tool. We hired three 30-something consultants from the Outrigger3[3] firm, who were experienced in campaigns in the private sector. More important, we knew they were nimble.

The college's referendum team assigned social media managing duties to two in-house staffers, who worked with several student interns, marketing instructors, and the consultants. One of our key targets was the media. We realized that the media in our area were beginning to use social media in very practical ways, in large part to keep tabs on the over-the-top races for U.S. Senate and governor. The college knew it needed the endorsement of every area paper and media outlet, and it eventually got them.

Working parallel to the college was the advocacy group, funded by community donors and led by Brei, a seasoned hospital administrator with deep roots in the community.

Madison College has more buoyancy than most higher education institutions, which are often mired in bureaucracy. However, it had not yet embraced the uncontrollable, somewhat chaotic world of Facebook, in which conversation is required as an engagement tool and commenters can criticize the college. The communication team leaders hired the college's student marketing club to educate the entire college community about how to use social media and to staff

(3) Link: outrigger3.com

the Facebook pages. We organically drew a gaggle of techie students, who joined with our consultants writing code and teaching others how to use innovative practices in social media. Our advocacy arm set up laptops in the hallways of the college, served pizza, and asked students to "like" the college's Facebook page.

"It was the Wild, Wild West of social media for businesses and organizations in 2010," said John Holcomb, consultant and principal of Outrigger3. "We learned under fire what types of tactics worked to maximize engagement, community development, and sharing of content."

Hitchhiking in Social Media Land

As we galloped to Election Day, the students did a great job of reverse mentoring. At the same time, some of the college communicators later said they felt isolated from this effort, and the team learned we should have been more inclusive (see "Lessons Learned," below).

While we were strategizing about Facebook, our consultants educated us about the power of email, which is still an essential social media tool. We started with an engagement survey that not only gave the college good information before the district board made its decision to go for the referendum, but also garnered media support[4] and helped educate community leaders and fellow employees about the issues.

We also learned to craft messages and calls to action that would prompt people to open the weekly Madison College emails that we began sending. Leaders learned from other area nonprofits how to get email addresses from public colleges and universities through open records requests. We began robust communication with UW-Madison and Madison College students districtwide. We began reaching out to the approximately 490,000 alumni.

As the 2010 election turned white-hot with very close races for the U.S. Senate and the governor's office, the advocacy group launched a "VoteYesMadCollege" Twitter channel, and the college started a Madison College account. Our tweeters shared posts in streams of endorsements and retweets from business, labor, UW-Madison, local bloggers, and influential tweeters who were busily covering other election races. Given that our message was about jobs and improving the economy, a message all candidates were addressing, tweeters picked up some of our messages, including ones touting that 89 percent of the college's graduates in those years were employed in six months and that the economy would receive nearly $4 for every $1 invested in Wisconsin technical colleges.

Our consultants taught us that the job of email was in part to

We learned under fire what types of tactics worked to maximize engagement, community development, and sharing of content.

(4) Available at mstnr.me/MadTech4

lead fans to the Smart Community Facebook page,[5] a growing powerhouse in social marketing and a linchpin of our strategy. We went beyond just asking people to "Join us on our Facebook page." The consultants helped us learn that the job of a Facebook page is to drive traffic to our website, where vibrant messages might convince them to vote for us. The customized Facebook page conveniently led users to multipage web content with links to our blogs and other college sites. To boost our reach in the compressed eight-week campaign, the college's foundation donated an iPad, and we offered it as a prize in a drawing for those who liked our page.

Our page likes spiked the first week to about 500 people, then stalled. But our analysis showed that by the second weekend, our Facebook page had 7,000 "lurkers," who were checking out but not liking the page. We realized that we needed authentic voices to keep traffic growing and to expand our online conversations on Facebook. The site's users didn't react to automatically generated content and preferred sites that offered customized material and maintained real-time conversations. We enlisted faculty, staff, and student leaders to help interns and the student marketing club ramp up engagement with authentic conversation.

By the second week, we noticed that students began engaging with our social networks, first by asking questions about general college issues. Then a few opponents joined the conversation and a robust discussion erupted. We knew we had engaged the student crowd when a fan posted an appeal about whether our veterinary assistant program could help her find a home for some stray kittens, and another asked about the best parking spot in the morning. By the end of six weeks, we had about 4,500 friends and 88,000 page views. Fifty-three percent of our traffic for the referendum's Facebook page came from users' general searches for college information, a statistic our consultants had never seen before.

We knew we were reaching the media and influencers because they would call us minutes after we posted social media messages. During October, November, and December of 2010—the months of the campaign and follow-up—the college's "earned media," which measures coverage by news reporters, was 71 percent greater than the previous year, another record-shattering number.

Swarming Social Media

These results did not come without quick decisions made on the fly. As Election Day approached, polls showed our support might be dropping a bit. Consultants brainstormed with the advocacy team about a last-minute "swarm" tactic for Facebook and Twitter, called "electronic lawn signs." The college advocates asked Facebook

> **The site's users didn't react to automatically generated content and preferred sites that offered customized material and maintained real-time conversations.**

(5) Link: facebook.com/madisoncollege

The referendum passed in the midst of major state and national financial crisis; educating the public about the value of the plan was key to its success.

friends to swap their profile photos for a thumbnail image that said "Be a Hero MATC Nov. 2" or "Vote Yes MATC referendum." Every time a Facebook friend replaced a thumbnail, his or her Facebook pals got an update about it. Every time that person posted a message on Facebook, the college-branded profile photo showed up in his or her friends' general news feed. Soon we had thousands of friend-ambassadors organically spreading and endorsing our message by their activity on their pages.

The consultants estimated that fans shared more than one million, and perhaps as many as five million, impressions about the campaign. This came primarily through Facebook users who had more than 500 friends. This was part of the strategy: The consultants searched for local Facebook users with large friend bases and asked them to reach out through comments or retweets. They did, in droves.

Finally, late in the campaign, the college used a crowdsourcing tactic that was brilliant but possibly launched too late. Called a digital "idea forum," FutureofMadison.org awarded scholarships for big community ideas. All suggestions for our community's future would be placed in a time capsule inside the foundation of the first building the referendum dollars would finance. The college received more than 350 ideas, and seven winners were chosen.

The Referendum Legacy

The buildings financed by the referendum now tower over the Madison campus, and a few smaller projects have opened at smaller campuses. While some citizens gripe in letters to the editor about the additional tax bill, the college still holds great respect in the community. It hosted a gala celebration of the new additions during the college's 100th year in October 2012. The Madison campus buildings are scheduled to finish construction in 2013.

Bales, the board chair during the referendum, predicted on election night that the referendum victory would resonate in years to come. "It's always nice to have your stakeholders affirm the value that you hope you're providing for them," said Bales, superintendent of the DeForest Area School District, in a post-election article.[6] "And I think this is a message from the community that they hope we're able to continue to provide that for a long time."

The college continues to engage in real-time communications to bring its neighbors along with the college during its multiyear building plan. This occurs most robustly in the foundation, where an alumni advisory board will direct the organization of an alumni association, a long-awaited and needed addition to this increasingly relevant college.

"The referendum created energy, which spurred the alumni effort to organize," said Melanie Kranz, a successful Madison business leader recently appointed to Madison College Foundation's Alumni Advisory Council. "It feels like the college is trying to grow up and not be the quiet school it has been over the last 25-plus years."

Lessons Learned

The strategy and marketing and communication efforts were deemed a success by President Barhorst in her statements to the board and to the press after the election and during celebrations that began the college's Centennial Year in 2011. "We have a good story to tell, and we have touched the lives of thousands of people in the district," she told the Badger Herald the day after the election.

One of the leading media observers, Deb Ziff, said in an election roundup,[7] "MATC leaders won people over by making a sophisticated but persuasive pitch: Yes, there's an immediate hit to the pocketbook, but the investment will have a long-term payoff in job training."

Some pundits said the college campaign had little visibility. Their comments indicated they were not on social channels where the college had targeted voters through the many communications tools.

The decision to wait until just eight weeks before the election to start the campaign was a smart political decision, but it was a communications and organizational challenge. The college excelled in the traditional channels in which its marketing department had great expertise. The college also performed superbly in the social space with strategies that were new to the college culture.

The consensus-building tactics used in the organizing phase

---

(6) Available at mstnr.me/MadTech6
(7) Available at mstnr.me/MadTech7

were lost during the pell-mell rush to Election Day when it came to social media. Some communication leaders later said they felt left out. Other leaders were confused about why trivial messages about crowded parking lots and abandoned kittens were part of campaign communications. With more time, the communications team could have shared more information about how social media works.

The communications team could also have been more effective with the metrics now available. "One of the most difficult things about working with an institution with social media is determining measurements for success that help leaders, alumni, faculty, the communications team, and advocacy groups understand the power of the tactics," said Holcomb of Outrigger3, who has also worked with teams at area United Way organizations and UW-Madison.

Holcomb said that after the victory, the college quickly moved on to the building process and didn't immediately leverage its teeming social audience. Social media's very nature contributes to it being underused for two reasons, according to Holcomb. "Social media can make executives uneasy," he said, pointing to the challenge it can offer to traditional marketing practices. Also, he said, the need to move fast flew in the face of the higher education culture of decision by committees.

"At the end of the day, a digital strategy more attuned to a nimble and adaptable militia rather than a well-organized army was necessary and ultimately most effective during the quick-strike, eight-week social media campaign," Holcomb said.

Steve Noll, a college instructor and a leader in the campaign's social media communications, said the role of social media was a "critical piece in passing the referendum with such a high margin." He applauded the student effort, saying that students were able to use their social media networks to reach out to their friends and family, who then reached out to more people. "Within minutes, this student-led message machine was able to reach the right audience with the right message," he said.

In engagement surveys in the research phase in 2010, the college found that most students did not have smartphones. I suspect this has changed if college users are trending with other national user studies. The increasing use of smartphones and tablets calls for new social media strategies. For example, customized Facebook developers are creating tabs that can be seen on smartphones, and Twitter has gained many new followers who look for up-to-the-minute news.

Also, the popularity of Pinterest and YouTube underscores the increasing reliance on visuals. This would need to be more integrally included in any updated social media strategy in a college setting today, as would texting, a widely used and effective communications tool.

Holcomb agrees that while the electronic lawn signs were

> One of the most difficult things about working with an institution with social media is determining measurements for success that help leaders, alumni, faculty, the communications team, and advocacy groups understand the power of the tactics.

a media hit, the team did not have enough time to properly pursue the crowdsourcing project, the Big Idea Challenge, on the FutureofMadison.com platform. He said he was disappointed that the effort was dropped after the victory but understood the college's need to get the building effort ramped up.

Student participation propelled the campaign for institutional reasons and practical ones. The college had limited resources. Figuring out how to tap a handful of students who are well-connected social media users rather than using many ill-equipped social users is a tactic for the next campaign.

The Madison College campaign lived up to its various names. It was *smart*, but its success will be improved by those who follow in this higher education community squeezed by budget cuts. However, its overarching lesson resounds: You can get by with a little help from your social media friends. **sw**

An Integrated Social Campaign Powers the Mascot Search at the College of William & Mary

By Susan T. Evans | @susantevans

Susan T. Evans is senior strategist at mStoner. Evans leads one of mStoner's consulting teams, developing communication strategies for clients. Evans also leads mStoner's social media and content strategy practices.

You know your new mascot has arrived when it gets a plug on "The Daily Show."

But more interesting than the mascot itself was the process that William & Mary used to encourage the community to weigh in on what, exactly, the college mascot should be.

The search began in 2009 when William & Mary's then-new president, Taylor Reveley, heard board members, students, and alumni alike bemoaning the fact that the college didn't have an official mascot to rally support for the college's athletic team, the Tribe. They believed that the athletic teams at William & Mary, the second-oldest institution of higher education in the United States (only Harvard is older), deserved better. So President Reveley created a task force to select a mascot for the college, charging its members to make the search open, engaging, and fun.

Then director of creative services at William & Mary, I planned and directed the communications for the mascot search. As project manager for the redesign of the William & Mary website, I had seen firsthand the power of social media: The re.Web blog,[1] which chronicled progress on a relaunch of WM.edu, was widely praised by colleagues and earned an eduStyle People's Choice Award in 2008. So I built a communications plan for the mascot search that relied heavily on social media—both for the actual search and for the announcement of the new mascot—knowing that the buzz would encourage people to engage with each other and with the college.

Opening the Channels

President Reveley announced the mascot search through an email message sent to the campus community and to alumni. Within

---

(1) Link: reweb.blogspot.com

days, nearly 400 individuals completed a general comment form on the newly launched mascot search website. As an unexpected benefit, the form included the option for alumni to provide their current contact information. Our team then made sure that all web forms used by alumni to submit official suggestions or participate in the feedback survey included the update option, and we shared the alumni data collected with the alumni association.

We used a William & Mary web page[2] as the outlet for more static content and as the hub for links to the many social channels. A blog,[3] a Twitter feed,[4] a Mascot Search Facebook Group,[5] and a YouTube channel[6] were augmented by Flickr sets, more email messages from the college's president, and an online survey, as well as some print materials.

Together, these channels formed the basis of a broader communications campaign that helped constituents find out about, stay up to speed with, and participate in the mascot selection process. The viral aspect of social media helped William & Mary reach individuals who might not otherwise have been paying attention to an announcement about a mascot search, and social channels meant more immediate and more frequent updates for those most interested. Plus, as the campaign got rolling, it got a real boost as it earned media mentions from print and broadcast outlets that were following the social channels.

Throughout the social media campaign, the tone was wacky. William & Mary decided early on to let social media demonstrate that there was fun to be had with a mascot search. Ebirt, the former, unofficial William & Mary mascot,[7] had his own blog and Facebook profile; he regularly weighed in on the search for his replacement. The informal tone and humorous approach encouraged participation and ultimately made the community more accepting of the finalists.

How the Channels Fit Together

The blog was the more traditional of the channels and functioned almost like the website. We used the blog to share information and to describe the kind of mascot we were looking for. A lot of the blog posts functioned like press releases. For example, the William & Mary team developed an "In Committee" feature offering background about deliberations in committee meetings. In total, there were just over 250 comments on the Mascot Search blog, not nearly the volume received on other channels like Facebook and Twitter.

---

(2) Available at mstnr.me/WandMmascot2
(3) Link: wmmascot.blogs.wm.edu
(4) Handle: @wmmascot
(5) Available at mstnr.me/WandMmascot5
(6) Link: youtube.com/wmmascot
(7) Link: wikipedia.org/wiki/Colonel_Ebirt

During the campaign W&M did not have a dedicated social media position. Rather, two members of the creative team devoted substantial time to the mascot search.

Facebook, on the other hand, was where a lot of the interaction happened. At the time we launched the mascot search, we had about 10,000 fans on the William & Mary Facebook page, so we co-opted it for announcements about the mascot search because we had so many people already engaged there compared to the other social channels. Members of a Mascot Search Facebook group were offered an early way to submit official mascot suggestions. The nearly 900 members of this group wrote more than 1,000 wall posts about William & Mary's search for a mascot.

Meanwhile, my colleagues and I used Twitter to break information. The 1,360 followers of the @WMMascot Twitter feed received the first notices about news on the search, and every day, one of the mascot suggestions was announced on that platform.

During the later stages of the mascot search, the team used Flickr to showcase concept drawings of suggested mascots designed by Torch Creative, Inc. And a Flickr set was used to unveil the final selection on the day of the campus event announcing the Griffin as William & Mary's new mascot.

Overall, YouTube was the most successful channel, though during the selection process it really only served as a distraction— albeit a useful one. During the process, we took suggestions for 90 days using SurveyMonkey and then accepted feedback about five finalists for a month. A transparent process that encourages a lot of participation takes time. So while the mascot search committee deliberated, the team used YouTube to host short videos about the William & Mary community's reactions to the search.

At the conclusion of the campaign, William & Mary posted a humorous video on YouTube[8] revealing the new mascot. "Get Me the

(8) Available at mstnr.me/WandMmascot8

The W&M mascot search was officially described as a "fun, inclusive, and carefully planned process."

Griffin," featuring President Reveley, helped to engage constituents who weren't able to join the 700 people who attended the campus launch event. In a very short time, there were more than 17,000 YouTube views of the announcement video. When the Griffin walked out into the crowd at the campus event, our simultaneous internet launch had many people involved via social media.

Twitter, however, was probably the fastest way to find out what the new mascot was, and the #WMmascot hashtag trended in the Northern Virginia area for the first 24 hours after the announcement. The internet launch of the Griffin meant that thousands of people who participated in the search but couldn't be in Williamsburg were able to hear the announcement within seconds of those who were on campus.

Response and Results

Before the campaign began, William & Mary did not define specific metrics for success. We didn't know what to expect, beyond having a goal of involving as many of our current students, alumni, faculty, staff, and parents as we could. We didn't even set targets for how many suggestions we wanted to get. We knew that mascot searches were often messy, so we hoped that by being inclusive and allowing people to participate we would get consensus. We wanted to build good will around our commitment to listen to suggestions and ideas.

The response was off the charts. More than 800 people

representing 44 states and the District of Columbia visited the website to suggest a mascot idea. Moreover, we had tremendous feedback when we narrowed down to the final five. On the day the five finalists were announced, there were nearly 17,000 unique visitors to the website. And, in the 30-day comment period that followed, more than 11,000 individuals offered feedback on the Griffin, the Pug, the Wren, the King and Queen, and the Phoenix. Members of the Mascot Search Committee were convinced of the power of social media when they learned that there were 22,000 comments to read through!

The engagement wasn't just comment-deep. I was surprised at how strongly people felt about their mascot suggestions. They took a lot of time to write their cases, many of which were very well documented and thoughtful. Some people even ran their own campaigns to promote the mascots they suggested—for instance, those who supported "Bricky the Brick" formed their own Facebook group.[9]

But the main lesson we learned was that the integration of these social media tools matters. We didn't realize at first that the power behind what we were doing was that we were using all of these channels together, but in different ways. The result was that we had a cohesive presence, which was the result of an integrated set of multiple community tools, a consistent concept and brand, and an informal and humorous tone.

Plus, we confirmed a key assumption we had that older alumni would use the internet to engage with the college. At the beginning of the campaign, some people were certain that alumni wouldn't participate via the web. That was hardly true! Alumni of all ages participated and visited the blog. They submitted suggestions regardless of their age; in fact, 20 percent of the alumni who submitted mascot suggestions were age 52 or older. Total participation was about 50 percent alumni—and a substantial number of those individuals were ages 50 to 80. Even prospective students submitted drawings. And a parent who was in Williamsburg visiting his son, a college employee, brought drawings of proposed mascots with him and personally delivered them to my office.

An unanticipated byproduct of the mascot search was the enormous amount of media coverage[10] it received. We did a little bit of media outreach. The athletic department used its email list, distributing information along the way to media contacts. But a lot of media got information directly from our website, blog, and social channels. The earned media included a segment on "The Daily Show"[11] with Jon Stewart, a William & Mary alumnus, along with stories in *The Washington Post*, *Sports Illustrated*, *USA Today*, and

I was surprised at how strongly people felt about their mascot suggestions. They took a lot of time to write their cases, many of which were very well documented and thoughtful.

(9) Available at mstnr.me/WandMmascot9

(10) Available at mstnr.me/WandMmascot10

(11) Available at mstnr.me/WandMmascot11

The Chronicle of Higher Education.

In 2009, social media was not mainstream. Using platforms like Facebook and Twitter for official university communications was not as widely practiced or accepted. A few campus administrators were initially a bit worried that the online communities William & Mary hosted for the mascot search were not moderated. But the mascot committee and the communications team in creative services wanted to step back and let the good, the bad, and the ugly appear. The vast majority of social media interaction was positive. Concerns began to fade after William & Mary's athletic director was asked to appear on ESPN's "First Take" and the mascot story was picked up by the Associated Press.

Ultimately, the social media campaign around the William & Mary mascot search won two 2010 Gold Awards from the Council for Advancement and Support of Education—one for best use of social media in the Website category, and one for creative use of technology and new media in the Alumni Relations Programs category.

Interestingly, William & Mary did not have a dedicated social media position during the campaign; in fact, it still doesn't. Two members of the creative services team—Joel Pattison, then associate director of creative services, and I—devoted the most time to the mascot search. We created the plan, designed the creative components, and developed the content for the social channels. We basically squeezed this in among the other responsibilities we had. Coming off a campus web redesign project, we were used to long hours. I recall sipping my morning coffee and posting an update to the blog or tweeting a mascot idea received the night before. That constant interaction was a key to the campaign's success. We gave people something to talk about, and we kept up our end of the conversation. **SW**

Infusing New Media into Admissions Marketing at Loyola University Chicago

By Nicole O'Connell | @noconnell

Nicole O'Connell is director of marketing and communications at Loyola University Chicago, where she is responsible for driving enrollment through the development of strategic integrated marketing and communications campaigns.

How do you break through the clutter and become a No. 1 choice to your prospective undergraduate students? What tools are in your tool box to uniquely engage your primary audiences on a one-to-one level? How do you integrate new media into your traditional marketing mix? These were just a few of the issues we faced at Loyola University Chicago in 2009, at the onset of the social media movement. At a time when most academic institutions still were hesitant to take initiative and embrace social media as a marketing approach, Loyola decided to venture out. We were eager to test new media and develop a communications strategy that effectively integrated social channels.

Ramping Up for Social Media

Lori Greene, director of undergraduate admission, recognized the need for a social media presence, particularly on Facebook, but wasn't quite sure where to start. Greene's department began by hiring a consultant, who led focus group sessions with the senior admission staff in January 2010. Long days full of lively discussion and idea generation resulted in Loyola's now well-known Class of 2014 Facebook group page.

"We took a big risk at the time by intercepting an already existing organic group page and creating an official Loyola Class of 2014 page," Greene said. "Fortunately, because the transition was so well planned, the new 'Class of' group was well received by both admitted students and Loyola administration."

Since 2009, nearly a year before hiring a consultant, we had been following Facebook and those groups affiliated with Loyola. Of note was the high level of engagement, as demonstrated in the posted comments, which informed our internal staff about mailings gone bad or policies that may have been negatively perceived. The popularity of the organic Class of 2013 and Class of 2014 pages was apparent—but also apparent were the absence of brand, the lack of faculty and staff interaction, and, in a few instances, cyberspace bullying. After serious study of the situation, we decided to launch an "official" Class of 2014 group. We began outlining Loyola's specific action steps to accomplish the transition from "organic" to "official" site in a manner that wouldn't offend any constituents.

"Our first step was to post a comment asking the organic group if they'd like an official Loyola logo—and they readily accepted," said Marketing Communications Specialist Melissa Niksic. "From there we took it one step at a time, with intermittent postings, so they could get to know me as the face of Loyola. Once I established trust with the group, I offered to create an official Class of 2014 page, and the concept was overwhelmingly well received." Loyola continues to successfully support "Class of" pages along with several additional platforms targeted to specific audience sets.

By April 2010, as part of the organic-to-official rollout process, we were hosting training sessions for faculty and administrators to garner their buy-in and encourage participation. At that time, many staffers did not yet use Facebook, so we had to start with the basics, such as how to set up an account.

Knowing we would have to overcome anxieties about people making posts they couldn't retract or that might shed negative light on the university, we had already developed Loyola's Social Media Policy. Drafted in April 2009, that policy addressed the most common concerns about privacy, interaction between faculty and students, and the potential for inappropriate posts. To this day, the policy is a concise five-page document that applies to any internal staff members who participate on undergraduate or graduate social media platforms. Initially this policy was distributed at launch meetings and, while it occasionally is reviewed and updated, its contents have changed little since April 2010—the only exception being the relatively new and strongly enforced rule that all Loyola employees use a professional Loyola account when engaging as a staff member with a constituent.

"Fortunately, none of our fears were confirmed, and by the time May 1 rolled around, we had almost 1,800 admitted student 'friends' of the Class of 2014 page—a huge success at the time," said Greene. "This gave us the confidence to move forward and consider testing new platforms as well. YouTube was becoming increasingly prominent, and I knew that the next best way to market the Loyola experience was through live video and use of personal storytelling."

Knowing that Loyola's marketing and communications strategy was shifting, we closely examined our staffing and resources to better manage these new platforms. We took a deep dive

Fortunately, because the transition was so well planned, the new "Class of" group was well received by both admitted students and Loyola administration.

LOYOLA CLASS OF 2017

Loyola converted from Facebook groups to Facebook pages in 2011 after careful analysis of access and use data on its pages. Afterward, it could offer more timely and engaging content.

into Loyola's organizational structure, job responsibilities, and evaluations of staff talent. It didn't take long to recognize natural "content creators" already on staff who had a zeal for social media and were excited about taking on new responsibilities.

"My job description was completely revised so I could focus on developing Loyola's social media platforms," said Niksic, who manages all of undergraduate admission's social media channels. "I personally enjoy spending my time in these channels, so it was a natural fit. I also get to work with people across the university, which makes my everyday work much more enjoyable and fulfilling."

Niksic was also interested in video production. She pitched the idea of hiring student videographers and purchasing good equipment. From April 2010 to August 2011, Loyola's video library grew from zero to more than 200 videos.

Developing an Online Brand

Once Loyola's presence on YouTube was firmly established, we quickly went on to master other social media channels that would lend themselves specifically to recruitment. This included the January 2011 introduction of the now well-known "From the Admission Director" blog, Twitter feeds, and a Flickr platform. We also began segmenting our Facebook pages by audience to be as relevant as possible in positioning and message to our respective audiences. We knew we were not serving all of our various student audiences equally by maintaining only one Facebook page, for incoming freshmen.

After the success of our Class of 2014 group, we turned our attention and resources to other market segments, specifically the high school sophomore, junior, and transfer populations. "Even Financial Aid needed a new brand image," said Niksic.

Loyola had already realized that Facebook and other social media were more than just communications channels; they had the potential to represent our brand. In 2011, after two fiscal years, our data showed that social media served as a highly visible communications platform for undergraduate recruitment. Analytics revealed that visitors spent significant time on our pages,

and we also confirmed that Facebook activity proved a particularly strong tactic to boost yield. The next step, then, was to transform the content and design to reflect specific timed events in the recruitment cycle. In other words, rather than using Facebook simply as a place to engage prospects and admitted students, we wanted to make it easy for them to find information that was relevant to them at a particular time in the admission cycle.

We decided at this point to convert from Facebook's group format to page format so we could customize those pages for both audience and content. "With detailed planning among our enrollment marketing and admission teams, we were able to radically transform our Facebook presence and bring our brand to life with updated design, relevant content, and live video," said Greene. "We created tabs for 'Apply Now,' 'Request Info,' 'Open House,' 'Financial Aid,' 'Residence Life,' and other events, along with a 'Deposit Now' app, with the goal being both engagement and conversion. We provided important copy points, but we also integrated video and posted links to relevant student blogs, tweets, and videos. Our data indicated that this model was successful in terms of both improving conversion and yield and, more important, generating engagement among our prospective and admitted students," Greene said.

Strategizing Across the Net

With Facebook and YouTube firmly embedded in Loyola's communications strategies, in 2011 and 2012 we shifted our focus to content, specifically blog content. Through studies by Loyola's Office of Enrollment Systems, Research, and Reporting, a new concept emerged for using blogs and Twitter together to create an informed PR strategy that both generated potential buzz about

Loyola's undergraduate programs and increased the number of followers for key "influencer" blogs.

"We mapped an annual publishing calendar of admission and financial aid content from traditional and new media sources, identified key media bloggers, and created an editorial calendar that synced up to the admission cycle and to Lori Greene's 'From the Admission Director' blog," said Tim Heuer, director of enrollment systems, research, and reporting. "We then strategically identified publications and writers in higher education who we wanted to take an interest in what Greene had to say about undergraduate recruitment. We built an integrated PR campaign with the goal of increasing the visibility of her blog and positioning it as one of national influence."

At about the same time, Twitter released a new product, Sponsored Tweets, whereby advertisers could target potential followers by buying targeted keywords. Loyola tested this by using the general undergraduate Twitter account paired with the face of Lori Greene, the goal being to increase her number of Twitter followers and thus the number of constituents reading her blog. This tactic increased follower numbers from 700 to more than 4,000 in four months' time. The "From the Admission Director" blog also rose to the No. 1 position on Loyola's blog site and was picked up by several media sources for commentary, including EDUguru.com. Probably even more important, this tactic brought high traffic to Greene's blog and garnered readership among prospective and admitted students and their parents.

With the growing importance of search engine optimization, Loyola realized that blogs were yet another way to fill the content supply bucket—a tactic to help feed the search engines and assist in improving Loyola's search rankings for key terms. "We also knew that our prospective students wanted to read about current Loyola students, so we identified six current students and hired them to blog," said Erin Moriarty, associate director of undergraduate admission. "We put them on a rotating schedule so content was always revolving and fresh, with a focus on organic and real storytelling, with very little editorial direction from our staff. We want our prospective students to be able to answer the questions, 'Do I see myself at Loyola?' 'Could I be friends with this person?' So we looked for a diverse set of bloggers."

What began modestly with six student bloggers has morphed into a group almost double that number, with analytics indicating tremendous growth in both traffic and time spent on page, indicators that our time and resources are well invested. According to Niksic, traffic grew 43 percent from May 2011 to May 2012.

The solid results gained from dedicating resources to blogging led Loyola to test a new video blogging tactic in fiscal year 2012–13.

"With use of a hired student intern who has talents in both video and storytelling, we plan to create a series of video blogs that focus on the student perspective," said Moriarty. "While the admission staff will certainly guide the intern in terms of content direction, video production and accompanying story will be organic and told from the student voice. We'll allow some fun to come into play with shots of dining and residence halls, student organization events, athletics, and so forth, but we want to be able to market this material to parents as well, so we'll also cover topics on academics, outcomes, and financial aid."

Integrating Media Resources

We attribute Loyola's successes in social media in large part to our concentrated focus on integration points within our overall communications strategy. We took inventory of what communications channels were already used and considered how we could integrate these new media into already successful marketing campaigns.

"We started with the central hub of communications—our website—which at the time did not have links on any pages to our social media platforms," said Niksic. Loyola launched a completely redesigned Undergraduate Admission website in August 2011. The new website was designed to bring social media to the forefront, with multimedia content highly visible on every page.

The website also provided a better way to manage Loyola's video assets. "We've found that YouTube serves as an excellent cataloging library for us," said Niksic, "but video hits weren't as high as we wanted them to be. Since we invested a great deal of time and money into growing our video library, we wanted a vehicle to push out what we knew was great interactive content. So we created a subsection of the site using video for virtual campus tours. Topics focus on academic facilities, sustainability, faith and community service, living and dining, and social and recreational life, along with the city of Chicago."

Another important channel that drew our attention was email. The volume of emails pushed out to prospective and admitted students has doubled since 2008. And with open rates topping over 50 percent with some market segments, we knew email was an excellent way to drive students and parents to new media. "We started with just the basics of an email template," said Moriarty, "and incorporated a fixed design where our social media icons lived permanently in the rail. Our No. 1 goal is to increase the number of likes on Facebook, so we permanently added the 'Like' button in the upper right header of all emails. This was probably the smartest and easiest way to help us meet that goal." In addition to relying on design templates, Loyola also uses the right and left rails of HTML templates to highlight relevant blog or other social media content.

> Since we invested a great deal of time and money into growing our video library, we wanted a vehicle to push out what we knew was great interactive content. So we created a subsection of the site using video for virtual campus tours.

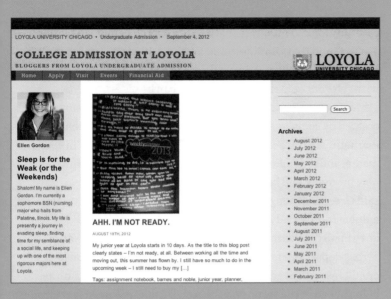

Loyola's staff, alumni, and current students all contribute content to the admission blogs.

Planning and Progress

Social media planning has now become an integral component of Loyola's overall enrollment marketing and communications strategy. "We spend the greater parts of the months of May and June evaluating past communication strategies, and, based upon data, we determine what stays, what goes, and what we are going to test," said Greene.

Loyola starts with an annual communications plan that is segmented by audience, channel, and topic. "We then break this down on a monthly basis," said Moriarty, who is responsible for the day-to-day execution. "This year we hope to be as granular as to indicate what day a strategic post or tweet needs to occur. We are also focusing on tracking and tagging to get a better idea of what type of content resonates best with our audiences—what topics garner engagement? We also hope to continue our focus on mobile marketing, which we just ramped up last fiscal year," said Moriarty.

Loyola's staff believes that the next wave of opportunity in enrollment marketing revolves around the synergy between mobile devices and social media. In Noel-Levitz's *2012 Mobile Expectations* report[1] (which surveyed 2,300 college-bound high school students), 52 percent reported viewing a school's website from a mobile device, and 76 percent said they access Facebook via mobile devices.

"We are just at the forefront of developing mobile-social strategies and are testing simple concepts, like using QR codes on print pieces that direct readers to video," said Moriarty. "Or, if a prospective student has opted in to receive SMS messaging, we'll

(1) Available at mstnr.me/Loyola1

carefully look to integrate texting into overall campaign tactics. We've found that, similar to social media, if you deliver an inviting 140-character text and direct a user to a mobile optimized page with relevant content, the open rates can be big."

Moving into 2012–13, Loyola is excited about the dynamic space created by social media and is concentrating on cross-channel marketing to further improve yield. "There are no rules in social media, and it demands instant creativity from marketers to test new products and keep pace with changes in existing platforms," said Greene. Among the greatest benefits of the Loyola's newfound emphasis on social media, she said, are that it challenges staff to keep up to date with technology and prompts communication across departments. In its May 2012 issue, *University Business* cited Loyola University Chicago Undergraduate Admission as being ahead of the trend with its use of social media in recruitment. Loyola intends to stay at the front of the trend—and at the top of students' choices. **sw**

How Video Helps Recruit Students to Rochester Institute of Technology

By Mallory Wood | @mallorywood

Mallory Wood is director of marketing at mStoner. Wood dreams up new marketing opportunities, works with potential clients to identify future project opportunities, and manages EDUniverse.org.

Rochester Institute of Technology has long understood that current students are the institution's best storytellers. In 2004, it created a blogging program through which current students could share their experiences, thoughts, and photos with prospective students. But with the growing popularity of YouTube and other online video platforms, the admissions office soon realized that video offered a way for RIT's campus ambassadors to deliver even more dynamic and interactive content to prospective students.

The 2010 Noel-Levitz E-Expectations survey[1] reported that 67% of prospective students and their families were interested in viewing videos made by both institutions and students. It also reported that the overwhelming majority of survey respondents wanted to see videos about student life—not surprisingly, prospective students are eager to discover what life is like on campus and whether they'd fit in. With this information in hand, Ashley Hennigan, assistant director of undergraduate admissions, started thinking about ways to expand the current student blogging program to take advantage of this rich medium.

It was one of the student bloggers, Emily Okey, who approached Hennigan in the fall of 2010 with the idea to develop video profiles for each on-campus student ambassador and post those videos on the site. "When I was applying to RIT, I loved reading the student blogs because it helped me get through the waiting period after I was accepted and before I arrived on campus in the fall," said Okey. "Once I got on campus, I knew I wanted to become a blogger. And I knew that introducing video content to the mix would allow me and the other ambassadors to connect with even more high schoolers."

_____

(1) Available at mstnr.me/Rochester1

The RIT Admissions homepage features current student blogs, Twitter accounts, and YouTube videos up front.

Hennigan liked the idea, but asked, "Why stop there? Why not use video to tell stories? Why not show what life is like on RIT's campus from the eyes of a student?" The result was the Social Media Ambassador team, through which student ambassadors interact with prospective students on social channels like Facebook and Twitter—and, especially, through video.

As their website[2] says, "We blog, we film, we tweet. But the big part of our project is 'RIT Behind the Scenes,' our weekly episodic webseries."

Selection, Training, Technology

Hennigan knew that she needed a mix of students that would be a good representation of the diverse student body at RIT, but she wanted to keep the size of the program manageable for its first year. Some of the applicants had backgrounds in journalism or took multimedia courses at RIT, but Hennigan decided that it was just as important to select high-energy students with strong school spirit.

"It was crucial to find students involved on campus, especially in leadership roles, because they are already attending events and club meetings and participating in service opportunities," Hennigan said. "I knew these students would be able to sustain a video series over time and continuously think of interesting content to feature."

(2) Link: youtube.com/user/5RITstudents

After reviewing applications from interested students, she selected five Social Media Ambassadors to help her and Okey get the program off the ground.

But before anyone picked up a video camera, Hennigan put the new Social Media Ambassadors through RIT's already established student ambassador training. This foundation allowed the students to understand RIT's broader brand and enrollment goals, learn key marketing messages, and see the bigger picture for why ambassador programs exist. The students were given a crash course on RIT enrichment programs and support services and were exposed to other areas of academics.

The ambassadors also received technical training. Because students were not selected for their prior social media experience or video expertise, there were a few learning curves to overcome.

Goals and Expectations

Hennigan involved the students in every aspect of goal setting and decision making. Together they determined that they'd launch the video series in January 2011 because it fit well with the enrollment cycle and gave the students time to learn the mechanics and to create video content. They also decided to publish videos on both RIT's website[3] and YouTube, for maximum exposure.

Hennigan encouraged the students to think about the admissions funnel when setting their production schedule. "When students are deciding whether to apply to RIT, they are looking for basic facts and general information about academics and student life," Hennigan said. "And as the year progressed and they started questioning if they'd be a good fit for RIT, we started to introduce more detailed topics. For example, we knew we should release a video about housing options around the time accepted students were going through housing selection."

It was important to Hennigan to set expectations from the start. The team members decided that they'd release one video a week from mid-January to mid-May to keep content fresh but not overwhelm the already busy student ambassadors' schedules. Hennigan set up office hours during the week for the students and a weekly staff meeting every Friday to check in and prepare for the following week's video release. The admissions office decided to pay the students by the hour, similar to how the institution's tour guides received compensation, to show appreciation for their hard work and encourage the students to take their new positions seriously.

The last hurdle before officially kicking off the program was to figure out what type of technology to use. Hennigan outfitted each ambassador with an iPod Touch. This enabled the students

(3) Link: rit.edu/emcs/admissions

to take photos and videos at any moment during the day. The admissions office also purchased a MacBook and an extra hard drive for the students to use for video editing. For editing software, iMovie proved to be the most robust choice with the lowest learning curve.

Reality TV, Campus Style

Why is reality television so popular? It is appealing to see real people react to real situations. Our emotions are engaged as we get to know the cast of characters and we are given an intimate glimpse into other people's lives. These principles guided the ambassadors as they created video content for the first year of "RIT Behind the Scenes."

Okey asked, "What if we follow five students around in their day-to-day life? What stories will we uncover? What do students, especially students from far away, want to learn about the RIT experience?" Answering these questions led the ambassadors to focus on creating a video series around the "big buckets" of college life, such as athletics, clubs, and housing. Okey took on the role of project manager and worked closely with Hennigan to make sure videos were on point and on schedule.

Taking more cues from television, on Nov. 12, 2010 (after months of planning and preparation), "RIT Behind the Scenes" posted its first video—a commercial introducing the team. "We are five RIT students on our adventure through college," they explained. "Join us for a behind-the-scenes look at what campus life is all about." The video was promoted and shared on social networks over the next couple of months to get prospective students excited about the webseries.

The first episode, simply titled "Pilot",[4] introduced viewers to the ambassadors and took a look at their morning routines and schedules. From the start, the ambassadors portrayed themselves as "your everyday college student." And, as expected, it was a hit! One prospective student commented on the video, "This is really creative. I can't wait to come to RIT!"

"The videos created by these students are extremely authentic," said Hennigan. "They are unscripted, candid, and uncensored." After three years, Hennigan can recall only one time when she decided to edit a video. Okey noted that prospective students often didn't even realize that the Social Media Ambassadors worked for admissions.

"What helped us the most was playing to people's strengths," said Okey. "One student was great with coming up with story lines, while others were more involved on campus and we could use their experiences as topic ideas."

As the semester progressed, the students touched on all the key aspects of being a student at RIT: programs of study, dorm

> The YouTube channel gained more subscribers and traffic than the official RIT Admissions channel. This demonstrated to Hennigan that the Noel-Levitz findings were correct; prospective students want to see video content created by college students about their life at the institution.

(4) Available at mstnr.me/Rochester4

5 RIT Students invites prospective students to take "a behind-the-scenes look at our college adventure."

rooms, clubs and varsity athletics, staying fit, spring break, and preparing for finals. On average, each video was 4 to 5 minutes in length, featured all five Social Media Ambassadors, and received thousands of views.

Results and Lessons Learned

"RIT Behind the Scenes" was declared a huge success by the undergraduate admissions office. The YouTube channel gained more subscribers and traffic than the official RIT Admissions channel. This demonstrated to Hennigan that the Noel-Levitz findings were correct; prospective students want to see video content created by college students about their life at the institution.

Accepted students often recognized the "stars" during campus visit programs and tours, so Hennigan started to bring Social Media Ambassadors to offsite admissions receptions in Washington, New York, and Boston to enhance the relationships being formed between the ambassadors and accepted students. Hennigan also realized the audience for "RIT Behind the Scenes" was much larger than just prospective students. Parents, current students, and even alumni were viewing the videos to stay up to date with campus life.

Still, there was room for improvement. "After reviewing YouTube analytics, we noticed that viewership dropped off significantly between the 2- and 3-minute mark," noted Hennigan. "We decided to make a concerted effort moving into Season Two to keep videos to 3 minutes or less."

Season One also taught the team that not everyone needed to be involved as a producer, actor, and writer each week. As new students were brought on the team to replace the graduating seniors, roles were divided up in advance for Season Two, based on people's strengths and abilities, and each episode had one point person to do the planning and pull in the necessary resources. The combination of creating shorter videos and a better focus on talent and resources allowed the ambassadors to create more video

What video subjects are most interesting to them?	
Student life	46%
Academics/classes	30%
Location/areas around campus	11%
Athletic events	6%
Faculty/program details	5%

What videos are most valuable to them?	
Videos made by the college	7%
Videos made by students	26%
Videos made by both	67%

The Noel-Levitz E-Expectations Survey Report encouraged RIT admissions staff to continue pursuing student-generated video content.

content, and they increased production from one video per week to two. In Season Two, the team decided to do a spin-off series to highlight academics, titled "9 by 9," featuring nine different students from the nine colleges at RIT.

On top of "RIT Behind the Scenes," the Social Media Ambassadors maintained personal blogs and Twitter accounts and participated in Facebook conversations with accepted students. Having seen the success of their YouTube channel, the ambassadors decided to post vlogs (video blogs) more frequently on their personal blogs. "It is easier to produce a vlog vs. write a thousand-word post. And the vlogs are easier to consume," Hennigan pointed out.

Three Years Later

As the series enters Season Three, "the biggest challenge now is sustaining 'RIT Behind the Scenes,'" said Hennigan. "I'm a critical consumer. I don't want to see web video where the subjects are wearing clothes from five years ago and there are outdated computers in the background." Hennigan recognizes that even though the same overarching messages are highlighted each year, the students change and updates are needed. "We need to look state-of-the-art, and highlight what is new, especially at a tech university."

Hennigan has also learned that managing students is a challenge. "You have to roll with the punches," she advised, "redistribute work and make changes, keep the drama out of the group, and make people feel like what they're doing is valuable."

Okey, who recently secured a UX design position at Carrot Creative, stressed that selecting the right students to participate is crucial to the success of the program. "This is a prestigious role on campus, but it is also a job, and students need to be willing to put in extra time," said Okey. "My experience as a Social Media

Ambassador changed my career goals and greatly enhanced my resume. It showed me career paths that I didn't know existed!"

This year Hennigan is looking specifically at the topics covered in the presentation RIT's admissions staff gives during group information sessions on campus and on the road. She plans to give the students more direction on video topics based on this breakdown and then will let the students run with it from there. The goal is to close the information gaps and introduce new topics to Season Three.

Hennigan is also encouraging her colleagues to repurpose the content created by the Social Media Ambassadors. For example, admissions officers are encouraged to mention the housing videos to prospective students. "Families like to hear that this 'real view' exists," said Hennigan. Admissions also incorporated a slide about the ambassadors into the group presentation. And the ambassadors' social content shows up front and center on the newly redesigned undergraduate admissions landing page on the RIT Admissions website.

Hennigan will also have the ambassadors focus on creating short Q&A videos for prospective students. They'll solicit questions from Facebook and other social networks and also address questions commonly asked at college fairs and high school visits. "These videos will serve as little public service announcements or highlights for each of our nine academic colleges," said Hennigan. "Our team is expanding from reality TV to true content producers for many different needs at RIT." **SW**

A Distinctive Print and Web Approach to College Marketing: Ampersandbox at the College of William & Mary

By Melissa Soberanes

Melissa Soberanes is a writer and editor at mStoner. She has more than 15 years of experience helping nonprofit organizations and education institutions increase awareness and tell their stories through effective communications, media relations, and web strategies.

The admissions officers at the College of William & Mary didn't want a regular viewbook; they wanted a spaceship. They wanted their new admission piece to zoom above the competition, right out of the mailbox and into the hands of both high schoolers and their parents. And, most important, they wanted teens to go online to WM.edu, where they could have a distinctive William & Mary experience and decide whether or not the college was the right place for them.

In short: "We wanted admission pieces that were different from the competition, and that would vie for attention in a stuffed mailbox—pieces with impact, interactivity, and integration with the website," said Henry Broaddus, associate provost for enrollment and dean of admission.

The William & Mary team, comprising the Creative Services department and the Office of Undergraduate Admission, worked together to create a new admission recruitment package. The result was the Ampersandbox, a campaign concept that tells stories of William & Mary through word pairs joined by the William & Mary ampersand, juxtaposed with candid photos from the college's Flickr feed. It breaks away from the traditional print and digital viewbooks by capitalizing on the interactive opportunities provided by online communications available today.

In print, the Ampersandbox is literally a box of cards that feature information on topics such as study abroad locations, clubs and organizations, and research or internship opportunities. Each card has a word pair representing a different aspect of the William & Mary experience, like Fire & Ice (the arts), Bread & Butter (the library), and Near & Far (study abroad). The cards include a url that links to the custom microsite,[1] where the encounter becomes truly interactive. On the microsite there are two settings, the Ampersandbox and Your Sandbox. The first includes the official word pairs shown on the cards, and the second is where visitors create and share their own word pairs and stories.

"The Ampersandbox is different from anything else out there. The concept of using word pairs—just as the title of the college is a word pair—to describe the William & Mary experience really identifies with our school," said Justin Schoonmaker, associate director of design. "And online, the word pairs are featured in a way that displays the beauty of the school, describes the culture of the school, and says that the school is willing to do something different and untraditional."

Different and untraditional seems to be the winning formula. Since its launch in August 2011, the Ampersandbox website has had more than 12,565 visitors (the college's undergraduate admission site received well over 1 million). Praise from other admissions officers and the media has also been overwhelming. Articles about William & Mary's innovative approach have appeared in both *The Washington Post*[2] and *The Chronicle of Higher Education*.[3] The Ampersandbox viewbook and microsite also received several awards within the field in 2012: The Council for Advancement and Support of Education granted it a Bronze Circle of Excellence Award, and the University and College Designers Association (UCDA) gave it a Silver Award for Recruitment/Viewbook and a UCDA Excellence Award for Campaign Strategy.

Integrating Print and Web

Schoonmaker explains that in developing the Ampersandbox, the team wanted to use content-driven components that were different but compatible, in this case the viewbook (print) and the microsite (online). They wanted to retain some of the sexiness of print, but also to have a robust online extension for discovery and engagement.

"All the components of the Ampersandbox work well together. They complement each other, but are not identical. And I don't think they should be the same," Schoonmaker said. "You have to consider that people read differently on the web and print, and people don't behave the same on the different channels."

To connect the print and web components, the designers included a url on every card that links to the online version of the same word pair. The design is the same in both versions, and the use of photos from William & Mary's award-winning photographer Stephen Salpukas adds another layer of consistency.

This focus on integrating the online and print experience was

---

(1) Link: ampersandbox.wm.edu

(2) Available at mstnr.me/WilliamandMary2

(3) Available at mstnr.me/WilliamandMary3

crucial to the success of the campaign. "In today's marketplace, a school as highly selective as William & Mary has prospective students that are just as selective, and in some cases even more so. By adding a web component to print, we were better able to capture their attention and stand out from the competition," said Wendy Livingston, associate dean of admission.

Bringing the William & Mary Experience to Life

While the cards can function by themselves, as can the website, one of the reasons the Ampersandbox is so successful is that it brings the William & Mary experience to life for prospective students in a way that goes beyond a traditional viewbook. It creates a robust online space for discovery and engagement.

"What's so great about this approach is that it involves interaction. Prospective students get the Ampersandbox cards in the mail, but that's not all. They can also go to the website and create their own word pairs. This allows prospective students to be part of the William & Mary community before they even apply," Schoonmaker said. "It gives them the privilege of adding to a discussion that most schools don't give you until you're accepted."

Current students and alumni rave about the Ampersandbox, saying that it perfectly captures the William & Mary they know and love, while prospective students and their families say that it makes the school stand out to the point that they want to apply. Following are a few of the accolades posted on Facebook:

> » "Received the box of conjunctions yesterday. Must say I was happy my son had planned on applying before they arrived and now I'm even more pleased. I noticed he had left a few highlighted on the table this morning with notes about why he felt William and Mary would be a good fit for him. Don't know if you are keeping records of favorites but if so here are his, Bread and Butter, Near and Far, Naked and Friendly, Show and Tell, Home and Away, Down and Dirty, and Leaps and Bounds. I'm quite impressed. I hope he makes it in. Thanks for the personal touch you have put into this college application process. Few colleges have attempted it as nicely as William and Mary."
> » "Just received a lovely box of conjunctions from you. The Admissions Board at William and Mary has officially made my day."
> » "Some colleges send comprehensive packages about their academics or fancy-looking letters. I read some, but really, almost all of them say the same things .... The ampersand box was simple in presentation, but incredibly intriguing. I loved that I could hear the voice of the school on the cards!"

Prospective students and other audiences also immediately

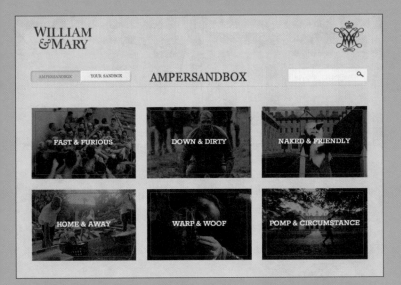

The collaborative website encourages visitors, "Take a moment to review the conjunctions that describe the lives and dreams of the W&M community and submit one of your own."

began posting their own word pairs and photos to the site. Following are a few of the admission team's favorite submissions from members of the Class of 2016:

» Loud & Proud, Caroline Dost: "At 4:27 on November 30, I was at school with my Mock Trial team, anxiously awaiting my ED email. I couldn't talk. I could barely breathe. Then my phone chimed. 'Good Things!' My ear-shattering scream could only mean one thing: I was in. My teammates swarmed around me in one big group hug, screaming right along with me. I have never been happier or LOUDER! in my life. I'm so proud to finally be a part of the Tribe!"

» Ready & Willing, Claire Tinsley: "I am ready and willing to try new things. I'm ready and willing to take on a challenge. And most of all, I'm ready and willing to experience everything William & Mary has to offer!"

» Friends & Family, Katie Conely: "If only one word could be used to describe the college, it would be community. Whether a student, alum, parent, visitor, or prospective student, you are treated with friendliness everywhere you turn. Never have I been on a campus with such a welcoming feeling. That is truly the William & Mary difference. Not only is it a place of academic excellence, it is also one of friends, family and community. Long live the Tribe."

» Search & Find, Katherine Oliver: "There is nothing like that moment when you realize that you have found the place you want to spend your college years. Stepping onto the William & Mary campus is like finding your schoolmate. Through all the daunting college searches it sometimes feels like you will never find a place where you fit in, then it happens: You step onto the W&M campus and can just tell. You breathe a sigh of relief, 'This is my home.'"

With the Ampersandbox, students are encouraged to "explore" and "connect" in addition to creating their own word pairing. (top)

The power of the campaign was that it combined both print and online media. (bottom)

Supporting Overall Communication Efforts

A vital part of the success of the campaign was having clear objectives in place to provide a benchmark for evaluating the campaign's effectiveness.

Targeting prospective students, the Ampersandbox campaign had three guiding objectives:

» To provide an effective web complement to the print component of the Ampersandbox. By having a web complement, the college uses current technology to better reach our prospective student base.

» To provide rich photography to prospective students in an interactive manner so that they can see what life looks like at William & Mary. William & Mary has a beautiful campus, so photography is an asset that the institution uses constantly.

» To digitally communicate the essence of William & Mary in succinct and poignant ways to a prospective student audience and their parents.

These objectives resulted in an innovative campaign that stood on its own, but at the same time supported William & Mary's overall communication efforts. While the Ampersandbox microsite has a customized design, it is reminiscent of the main website, which helps visually unite the two sites and makes linking between the two a natural transition.

The Ampersandbox word pairs also communicate the overall messaging of the college. "The Ampersandbox supports the message that William & Mary is an interesting, lively place to get a serious education. It's serious content in a fun wrapper," said Schoonmaker.

The campaign's favorable response by William & Mary administration has also started high-level conversations about other ways to leverage the ampersand in the college's name.

"The idea of using word pairs and what it means to us conceptually is carrying over to other marketing and communication endeavors," said Schoonmaker. "For example, the 2012 Miss Virginia, Rosemary Willis, is a senior at William & Mary. We're going to place an ad in the Miss America magazine for the 2013 pageant using a word pair to wish her well; maybe Brains & Beauty."

The Challenges of Producing a Spaceship

The William & Mary team had a unique challenge when producing the print component of the Ampersandbox: How do you print and mail something so completely unorthodox?

"From a print perspective, the box was a wonderful device. The writing and photography was really good, and the box was so different from what anyone else gets in the mail. It was so unusual that it led prospective students to read the cards and go to the website. But practically, the box was a nightmare," said Cindy Baker, associate director of creative services.

The cost of mailing the boxes of cards was close to double the expense of any previous viewbook campaign. The package also wasn't flexible or sturdy enough, and it got damaged in the mail. To address these issues in the second iteration, Baker said the staff decided to work with a packaging company. The result was an envelope with the same cardboard box feel, but one that was sturdier and cost less to mail. In fact, mailing costs dropped from $1.38 per piece to $.17 per piece.

There were also several design changes made to the online component. Schoonmaker explained that the pagination circles on the site didn't work well as a navigation tool for an increasing number of submissions. So, capitalizing on the "box" part of the name Ampersandbox, he changed the circle motif and made everything on the site square and boxy. In the second iteration, Schoonmaker also revised the layout to address some problems with text overlay on the photos, and to allow for greater use of photography. Another major change included the design of a mobile version. It's pared down to the most essential elements and remains focused on the content, so reading it on a mobile device is not cumbersome.

"For 'Your Sandbox,' user submissions are growing all the time. In the initial design, there was no plan for what to do with so many

> From a print perspective, the box was a wonderful device. The writing and photography was really good, and the box was so different from what anyone else gets in the mail. It was so unusual that it led prospective students to read the cards and go to the website. But practically, the box was a nightmare.

user submissions. We didn't know what we would get. But it's a good thing that we had so many people participating that we ran into design problems," said Schoonmaker.

Looking to the Future

With the second iteration of Ampersandbox complete (it was mailed in September 2012), Schoonmaker said that he and his colleagues are still looking at ways to address ongoing challenges and increase engagement.

One way they've boosted engagement is by adding a share function for all user-generated submissions. Anyone who creates a word pair on Your Sandbox can now share it on Facebook.

"Because prospective students live online, we're always looking for ways to engage them where they live. This sharing feature makes the Ampersandbox even more interactive and expands our reach," said Broaddus.

With the continuing growth in user-submitted word pairs, there is now a new challenge to address: How do you handle site contributions from students who ultimately are not accepted to William & Mary?

"Whenever you allow prospective students to become part of your community, even if it's just digital, you run the risk of having contributions from students who are ultimately not accepted. We have word pairs that are approved by admission, but what do you do with word pairs from unaccepted students? You should have some sort of exit strategy for how to deal with these students after the admissions season is over," said Schoonmaker. He added that nothing like this has happened yet, but the college wants to be prepared in case it does.

An evaluation of the campaign's effectiveness in recruiting undergraduates is also under way. Creative Services and the Office of Undergraduate Admission are developing a plan to garner feedback from the 2012 freshman class to find out how the Ampersandbox affected their decision to attend William & Mary. This feedback will also be instrumental in honing the campaign messaging to more effectively communicate with prospective students in the future.

While every campaign has its challenges, Schoonmaker advised to keep pushing through these obstacles: "One of the things I appreciate about William & Mary is the administration's willingness to take a risk and try something new that shows we're not like the competition. If you have a good idea and know you have a good idea, keep pushing forward. Try something new and different, and create your own spaceship." **SW**

Student-Powered Relationship Marketing in Admissions at Saint Michael's College

By Mallory Wood | @mallorywood

Mallory Wood is director of marketing at mStoner. Wood dreams up new marketing opportunities, works with potential clients to identify future project opportunities, and manages EDUniverse.org.

Current students are the best brand ambassadors for our institution. We already know this is a fact—why else would we use them as tour guides? Students live the story. And telling good stories can help institutions communicate more effectively with key audiences. So why do we limit students' connectivity to guiding campus visitors?

Saint Michael's College in Colchester, Vt., has let students tell the institution's story through many of the communication channels that today's audiences use in the new online world. The effort began in 2001, when the Office of Admission kicked off one of the earliest institution-sponsored student blogging programs, with just four bloggers. In 2006, the program doubled in size, acquired the title "SMC Bloggers," and became the face of St. Mike's online student-to-student recruitment efforts.[1] And in 2009, other social media tools entered the mix as the blogger program officially expanded into an online student ambassador program, overseen by the Office of Marketing and Communications. Today there are 15 SMC Bloggers, and they manage Blogger, Twitter, and Formspring accounts. They also participate in live chats with prospective students, create videos, connect with prospects on Facebook, and use mobile apps like Foursquare and Instagram.

"The goal driving the expansion of the program was centered on the idea that effective enrollment marketing comes from building relationships with prospective students," I said in 2009, when I was Saint Michael's assistant director of marketing, calling on the Bloggers to broaden their use of social media tools. "An ambassador can 'meet' a prospective student in one space and then reconnect with him or her in another, making that prospective student more likely to engage

---

(1) Available at mstnr.me/StMichael1

Training student ambassadors on social media tools helped to increase their effectiveness.

Alexandra Elena
@HeartsHalo92

Follow

PEOPLE RECOGNIZE ME FROM MY BLOG!!!!! #bestdayever #ithoughtnobodyreaditexceptmyparents

↰ Reply ⇄ Retweet ★ Favorite ⥥ Buffer

because he or she has built a relationship with the current student."

What does St. Mike's look for in an online ambassador? A student who:

- » is passionate about the college experience
- » cares about connecting with future students on behalf of the college
- » can highlight the academic experience in a compelling way
- » participates in clubs and organizations
- » exhibits leadership qualities
- » gets excited about new technology and social media.

Blogs

The blog continues to be the cornerstone of the program and the place where the ambassador can take greatest ownership of the space. Saint Michael's allows the Bloggers to select the layout and design of their blogs. Christian Camerota, assistant director of marketing for social media, believes this approach not only gives the students a greater sense of ownership of their blogs, but also encourages them to take more responsibility. And readers get a sense of the individual personality of each ambassador.

Camerota encourages students to write what they're thinking but to take a well-balanced, journalistic approach. "The ambassadors are welcome to offer criticism," he said, "but they have to show all sides of the issue."

"I try to be as honest as possible in my blog posts," said Gabbi Hall, the SMC Bloggers' current student coordinator. "I'm aware that St. Mike's is using my blog as a marketing tool, but it's important that I portray the SMC experience authentically."

Hall helps Camerota develop strategy for the program, keeping her own experience as a prospective student in mind: "Being from California, I couldn't drive to campus for a visit whenever I wanted or even attend summer registration day. Reading the student blogs gave me a sense of life on campus and what the students were like." For this reason, Hall strongly encourages the Bloggers to add photographs of campus and the surrounding area to their blogs. She also maintains a list of blog topic ideas to inspire the other ambassadors.

About 40 percent of the traffic to Hall's blog is from returning visitors. "By generating consistent and interesting content, I've developed a solid base of loyal readers," she said. Hall regularly reviews the search keywords that drive new traffic to her blog and selects new blog topics accordingly. Each ambassador can access his or her Google Analytics and regularly review the data to see what's working and to identify areas of improvement.

Twitter

In 2009, and against the advice of *The Chronicle of Higher Education*[2] and the Noel-Levitz *2011 E-Expectations Report*[3] — which both noted that teens showed low Twitter usage and little interest in using it as a tool to learn more about colleges—I required the ambassadors to use Twitter. The goal was to showcase life at St. Mike's in the moment.

Twitter became the micro-blog for the ambassadors, where they give a quick 140-character snapshot of their daily life on campus. Their tweets are accessible from the college website and their own blogs, so prospective students aren't required to create an account in order to see the content. Each year the Bloggers see increased interaction with prospective students and their families, but Camerota warns that follower count doesn't determine success or tell the whole story. Camerota sees value in retweeting what the ambassadors say from the official Saint Michael's Twitter account.[4] "The way they develop interactions and relationships with each other, with prospects, and with the outside world is extremely important. Their tweets give the college exposure in a positive way," he said.

Twitter also initially helped build a community among the ambassadors and increased Twitter usage on campus as ambassadors influenced their friends to sign up. Unexpectedly, it's also been an educational tool for the students as they started to follow leaders in higher education and marketing thought and participate in weekly Twitter chats like #HigherEdLive.

What I didn't expect was that an increase in the ambassadors' personal social networking activities would make the students better and more frequent bloggers. Using Klout,[5] a tool that claims to measure one's influence and reach across the web by producing a "score" for users, I determined which SMC Bloggers were considered to be the most influential and active on Twitter. When I compared

The way they develop interactions and relationships with each other, with prospects, and with the outside world is extremely important. Their tweets give the college exposure in a positive way.

(2) Available at mstnr.me/StMichael2
(3) Available at mstnr.me/StMichael3
(4) Handle: @saintmichaels
(5) Link: klout.com

the highest Klout scores with blogging metrics, via Google Analytics, I was pleasantly surprised to see that the Top 5 tweeters directly correlated with the Top 5 blogs as measured in unique blog visits, and four of the five saw the highest average page views.

Google Analytics also showed that Twitter ranks second among traffic sources to individual student blogs, at 16.2 percent, higher than any other social channel and even higher than direct traffic, at 13.5 percent. (The most traffic to individual blogs, as one might expect, comes from the college website at 46.5 percent.)

Formspring

Formspring,[6] Hall's favorite tool, is a Q&A social networking platform where anyone (with or without an account) can ask questions to users—anonymously, if they wish. Each online ambassador maintains a Formspring account. After just one year of use, the ambassadors had answered over 1,000 questions from prospective students and families via Formspring, ranging from "What is the honors program like?" to my favorite, "Is there toilet paper in the dorm bathrooms?"

Many admissions professionals express frustration that students rarely ask questions on the campus tour. They may feel too nervous to speak up, or they may have questions they're embarrassed to ask. Formspring gives prospective students and families a safe place to ask a question to an ambassador with whom they feel a connection. "The questions often are around sensitive topics, like the drinking culture on campus," said Hall. "Prospects want to hear honest answers from current students. It's better that they ask us, ambassadors who've been trained to respond appropriately and authentically, than someone else." And because Bloggers can feed Formspring answers into their blogs, other prospective students can benefit from the exchanges.

Facebook

The SMC Bloggers' approach to Facebook changes nearly as often as Facebook's privacy settings do. Current emphasis is placed on interacting with accepted students in their "Class of" Facebook group. This is a private group that each year's accepted students are invited to join, set up jointly by the Office of Marketing and Communications and the Office of Admissions.

Camerota's strategy is to let the SMC Bloggers facilitate and participate in conversations on the "Class of" group with the goals of building a community, driving traffic to the blogs, and sharing important information. "The SMC Bloggers are empowered to answer all of the accepted students' questions. They do an excellent

---

(6) Link: formspring.me

By Matt Connolly @MattC_TKHW

Traditionally dismissed as a tool for older audiences, Twitter is popular with SMC students and future students.

job because they have firsthand knowledge," he said.

Camerota said he sees his role as a moderator and answers sensitive questions but, for the most part, he tries to stay off the page. "We want this to be the students' space. The 'Class of' group isn't a place where we should hit them over the head with information or try to be their RA. Students should feel free to share anything in the group, but it is still an official college space, so there is some regulation necessary." At present Camerota is looking at ways to start using Facebook advertising to reach prospective students.

Other Social Media Channels

The SMC Bloggers are encouraged to participate in and supply content for other social media channels, like YouTube. While the ambassadors are not required to create video content, they're able to feed information about campus life to Camerota and the rest of the marketing and communications staff to let the team know what videos to create. "The ambassadors help us examine the quality of the videos we create in the marketing office," said Camerota. "It's good to get that type of feedback before releasing a video on our website or YouTube channel." And some Bloggers, like Hall, star in the videos. Hall has also experimented with video blogs and platforms such as VYou.[7] "I encourage the Bloggers to post video content because it engages our audience in a more dynamic way," she said.

Photography is another way of sharing visual content with prospective students. While the SMC Bloggers have historically used Flickr to upload and share photos, the ambassadors are now

---

(7) Link: vyou.com

spearheading a focus on Instagram. Many of them started using the tool on their smartphones to take photos of campus for their blog posts. "With Instagram we now have a really easy way to take cool photos of campus, share them, and build a community around them," said Hall. Camerota is still developing a strategy around the tool, but he anticipates asking Bloggers to tag campus photos with the official hashtag #SMCVT.

Payoffs and Lessons

Has the effort been worth the trouble? The Saint Michael's team believes it has. The Noel-Levitz *2011 E-Expectations Report* questions whether blogging is an effective recruitment tool, stating, "More than 75 percent of both parents and students said they never or only rarely read blogs on college sites." I question this statistic. If you look at the report, the reality is that 33 percent of students and 35 percent of parents admit to looking at blog postings on a college website. How many student recruitment efforts touch at least a third of your prospective pool? Very few.

While I managed the program, I routinely looked at Google Analytics on the college website and on individual student blogs to determine the program's effectiveness. In a presentation at the 2011 National HighEdWeb conference in Cincinnati, Ohio, the annual conference for higher education web professionals who want to explore the unique web issues facing institutions, I reported that the blogs saw over 70,000 visits each year and that the aggregator page itself had over a 20-minute average time on page. Students applying were asked on their application supplement if they'd interacted with the SMC Bloggers, and on average around 25 percent of applicants checked "yes." A few months later we'd ask the same question to entering freshman. Usually the number increased to 80 percent or more.

Here are some of the lessons we learned along the way.

Train, train, train! Camerota believes you can't train online student ambassadors enough. "We do our best at the beginning of every year to give a refresher course to the students. And we reiterate those messages over the course of the year to remind students about what is authentic versus inappropriate, what they can and can't blog or tweet about, and how to best avoid spammers."

With Instagram we now have a really easy way to take cool photos of campus, share them, and build a community around them.

Training topics include:

» best practices for writing for the web
» Saint Michael's messaging and branding
» how to understand and synthesize metrics in Google Analytics
» how to use each social media tool effectively.

It's no surprise that social media tools change frequently, with new ones seemingly being added to the mix every day. Adapting to and informing ambassadors of those changes is increasingly important. But training doesn't happen just during scheduled sessions. Camerota has learned to use teaching moments effectively in his daily interactions with the ambassadors in order to empower them to the greatest degree.

Find the right students. On campus, the SMC Blogger program is becoming a popular extracurricular activity for students. On average only four to seven spots open up for new ambassadors each year, and usually the number of students interested in filling those spots is four or five times what is available.

The students who make up the SMC Bloggers represent different examples of the Saint Michael's student. But when you're selecting new ambassadors, is it more important to fill a niche or find a student who'll do a good job? Of course you'd like to represent every niche of the campus community, but most importantly you need to hire students who'll remain motivated all year. Hall confirmed that finding a committed student is the top priority: "Finding new things to write about after participating in this program for three years is hard."

The application process to become an SMC Blogger is rigorous. For current students, the process takes a month, and for first-year students, it lasts an entire semester. Students are asked to create and manage a blog, Twitter account, and Formspring account as if they were an online ambassador. This allows Camerota and Hall to evaluate the quality and frequency of their content, their desire to participate in the program, their fluency with the various social media tools, and their willingness to learn.

Remember that this program affects more than just recruitment. The program also has an impact on the lives of the students participating in it. Camerota noted, "The No. 1 goal at Saint Michael's College is to educate students. We want to graduate good people who go out into the world and are successful in every sense of the word."

The SMC Bloggers receive a résumé-enhancing experience and learn valuable skills that employers will find desirable. In fact, many graduates of the program have received job offers largely because of the work they did and the knowledge they gained as an SMC Blogger. "And hopefully former SMC Bloggers will be more willing to give back to the institution in the form of prospective student referrals, donations, internships for current students, or jobs for future graduates," added Camerota. **SW**

How Social Sharing by Students Boosts Awareness for University of Wisconsin–River Falls

By Jennifer Connally | @JennConnally

Jennifer Connally, customer marketing leader at readMedia, focuses on the first-year experience, content strategy, and transforming client success into compelling stories.

For the University of Wisconsin–River Falls, the westernmost institution in the University of Wisconsin state system, standing out among 13 sister colleges, 26 campuses, and the Twin Cities market just across the border was a challenge. UWRF was determined to develop a social media strategy that would demonstrably support its institutional goals for enrollment, retention, and development.

UWRF's University Communication team observed that traditional marketing methods such as viewbooks, billboards, and print advertising were costing more than ever, yet lacked the tangible return on investment that senior decision-makers demanded. This trend, coupled with research[1] that showed Millennials are updating social networks several times per day, led University Communication to explore the possibility[2] of shifting dollars and resources into a measurable social media strategy that would deliver the accountability and results that legacy tactics could not.

According to Amy Luethmers, UWRF marketing specialist, research[3] shows that as many as 80 percent of prospective students learn about colleges from family and friends, and often those contacts occur through social media. "Students are using Facebook, and so are their parents," she said.

UWRF's key insight was that its student body represented the organic, authentic, and compelling "capital" it could invest in its social media strategies. Students' accomplishments, activities, and outcomes were both a testament to the value of the UWRF experience and the elements of a content marketing strategy. By

---

(1) Available at mstnr.me/UWRiverFalls1
(2) Available at mstnr.me/UWRiverFalls2
(3) Available at mstnr.me/UWRiverFalls3

leveraging the power of its student capital, UWRF launched a strategy that united content marketing and social media in a way all of the university's stakeholders could understand and support.

The Challenge

University Communications analyzed the competitive pain points for UWRF and identified three areas to address.

Competition. UWRF knew, early on, that it needed to segment messaging while maintaining a consistent institutional brand at all points of contact. Recognizable branding would help distinguish UWRF from other UW universities and, if executed properly, would resonate with audiences across state lines—long after exposure.

Reach. UWRF was in growth mode and seeking to attract applicants beyond its historic markets in northwestern Wisconsin, particularly from neighboring Minnesota and Illinois. However, it was expensive to build brand awareness from a standing start in remote markets.

Technology. University Communications consolidated messaging and channel communications to get the most bang for its branding bucks. Yet although UWRF budgeted 15 percent of staff time (at a cost of almost $10,000 per year) to managing and maintaining the institution's social media channels, including Facebook, Twitter, and YouTube, its social media strategy did not fully map back to the goals of the institution. Social media success boiled down to the traditional method of measurement: counting "likes," posts, and comments.[4]

Solving these three pain points became the social media strategy's mandate: stand out in a crowded market, build brand affinity in target markets, and replace traditional, low-value spending with measurable, higher-return social media where possible.

"We wanted to wrap social media into a new and improved communications strategy, but it was especially important to seek out cost-effective ways to manage, measure, and justify our social media efforts," said Luethmers.

The Solution

University Communications kicked off its project in January 2012. Serendipitously, colleagues in Admissions were reviewing software from readMedia that validates, promotes, and measures engagement in student achievements and activities on campus and aggregates these personalized stories online and in social networks. Admissions brought in University Communications as a natural sponsor.

"Our office was so impressed with readMedia that when

---

(4) Available at mstnr.me/UWRiverFalls4

we brought the solution to the attention of University Communications, we offered to use some of our own budget to offset the cost of purchasing the service," said Jennifer Sell, UWRF admissions counselor.

The readMedia approach challenged UWRF to think of students as natural brand ambassadors who would reach geographic and social media audiences organically. The key was having the tools to turn these brand ambassadors into engaged, enthusiastic, and measurable marketing assets.

The Strategy

The readMedia software combined a content-marketing strategy with the tools to conduct and assess each campaign. To launch, UWRF needed only a few assets of its own in place:

> » an initial "achievement strategy" citing activities and accomplishments that UWRF would validate and promote, each designed to continue a compelling narrative about the university's distinctive character
> » "badges" for each achievement, which were designed as high-affiliation brand artifacts that students and their families would share.

For its part, readMedia provided UWRF with a strategic framework and software to deploy and measure the campaigns conducted with it. It included these components:

> » a benchmark editorial calendar of achievements throughout the academic year that UWRF customized to map to its unique programs and traits
> » guidelines for identifying and extracting personalized achievement opportunities from generic, low-performing stories that had already been created within the news organization
> » the Attention Matrix, readMedia's tool to correlate audience and engagement traits to campaign goals
> » ReadAboutMe, a site hosting branded, personalized versions of each achievement UWRF awarded as well as achievement profiles of each individual student
> » benchmarking reports prepared by readMedia's senior strategist to measure UWRF's campaigns.

UWRF met with readMedia's senior strategist during a live online consulting and training session and used readMedia's software to award the Fall 2011 Dean's List in February, two weeks after purchasing the software. The Dean's List achievement generated 1,305 personalized student stories, with almost two-thirds of students engaging with them. In total,

Our office was so impressed with readMedia that when we brought the solution to the attention of University Communications, we offered to use some of our own budget to offset the cost of purchasing the service.

readMedia software helped to power awards such as the Dean's List each semester. (top)

Personalizing stories created more buzz and organic interest in UWRF news and events. (bottom)

246 students carried UWRF's brand into their social networks, prompting more than 4,000 additional readers to discover the university's content. Finally, readMedia's software delivered the students' stories to more than 453 media outlets in dozens of media markets—including UWRF's key out-of-state targets.

The Revised Strategy

UWRF quickly ramped up its strategy to actively promote the achievement strategy to the students themselves.

"While acknowledging larger achievements was not new to UWRF, the readMedia method itself was, and we knew we had to educate our stakeholders," said Luethmers. "So, we devised a communications strategy that would let faculty, staff, and students know that what we're doing isn't new, it's just better."

University Communications' iterative approach to promoting the readMedia-enabled social media campaign helped the staff learn quickly what tactics resonated with students and which did not. The least effective approaches were simply to present and talk about the new strategy and to make Facebook posts or Tweets from institutional accounts. Much more effective were these:

» dedicating a page to readMedia on the UWRF website[5]
» making an explanatory YouTube video[6]
» featuring readMedia and ReadAboutMe on the campus

---

(5) Available at mstnr.me/UWRiverFalls5
(6) Available at mstnr.me/UWRiverFalls6

By using students as natural ambassadors, UWRF sought to distinguish itself among peer institutions nearby.

media page[7]

» pitching articles to the student newspaper about readMedia and student success.[8]

The recurring theme in the effective tactics was that students, faculty, and parents wanted to know that the stories, badges, and validated achievements were institutionally sponsored. Once they knew that, they enthusiastically adopted the idea. The act of recognizing and awarding accomplishments did not begin with the current generation of college students. What is new is how immediate, personal, and digitally portable the readMedia-powered awards were. The fact that UWRF was validating and promoting the achievements made them not only more credible but also more desirable.

The Results

According to the *Email Marketing Metrics Report*,[9] the average email open rate in education is 11.5 percent. By implementing a new platform and strategy for publicizing students' activities and academic accomplishments online, UWRF far surpassed the average, with a current open rate of 58 percent. Using readMedia software, UWRF staff members can track how many stories are emailed to students, parents, and media outlets. They can also view delivery reports for each achievement, so they can monitor, measure, and improve their reach.

In less than one year, UWRF promoted 20 achievements, generating 5,023 individual stories that were published online and to 5,023 students and parents. Moreover, 502 of those individuals

(7) Available at mstnr.me/UWRiverFalls7
(8) Available at mstnr.me/UWRiverFalls8
(9) Available at mstnr.me/UWRiverFalls9

shared these institutionally branded accomplishments on Facebook, reaching an audience of approximately 687,400. The Facebook shares and social media activity alone drove 7,487 friends and family members to the original student stories and profiles on ReadAboutMe.

UWRF is preparing to distribute its fall 2012 enrollment achievement to an incoming class of approximately 2,472 freshmen. These stories are expected to reach 321,000 Facebook news feeds, bringing UWRF's Facebook audience to over one million viewers. A projected 1,500 additional friends and family members will follow the link back to the full story, bringing readership to nearly 9,000.

While UWRF has garnered attention for its unique brand attributes, other institutions have successfully used the same approach to support their own brand positioning. For example:

» James Madison University in Harrisonburg, Va., promoted 10 achievements in three months. These generated 15,516 individual student stories that reached more than 36,082 students and parents, prompted 2,253 social media shares that reached a Facebook audience of 2,129,400, and drove 40,693 readers to view the original stories.

» The Berklee College of Music in Boston awarded six achievements within a month. The resulting 3,415 stories were brought into 546 personal social networks, reaching an audience of more than 770,000 viewers nationwide, 11,594 of whom then read Berklee's branded stories in depth.

Personal Marketing

David Moteelall, a student at UWRF, is from Cologne, Minn., a small township in Norwood Young America, located 40 minutes southwest of Minneapolis—right in UWRF's target market. In April 2012, Moteelall received a scholarship from the UWRF College of Business and Economics. To celebrate this accomplishment, UWRF used readMedia to distribute a personalized story. This appeared on ReadAboutMe, and Moteelall shared his success with family and friends on Facebook. The UWRF-branded story was promoted in the news feeds of over 400 friends in Moteelall's network, 11 of whom imported UWRF's brand into their own social networks by "liking" the achievement; seven others left encouraging comments for Moteelall that in turn became visible to their own networks.

All told, the PR effort announcing the 18 scholarships awarded at this time to students at UWRF drove 45 family members and friends back to ReadAboutMe to read the full story. This is powerful word-of-mouth marketing that is scalable, predictable, and measurable. **SW**

Using Social Media and a Rap Video to Increase Visibility for Murray State University

By Dana Howard | @DanaMSUalum

Dana Howard is the social media marketing manager at Murray State University in the office of University Communications.

W hen the 2011–12 Racer basketball season opened, we knew it was going to be a special year at Murray State University ... but we had no idea what was about to happen.

Suddenly, positive national exposure was knocking on our door, and we had to answer immediately. Our University Communications team pulled together quickly to capitalize on the growing attention the world was showing our small town of Murray, Ky., and our "Cinderella story" basketball team.

Social media platforms were exploding with people talking about our basketball team, the Racers. At first, most discussion came from the university community, but soon others, like ESPN reporters, started talking daily about the team. With a star point guard and new head coach, both standouts in the nation, people began asking, "Who are the Racers?"

Building on the Excitement

Our plan to promote the basketball team began with simply responding to those with an interest in the team. Social media monitoring and response, primarily on Twitter, was a constant job. We pushed branding hashtags, such as #WeAreRacers (later #WAR) and #RacerNation, and this became very important through the rest of the season and marketing campaign.

The next phase of the media plan came as a complete surprise. Our communications team discovered that a student rap duo, TrubzNMatlock, had written a rap about the magic of the basketball season, and it was quickly becoming popular among the students. We told the two rappers that we would make a professional video for their song if they would let us use it to promote the team and university. Planning for the video started in

December, we shot it in January, and we released it right after the students returned from holiday break. Although we planned the timing of the release, we had no idea it was going to be right before we became the nation's last undefeated men's NCAA Division I basketball team, one of the peaks of exposure for the university.

The "Murray State Anthem" was an instant hit among Murray State supporters and became the anthem of the season. The video highlights our students, the basketball team, the mascot, faculty and staff, and campus traditions. During the two weeks of shooting, we released behind-the-scenes videos and pushed these teasers out with the hashtag #MurrayStateAnthem to get people talking. This got the students excited about sharing the Anthem and encouraged them to come to the home game early the night of the Anthem debut.

At the same time that we were working on the Anthem video, we designed a special edition t-shirt that added a new twist to our branding. Our current branding is "We Are Racers," but since many universities have started using the same type of slogan, we wanted a unique version of it. The communications team came up with WAR. We believed this represented all facets of being a Racer: from current and former students fighting their way through life, academically or in their careers, to a small-town team determined to show the world what they were made of. We released the new WAR campaign at the same time as the Anthem. The original plan was to use the shirts as giveaways for people sharing the video online. However, the shirts were such a hit that the university bookstore decided to reprint them for sale, and they quickly became a top seller.

The new shirt said "WAR" with "We Are Racers" below it to get people used to the new logo. The back of the shirt was a word cloud of hashtags being used on Twitter throughout the season. We had created some of the hashtags for branding purposes, but most of them came from our university community, including students, faculty, and staff. To gather these, we went through the history of tweets referring to Murray State and decided which hashtags were most used or most important to the season. The hashtags provided a timeline of the season up to that point, referring to our standout players, rivalry games, places we had played, and other things that stood out to our affinity groups.

We revealed the shirts the same night we premiered the Murray State Anthem video. University Communications staff and TrubzNMatlock and their team wore the shirts to the home game. When TrubzNMatlock were introduced on center court after the video, people wanted to know where they could buy a shirt, and we spread the word that they could win a shirt by sharing the video with their friends online.

> The "Murray State Anthem" was an instant hit among Murray State supporters and became the anthem of the season. The video highlights our students, the basketball team, the mascot, faculty and staff, and campus traditions.

Murray State University Presents...
Murray State Anthem
Featuring TrubzNMatlock

Check it out NOW
www.youtube.com/murraystateuniv

Download the song now on iTunes

@MurrayStateUniv
@TrubzNMatlock

TrubzNMatlock describe themselves on Twitter as "chasing dreams too big for most."

Marketing the Video and Measuring Success

The video,[1] featured on the Murray State YouTube page,[2] was released online at halftime of that game with notification via Twitter and Facebook. Within the same hour the video was released, 50 people had shared it from the Murray State Facebook page, and 4,000 people had viewed the video from Facebook. In less than 24 hours, the video had 10,000 hits. The following Monday we announced the giveaway of the shirts on our Facebook page with a picture of TrubzNMatlock's team wearing them and had 147 immediate shares. The video views were well above 30,000 in three days. In 10 days, the video had more than 80,000 hits, there were 1,500 mentions of the official name "Murray State Anthem" on Twitter, and the video was shared 400 times on Facebook. In the next week, the video was embedded and discussed on many national blogs, including Yahoo Sports, CBS Sports, SBNation, NBC Sports, and USAToday. On top of that, countless sports bloggers continued to tweet about it all the way through March Madness.

To gain more student attention and provide easy access to the video, we relied on traditional marketing with a twist. Using pictures of scenes from the video, we printed a standout poster that included a QR code embedded with the video link. TrubzNMatlock took their team around campus, promoting the video as they went, and covered the campus in posters. People walking by could scan the QR code with their smartphones and see the video.

The Anthem video continued to bring exposure to the team

---

(1) Available at mstnr.me/MurraySt1
(2) Link: youtube.com/murraystateuniv

and the university through the remainder of the season and well into the NCAA tournament. CBS called to get original copies of the video to use in promos leading up to and through the tourney. On national blogs, the video was compared to videos from other universities in much bigger conferences. We knew we had something big when one blogger had a competition between our video and the Giants Super Bowl Anthem, and our video won. We used these opportunities to continue to publicize the Anthem through our own social media platforms, asking people to watch, vote, and share. With all the attention the team and the video were receiving, it was easy to keep the name, hashtags, and url in the mix of conversations across all social media platforms throughout the next couple of months.

As the season continued, the marketing from the Anthem campaign made its way into other, sometimes more traditional, marketing. Printed pieces, banners, and visuals that were used throughout March to market the university reflected the hashtag timeline used in the WAR shirts, including #MurrayStateAnthem and #HoopSquad, which were direct references to the video.

The Murray State Anthem exceeded all of our expectations. What took three months to achieve with previous viral videos (30,000 hits), took three days with the Murray State Anthem. In a month's time, the video had 100,000 views.

Another Social Media Campaign

The final social media piece of the season led to one of the most historic events in Murray State athletics history. Earlier in the season, we'd noticed that legendary sports announcer Dick Vitale was a fan of our team and coach and mentioned Murray State consistently during his ESPN broadcasts. As the season continued, he started tweeting about us, and he seemed to want to come to Murray State for a game. Our fans noticed this as well and tweeted frequently about his mentions. One fan decided we could influence him and his managers if we kept tweeting invitations to Vitale, so he started the #BringDickieVtoMurray hashtag. We immediately retweeted it, begging Vitale to come to our town.

But we didn't stop there. In collaboration with our athletics marketing team, we dove headfirst into another social media campaign. Athletics created images of the hashtag that people could use as their Facebook profile picture, and we asked our fans and followers on all platforms to keep using the hashtag as a plea to ESPN. Athletics also incorporated large signs of Vitale's picture and the hashtag into the student section during our televised games to show the nation we were inviting him.

A couple of games passed, and we kept hearing Vitale talk about all the people from RacerNation tweeting him, so we knew our

voices were being heard. He was well aware that we wanted him to announce a game, and we would do whatever it took to get him here.

A couple of weeks later, we finally lost our first game, and we were afraid we were not going to get Vitale to come to Murray, so we took the campaign a step further. We decided that our best chance to have him as an announcer was for the ESPN BracketBuster game at the end of the season, which was also our only prime-time ESPN broadcast game. We only had two home games before that night, and we wanted to use them to make our final plea. Using the hosts and crew from our TV show, RoundAbout U (also part of our University Communications team), we posted on Twitter and Facebook that we would be at the doors of the basketball arena before the game and asked people to bring their Racer spirit and do their best Dickie V impersonation. People dressed up, made signs, and showed off their best Dickie V impersonations as we walked through the lines. Our team quickly put together a montage of the community invitations to Vitale and pushed out a YouTube video[3] through our Facebook and Twitter accounts the following Monday. We asked people to continue sharing it using the hashtag #BringDickieVtoMurray. Then, using Twitter and Facebook again, we shared the montage with Vitale and several ESPN staff and invited them to keep looking at the hashtag trail of Murray State fans begging to have Vitale at our ESPN BracketBuster game.

At the final regular season home game of the year, Dick Vitale announced live on TV that he would be coming to Murray State as the announcer of the ESPN BracketBuster game. We believe that the social media push behind our winning team was a big part of

---

(3) Available at mstnr.me/MurraySt3

One of the rap's more prominent lines: "Got the whole world watching, asking 'bout the OVC. See us on the television; 'What up, Dickie V!'" (top)

The TrubzNMatlock lyrics helped inspire the #BringDickieVtoMurray campaign. (bottom)

ESPN flying Vitale to Murray, Ky., for what ended up being the most national exposure Murray State has ever seen.

Lessons Learned

Timing is important! You don't always have a year to plan a marketing campaign. Sometimes you just have to jump on things as they happen. The success of the Murray State Anthem and the Dick Vitale visit involved a little bit of luck, but we knew with each that we had to move quickly. Again, luckily for us, we became the last undefeated team in the nation immediately following the release of the Anthem. So, if we had waited much longer to release the video, we would have missed that peak point in the national exposure we were about to experience.

We are learning how to create our own campus trends. We picked up on this with our previous viral video project, the Racer Shuffle, in which we customized a pop culture trend, FMLAO's Party Rock Anthem/the Shuffle,[4] to our affinity groups. When you find something trendy that students and staff not only grasp but continue using for an extended time, you realize your effort was worthwhile. We started noticing people were using the Anthem song, the video, and the WAR shirts to support the team and show their Racer Pride. Many on Twitter used the Murray State Anthem to refer to the magical season. Months later, we are still seeing those references in tweets and Facebook comments, such as "So ready for basketball season to start, already blaring #MurrayStateAnthem with the windows down." It has become a part of the culture and tradition of

---

(4) Available at mstnr.me/MurraySt4

Murray State and our basketball program.

Integration is the key to a successful campaign. Although the Anthem campaign was primarily marketed using social media tactics, we used traditional marketing to create an overall presence online, on campus, and in the community. This included the shirts, posters, banners, and other printed pieces. Going outside of the internet to bring the theme and content to life created real connection for our audiences.

Naturally, some people were concerned that older alumni and supporters would not be impressed with this rap video we were using to represent the university. Of course, there will always be a few negative comments with anything you do, but overall, Racers from every generation not only enjoyed the video but also shared it with their online connections. We kept the video fun, clean, classy, and positive while integrating campus traditions into the video. So far, even though our videos have all been based on pop culture, the majority of our supporters enjoy them and continue to help us make our social media campaigns successful.

Finally, the content produced in a campaign matters. The Anthem was so special with all of our audiences because it was 100 percent Murray State. The song and video highlighted the team but also the culture and spirit of our campus and the following our basketball program has had through the history of the university.   **SW**

Employing Social Channels to Increase Institutional Support for a New Athletic Venture at Vanderbilt University

By Kylie Stanley Larson | @kylieslarson

Kylie Stanley Larson is a project manager at mStoner, where she serves as a primary point of contact for clients working with her consulting team. She has a broad background in higher education, including policy research, fundraising, and college admissions counseling.

I n July 2010, Bobby Johnson, Vanderbilt University's football coach for eight seasons, retired and left Nashville with a 29–66 win-to-loss record, 12–52 in the Southeastern Conference (SEC). Vanderbilt's offensive line coach, Robbie Caldwell, was named the interim head coach immediately, and within weeks he became the head coach, sans "interim." Caldwell led the Commodores through a disappointing season and ended the year with a 2–10 record. At the end of Caldwell's season, the message on blogs, on Twitter, on Facebook, and in emails to campus administrators was clear: The Vanderbilt community was tired of losing.

However, the 'Dores (as they call themselves) needed to find a way to win on the field while still adhering to Vanderbilt's central mission to be "a center for scholarly research, informed and creative teaching, and service to the community and society at large." The university needed to find a coach who understood that athletic excellence must coincide with academic excellence, rather than exist as a separate phenomenon. The search for such an individual began in late November 2010.

At the same time, Beth Fortune, vice chancellor for public affairs at Vanderbilt, and her team were charged with orchestrating the announcement and introduction of a new coach to the institution's community and friends. The strategic planning for that campaign began alongside the administration's search for the right coach, which meant that the Athletics Media Relations and News & Communications offices were engaging in planning sessions to announce an unknown individual at an unknown time.

Setting Strategy

Melanie Moran, then associate director of News & Communications, managed the day-to-day online campaign operations in close partnership with Athletics under Fortune's direction. The specific instruction to the communications team was to "change the conversation about Vanderbilt football and leverage all of the strengths of Vanderbilt in doing so," Moran said.

The News & Communications team understood that the hire would happen quickly, if possible; Chancellor Nicholas S. Zeppos and Vice Chancellor David Williams spent 21 days straight interviewing and weeding through candidates in November and December 2010. Strategy informed all actions. Moran noted, "We wanted to mark this as a university priority and make sure everything we did was consistent with that and reflected the rest of the messaging: We don't compromise on academics, and our student-athletes are integrated with the rest of campus life."

Based on that focus, the News & Communications team carefully constructed a rollout plan. Although the traditional approach would be first to hold a press conference and issue a press release, Moran noted, staff members looked instead at an online-first approach, considering which tools they had at their disposal and where their audiences lived online. Ultimately, the team decided to make the initial announcement on Facebook, "where our audience was most engaged," Moran said. Moreover, making the announcement via social media would meet fans where they were comfortable, and the university "wanted to give something back to our fans, directly," said Moran.

The plan for bringing in a new coach extended far beyond the initial hiring announcement. The team also had to introduce the individual and help drive the conversation. In keeping with the philosophy that this was a university announcement and not solely athletic news, the News & Communications team pulled in faculty and staff from all over campus to help with the rollout. Members from Athletics, Web Communications, the central video team, the central news team, Creative Services, Development and Alumni Relations, and the Dean of Students' office assisted in the planning, pre-production, and production phases.

Deploying the Message

On Dec. 17, 2010, the right individual emerged, and campus leaders were ready to announce a new head football coach. While rumors flew across various social media channels, Vanderbilt's News & Communications team took to Facebook[1] and posted: "Vanderbilt fans, we want you to be the first to get the official news on the new head coach of the Commodore football team. Once we have the confirmed information, we'll post it here. Stay tuned!" That post received 87 likes and 172 comments nearly immediately. Shortly

> The specific instruction to the communications team was to "change the conversation about Vanderbilt football and leverage all of the strengths of Vanderbilt in doing so."

_____

(1) Link: facebook.com/vanderbilt

Vanderbilt University
December 16, 2010 ⊕

Vanderbilt fans, we want you to be the first to get the official news on the new head coach of the Commodore football team. Once we have the confirmed information, we'll post it here. Stay tuned!

Like · Comment · Share   👍 87   💬 172

Vanderbilt Web Communications skipped a traditional press release and made the coach announcement on Facebook first.

afterward, the Vanderbilt Facebook feed displayed its official announcement: "Commodore Nation: We have a new head football coach. James Franklin will leave Maryland to lead Vanderbilt. More details later today at a news conference scheduled for 1 p.m. and streamed live at http://www.vanderbilt.edu/coach." Short, simple, and action-oriented, the message drove fans to the new university-created website for Coach Franklin.

The immediate reaction to Coach Franklin's hiring announcement was largely negative. Days earlier, high-profile Gus Malzahn, offensive coordinator at Auburn University (whose team went on to win the BCS Championship that season), looked likely to score the gig, and 'Dore fans were jazzed at the opportunity to bring in such a big name. In contrast, Franklin lacked the immediate cachet of Malzahn (and others in the running). One of the first comments on the official Facebook post said, "This would be a great time for a dislike button." Other comments included these:

> » "The absence of Ron Prince is disheartening and likely brings an end to my lifelong love of Vanderbilt football."
> » "Why not go for Terry Bowden?????????"
> » "I won't go as far as 'Like.' I'll 'Tentative Optimism' it, though."
> » "BOOOOOOOOOOOOOOOOO!"

Reading the initial negative commentary was tough for Fortune, Moran, and the rest of the News & Communications team, but they stayed in line with the Vanderbilt News Comment Policy:[2] "Comments that disagree with or criticize Vanderbilt are approved." Following that policy, they did filter out any comments that used vulgar language, hate speech, or personal attacks. Moreover, the media team tried to reach out to individuals who were spreading inaccurate information by messaging them directly with the facts, as is the office's normal practice. The team worked

(2) Available at mstnr.me/Vanderbilt2

Vanderbilt's News & Communications team emphasized the Franklin family joining the Nashville community.

throughout the day and continued driving Vanderbilt's central messages: (1) This is a new beginning for our football program, and (2) The entire institution is behind this announcement.

The Vanderbilt Twitter feed, @VanderbiltU, posted a photograph of James Franklin, his wife, and his two young girls arriving at the Nashville International Airport that day. The feed quickly followed up with a video interview[3] News & Communications had done with the coach just that morning. Moran praised the team that pulled it off: "We have the absolute best video team in higher education. They are absolutely phenomenal, and video is an incredibly compelling tool."

In the official press conference later in the day, Chancellor Zeppos drove home the university's central message with zeal:

> We win everywhere at Vanderbilt. We win athletically. We win academically. And there's no darn reason we can't win in football, and we're going to do it…. I told Coach Franklin that he has my full support. If I need to be pulling the tire with him, if I need to be running with the parachute on my back, if I need to be with the kids lifting weights, I'm all in, and Vanderbilt is all in.

The press conference was streamed live on Vanderbilt.edu/coach,[4] and the YouTube video[5] was posted only a day later. Glued to social media monitoring tools, the Vanderbilt News &

(3) Available at mstnr.me/Vanderbilt3
(4) Available at mstnr.me/Vanderbilt4
(5) Available at mstnr.me/Vanderbilt5

Communications team slowly saw the conversation turn in a positive direction. The hiring became a trending topic on Twitter, and after the conference Twitter fans began to adopt Zeppos' phrase as a hashtag: #VUAllIn.

Amusingly, the followers started telling the leaders how to speak to them: @diezba tweeted "Hey @VanderbiltU @VandyFootball tell yr followers to tweet w/ new hashtag based on Zeppos/ Franklin's presser: #vuallin." So the News & Communications staff did—they retweeted and adopted the hashtag. Facebook fans also adopted the slogan, and the tone turned positive there as well, as some of the later comments demonstrated:

> » "I plan to love Coach Franklin if he takes good care of the student athletes!"
> » "Let's go Vandy!"
> » "welcome to my alma mater—and my father's and son's and daughter's—we are all hopeful—it's a great place"
> » "welcome coach. Come meet us at Hoops tomorrow night"
> » "I'll be there this fall to cheer on the 'Dores and welcome Coach Franklin!"
> » "come on guys give him a chance"

In the days and weeks that followed, the News & Communications team continued to steer its optimistic and supportive message. On December 22, the CloserVU video[6] allowed "a personal look at the first hours Head Football Coach James Franklin and family spent as new members of the Commodore Nation." There was a conscious decision to present Coach Franklin and his family as part of the Vanderbilt and Nashville community. It helped that the new coach was great with media and, as Vice Chancellor Williams put it, "dynamic."

Fortune and team felt it was important to put Coach Franklin and family front and center in the weeks and months that followed his hiring because the Vanderbilt community talks about itself as a family. The News & Communications office also sensed his charm on film. "He is who he is. He is extremely charismatic and good on camera and is that kind of public figure," said Moran.

Building Beyond Athletics

Despite an initially negative and confused reaction, the Vanderbilt community as a whole eventually embraced Coach Franklin and the new direction. The social media conversations shifted,[7] and when the next football season rolled around, ticket sales increased.

---

(6) Available at mstnr.me/Vanderbilt6
(7) Available at mstnr.me/Vanderbilt7

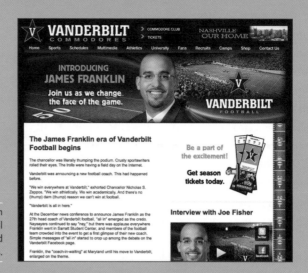

The Vanderbilt.edu/coach website aggregated social media and displayed institutional news stories.

In James Franklin's 2011 season, the Vanderbilt 'Dores had a 6–7 record and went to the Liberty Bowl.

The wins on the field and the bodies in the seats represented concrete examples of success, but Moran defined success more broadly: "We had a full-court media-rich welcome so that all audiences could get info in a way that made sense to them and left them with a positive impression."

The Vanderbilt football program's rejuvenation, in part due to James Franklin's successful hiring and introduction to the community, led to the new Game Changer campaign[8] presented in the 2012–13 academic year. The first in a series of videos[9] set the tone, starting with an image of the sun rising over Vanderbilt stadium as the background voice extols, "Change doesn't happen on its own. There is no magic wand, no silver bullet. Change is not for the weak. To change the game takes time, a willingness to challenge the status quo, but most of all it takes tenacity, to believe that you can win on your own terms—in academics, in life, and on the field— to be a game changer."

The Game Changer campaign begs the community to hang on and maintain enthusiasm even as the program rebuilds and experiences growing pains. Beyond the Game Changer campaign, the News & Communications team works closely with the Athletics office at Vanderbilt. The resulting plethora of multimedia aims to show Vanderbilt observers what really goes on at an SEC program and what's possible when you marry your athletics and academics. Fully in support of that goal, Coach Franklin gave unprecedented access to his signing day activities,[10] scholarship

(8) Available at mstnr.me/Vanderbilt8

(9) Available at mstnr.me/Vanderbilt9

(10) Available at mstnr.me/Vanderbilt10

decisions on the team,[11] and post-game reactions.[12] Vanderbilt's social media successes with the football program have inspired other coaches on campus and at peer institutions to take a similar approach to publicity.

Back on Dec. 17, 2010, as Vice Chancellor Williams kicked off the press conference, he told the Vanderbilt community the administration would do three things: change the culture of Vanderbilt football, increase the quality of Vanderbilt football facilities, and hire a dynamic football coach. Looking back at the James Franklin announcement, the subsequent introduction, and the continuing campaign for support, it's clear that the strategy set in late 2010 is still part of the messaging two years later.

Drawing Lessons

Based on Vanderbilt's experience, there are takeaways for other PR officers charged with carrying the message of a major program change:

» Always start a campaign with a clear strategy. What are you trying to accomplish? Who are you trying to reach? Where does your audience engage most with that topic? Which tools do you have at your disposal?

» As part of developing your strategy, research your audience extensively. Understand the conventions of your audience members, the conversations they are already having, and where they are most likely to go to have those conversations.

» Remember that you cannot control negative commentary. You can, however, create rich positive experiences for your community that help to balance the negative voices. You can also reach out and attempt to directly correct factual errors.

» Put a social media handbook and news comment policy in place now. They will support you through the hectic lifecycle of campaign or crisis communication.

» Empower your fans by adopting the topics and media they are interested in. Stay true to your central message and strategy, but be willing to go off course on the "how" if someone in the audience has a better idea.   **SW**

---

(11) Available at mstnr.me/Vanderbilt11
(12) Available at mstnr.me/Vanderbilt12

How Gamification Boosted Participation at Johns Hopkins Alumni Weekend

By Melissa Soberanes

Melissa Soberanes is a writer and editor at mStoner. She has more than 15 years of experience helping nonprofit organizations and education institutions increase awareness and tell their stories through effective communications, media relations, and web strategies.

The success of Fantasy Reunion at Johns Hopkins University demonstrates that online gaming and social media have an important role to play in alumni engagement.

The alumni relations staff at Hopkins wanted a new approach to increasing participation at its annual alumni weekend, May 4–5, 2012, and turned to the popular online game Fantasy Football for inspiration. What they came up with was an innovative alumni engagement initiative called Fantasy Reunion.

Capitalizing on the renowned competitive drive of Hopkins alumni, Fantasy Reunion brought aspects of fantasy sports leagues to a reunion-based game. Instead of emphasizing loyalty to Johns Hopkins as a basis for alumni participation, the game encouraged friendly competition among alumni, focusing on their shared experiences while they attended Hopkins. It opened the door to engagement with peers and the university, and it provided a meaningful opportunity for participating in Alumni Weekend.

So how do you play the game? The Johns Hopkins Alumni Weekend program focuses on the undergraduate alumni from the Krieger School of Arts and Sciences and the Whiting School of Engineering located at the main Homewood campus. Fantasy Reunion targeted alumni in their five-year cycle from both schools, totaling nearly 7,000 alumni. To play the game, alumni signed up as captains; to create a team, they submitted the names of 15 fellow alumni whom they wanted to see at Alumni Weekend and with whom they shared a common Hopkins experience. (Common experiences were broadly defined to include categories such as dorms, sports, study groups, clubs, organizations, and sorority or fraternity affiliations.) Captains registered their teams online at a special Fantasy Reunion website.

The captains earned points by motivating teammates to register for Alumni Weekend and give class gifts. For example, captains received one point for each week in advance of the deadline a teammate registered for Alumni Weekend, double points when a teammate gave a class gift, and bonus points for anyone traveling from out of state. The captain whose team accumulated the most points won the grand prize: an Apple iPad. Additional prizes were awarded for second and third place and to point leaders from each reunion class.

In all, there were 245 Fantasy Reunion teams with 3,576 alumni participants. There was no limit on how many teams alumni could participate in, which meant alumni could form their own team serving as a captain, and also participate in another friend's team. But Pat Conklin, senior associate director of the Homewood Reunion Program, which manages Alumni Weekend, said that there wasn't much overlap due to the way teams came together. There was also a rule that prevented teams from having more than seven people who shared the same Hopkins experience. Conklin attributes Fantasy Reunion's success to its focus on shared experiences and the powerful reach of social media.

"Fantasy Reunion works so well because it calls our alumni into action. It gives them the power to create their own teams and generate excitement and participation among their teammates," said Conklin. "I've been working in the Alumni Relations office for 11 years, and we've found that what brings alumni back to campus is encouragement from friends. It's the emotional appeal of friend-to-friend engagement, and social media is an effective channel for making that happen."

The Right Channel for the Right Audience

Using a multi-channel approach was essential to spanning the vast age range of Hopkins alumni. It allowed the alumni relations team to use the channels that different age groups of alumni would respond to best. Facebook was the primary social media channel used, but other channels included email, print, web, and phone.

"We found that social media were more effective for younger alumni. They were more focused on Facebook," said Conklin. "For older alumni, we personalized communications through phone and email. That personal call made a difference and was an important engagement tool for older alumni."

Alumni relations sent an initial email and postcard to all reunion alumni about the game. The department also created the Fantasy Reunion web page and posted information about the game on the alumni association website.[1]

---

(1) Link: alumni.jhu.edu

As the main social media channel used throughout Fantasy Reunion, Facebook was instrumental in publicizing the game to the greater alumni audience. There was no dedicated Facebook page for Fantasy Reunion, but staff incorporated information into both the Alumni Weekend Facebook page[2] and the alumni association Facebook page,[3] as well as class reunion Facebook pages for several class years. Leaderboards and scoring tips were posted on Facebook pages. High-scoring teams were tagged, and their progress in Fantasy Reunion was publicized on their online networks.

Personal communication was also key to the success of the game. Alumni committee chairs assisted in promoting the program with alumni. And, of course, team captains encouraged their teammates to register, make a gift, and create their own Fantasy Reunion teams.

"It was crucial that participants shared their experiences with their peers as opposed to Hopkins as an institution. The game was completely alumni driven and managed by Hopkins staff. This is what made the team captains so valuable. They were the ones getting in touch with the people with whom they shared fond memories, not Hopkins staff," explained Eta Flamholz, coordinator for the Homewood Reunion Program.

Opening the Door to Engagement

Fantasy Reunion opened the door to future engagement and enriched the alumni experience by providing a fun and competitive way for alumni to reconnect with former peers and the university. Equally important, it provided a valuable opportunity for alumni relations staff to discover and connect with previously unreachable alumni.

"There are a lot of alumni we don't have contact information for, and social media help us reach these lost alumni. They might not be in contact with Hopkins, but their friends on social media are connected and involved," said Flamholz. "It's a really beautiful thing when people whom we don't have contact information for are getting back in touch with us."

Alumni relations staff members, acting as game managers, played a key role in engaging with alumni and gathering valuable information. Throughout the game, alumni relations staff connected with team captains weekly through phone, email, and Facebook to discuss the team's shared experiences and provide updates on the team's progress. This one-on-one communication benefited both the alumni and the university by facilitating networking, community building, and alumni

> It was crucial that participants shared their experiences with their peers as opposed to Hopkins as an institution. The game was completely alumni driven and managed by Hopkins staff.

(2) Link: facebook.com/JohnsHopkinsAlumniWeekend
(3) Link: facebook.com/johnshopkins

"Who's on your Reunion Dream Team?"

Game participants received points for early registration, class gift participation, and out-of-state travel to Alumni Weekend.

giving. Alumni had the opportunity to voice ideas, stories, and even concerns to alumni staff, while striving to gain points and win the game. In turn, staff gained valuable insight into the types of communities and experiences that participating alumni felt were meaningful during their undergraduate years.

Conklin stresses the importance of staying in touch with participating alumni once the game is over: "Sometimes we have a hard time engaging alumni and keeping the channels of communication open and alive. The team captains can help us keep the fires burning. We want them to use those great memories to become good stewards with their friends."

And that's exactly what this year's winner did. Evelyn Jerome Alexander, Arts and Sciences '92, was the grand prize winner of the 2012 Fantasy Reunion. Her team's shared experience was the Alpha Phi sorority. She said she used both email and Facebook to communicate with her team. Half of her team registered in the first few weeks of the game, giving her an early lead. As one of the gift committee chairs for her graduating class, Alexander saw Fantasy Reunion as an additional opportunity for asking her classmates to contribute to Hopkins.

"Part of the responsibility I have taken on is to ask my classmates to donate every five years. The game provided me with the opportunity to reach out to my classmates and encourage them to make a donation," said Alexander. "As someone who has been a very active alumna for many years, I think any game that engages alumni, gets them talking to each other, and gets them to come back to Homewood is a tremendous success!"

An Overwhelming Success

Fantasy Reunion proved overwhelmingly successful: It promoted early registration for Alumni Weekend 2012, increased class gift donations, engaged previously inactive alumni, and fostered

Participating players became Facebook friends with "Johnny Hopkins" and the game moderator used Facebook to encourage continued participation and post updates.

existing alumni relationships. The campaign also won a 2012 Circle of Excellence Gold Award from the Council for Advancement and Support of Education in the Best Uses of Social Media category.

Here are some of the results:

» In 2012, 572 alumni registered for Alumni Weekend within the first six weeks of registration opening, a 49 percent increase over 2011.
» Of those who registered in the first three weeks, 40 percent were captains or teammates in Fantasy Reunion.
» Total alumni registrations increased by a record 21 percent.
» Of Fantasy Reunion participants who donated, 6 percent were first-time givers, and 15–17 percent had not given in five or more years.
» Through Fantasy Reunion, alumni staff captured or updated contact information for 960 individual alumni.

Just as impressive are the type of connections that Fantasy Reunion helped foster. For example, one team captain—a 76-year-old engineer— flew in from Florida to attend his first reunion in years. And two fraternity brothers of the same class year—one a team captain and the other a member of his team—reconnected through Facebook with others from their organization, and planned an unofficial fraternal reunion during Alumni Weekend.

Based on this experience, the alumni office launched a Young Alumni Fantasy Reunion targeting graduates just one to four years out of Hopkins. The duration of the game was shorter, and

More thoughts on the topic...
Fantasy Football: In a League of Its Own

Just what is Fantasy Football? The short answer: an online game in which players assemble and manage an imaginary team of players—real-life football players—and score points based on the on-field performance of those players.

So how do you play it? First, you decide what kind of league you want to join. Then, as the general manager and coach of your team, you pick your roster from current NFL players through a draft, just like in real football. Typically, players have eight slots to fill on their roster. In most leagues, no player can be owned by more than one fantasy team. Each week throughout the entire NFL season, you set your lineup in hopes of gaining the most points. Your players' performance in their real games determines your Fantasy Football point total and overall success. Points include touchdowns, field goals, sacks, yards gained, interceptions, and more.

Whether you win or lose depends on how well you manage your team and maximize your roster. In leagues that cost money, winners get money prizes, and in some leagues, like those run by the NFL, winners get exclusive prizes. For Fantasy Football 2012, the NFL is offering a Super Bowl package as a grand prize.

If you're interested in playing Fantasy Football, you'll find an overwhelming array of choices. You can join a free, non-gambling league or one that costs money to enter. You can create your own league or join any number of leagues run by Yahoo! Sports, ESPN, CBS Sports, and the NFL, among others. But no matter how people choose to play this popular online game, one thing is certain: They love football.

"I joined a league on a lark and I found myself roped into the competition. It's a fun, casual venue for guys I know to enjoy a game that we love. But weekly, it's the competitive nature of 'my manufactured team can beat this guy's manufactured team' that really makes Fantasy Football so popular," said one player from Royal Oak, Michigan. "Most participants have not had much exposure to the nuts and bolts of the NFL. They relish the chance to play general manager and coach."

According to a recent study by the Fantasy Sports Trade Association, more than 34 million people will play fantasy sports in 2012, with three-fourths of them playing in Fantasy Football leagues. This is a significant change from the early days of Fantasy Football, when stats were recorded and tallied from newspaper box scores. In 1997, CBS launched the first free, public website for Fantasy Football, changing the game forever. Within three years, other online sports media launched competing Fantasy Football sites. Taking the game online provided an easier, more convenient way to play, enabling players to make connections, get stats, track components, and follow multiple games at once. Most sites also have forums where players can chat about anything from general thoughts about the game itself to trades and other strategies.

Whether players are in it for the love of the game, the competition and prizes, or the chance to be a virtual manager and coach, most say Fantasy Football changes the way they watch football. Scott Griffith, a player from Chicago, said it got him interested in the broader game of football rather than just one team.

"Playing Fantasy Football really keeps me interested in all the games throughout the season. Before I started playing, I was only interested in the Chicago Bears, but now I really watch the game and pay attention to other games. It makes you look at other aspects like how well players perform on other teams."

Want to learn more? ESPN has a great series of videos that can help anyone get started playing Fantasy Football.

---

culminated during Young Alumni Weekend (Oct. 5–6, 2012). Conklin reported that 225 alumni participated in the Fantasy Reunion game. Preregistrations were also up 22 percent from 2011, and 1,600 alumni registered for the Young Alumni Weekend, both of which she suspects were due to Fantasy Reunion.

Moving Forward

While Fantasy Reunion was an immense success, both Conklin and Flamholz saw room for improvement.

For the 2013 Fantasy Reunion, they're simplifying the game rules to make it easier to understand and easier to post on social media. Plus, more alumni will have the opportunity to participate in Fantasy Reunion. They're opening up the program to all Krieger and Whiting undergraduate alumni from the Class of 1938 to the Class of 2012—approximately 38,000 alumni. Conklin also plans to interview some of the 2012 participants and create a short video to accompany the initial mass email announcing the 2013 game.

But the biggest change is the creation of a Johnny Hopkins profile page on Facebook.[4] The same approach was used for both Twitter (@JohnnyQHopkins)[5] and Reddit.[6] While the Johnny Hopkins profile is not exclusive to Fantasy Reunion, Flamholz said it's helping spread the word more efficiently on Facebook.

"We've been able to test out the Johnny Hopkins Facebook profile during the Young Alumni Fantasy Reunion. We're had a great response so far, and it has been a nice tool to have. It's enabled us to have scoreboards and tag people, which comes up on participants' news feeds," said Flamholz.

One of the new rules for Fantasy Reunion, tested out during the Young Alumni Fantasy Reunion, was that all team captains must friend Johnny Hopkins on Facebook to participate. Team captains must notify the alumni relations office if they choose not to friend Johnny Hopkins. Conklin explained that their goal is to be inclusive, not exclusive, and they plan to review this stipulation for the 2013 Fantasy Reunion.

Conklin said she, too, is thrilled with the responses so far for Johnny Hopkins, and for the Fantasy Reunion campaign in general.

"This is all so new and fresh, and is constantly evolving. Our numbers of alumni who come back for homecoming and reunion weekend go up every year. Using social media gives us a great tool to make that happen. It allows us to change things subtly, and create more interest and affinity with our alumni," said Conklin. "Most importantly, through Fantasy Reunion, we're getting alumni back on campus to make the connection that builds a lifetime relationship with Hopkins." **sw**

(4) Available at mstnr.me/JHopkins4
(5) Handle: @johnnyqhopkins
(6) Link: reddit.com/user/JohnnyQHopkins

Strengthening Alumni Connections Through Photography at Rensselaer Polytechnic Institute

By Melissa Soberanes

Melissa Soberanes is a writer and editor at mStoner. She has more than 15 years of experience helping nonprofit organizations and education institutions increase awareness and tell their stories through effective communications, media relations, and web strategies.

L ike motivated alumni at other institutions, Rensselaer Polytechnic Institute (RPI) alumni have an unwavering pride in their alma mater, the nation's oldest technological university. Building on this inherent pride, the office of alumni relations launched the first-ever RPI Spirit Day and Photo Contest on Feb. 3, 2012.

Spirit Day was held the day before the 35th Annual Big Red Freakout, which was created as a "homecoming" of sorts to boost enthusiasm for RPI men's hockey. The RPI community, including alumni, was asked to show spirit by wearing RPI gear at work, at school, around the house, or anywhere else they might be on February 3.

But the real focus of Spirit Day was the alumni photo competition. Since pictures are almost always the most engaging items shared on social media, RPI asked alumni to take photos of themselves in their RPI gear and then submit their photos via email or post them on Instagram or Twitter, tagged with #RPISpiritDay.

To boost participation in the photo competition, alumna Meg Lenihan, '10, initiated a corporate challenge. An employee at GE Aviation in the Boston area, Lenihan challenged other alumni to see which company could be the most spirited. She posted, "Meg Lenihan, '10, Dave Eldridge, '09, and the rest of the RPI alumni at GE challenge you to a friendly Spirit Day photo competition! Upload a picture of your group showing their RPI Spirit (wearing and holding RPI gear) via Twitter or Instagram on Friday, February 3, before 1 p.m. EST. Photos must be marked with the hashtag #RPISpiritDay."

The goal of Spirit Day was engagement. "Our alumni love to show how proud they are of RPI. This was our first Spirit Day and the first time we used a photo contest to show our pride," said Michael

O'Neill, program administrator for the Office of Alumni Relations. "In the end, we thought it was incredibly successful, but I think the photo contest really made Spirit Day: It became Spirit Day."

Senior Communications Specialist Ellen Johnston also attributes Spirit Day's success to the seamless integration of the campaign across all communication and social media platforms.

"With any marketing effort, you have to communicate to your audience when they are ready to hear the message and in the way they are willing to hear it. Using a variety of channels allows you to reach multiple audiences in different ways and engage more people. The manageable bites of information that come out of social media are less daunting, more inviting, and more accessible," said Johnston.

A Multi-Channel Approach

The alumni relations team selected a variety of communication channels to help promote Spirit Day and encourage alumni participation in the photo contest.

For Spirit Day in general, channels used included more traditional modes of communication, starting with email and newsletters. The staff also created a Spirit Day web page[1] on the RPI Alumni Association website.[2] Serving as the main repository of all Spirit Day and photo contest information, the Spirit Day web page included links to social media channels, as well as a library of RPI images that could be downloaded and used as Facebook profile pictures.

Alumni relations reached out to regional alumni chapters, local businesses, and other university departments. Johnston said this collaboration and outreach was crucial to successfully promote Spirit Day and engage the entire RPI community.

"We worked closely with the athletic department, since Spirit Day was centered around the last home hockey game of the season. We even got coverage on NBC Sports for the night of the game," Johnston explained. Since the game was being broadcast, alumni regional chapters could set up parties to watch it. "And we had great support from local businesses. The bookstore gave 10 percent off on Spirit Day, and a local bank had a prize drawing for anyone who came in wearing RPI gear."

Facebook,[3] Instagram, and Twitter were the primary channels used for the Spirit Day photo contest. Of these channels, Twitter and Facebook were the most successful and engaging. "We don't have a very big network, but we have very active and engaged alumni on these channels, especially on Facebook." In fact, the Spirit Day event created on Facebook was the most popular post and the most viral. Almost 95 percent of the people saw the event as

With any marketing effort, you have to communicate to your audience when they are ready to hear the message and in the way they are willing to hear it.

(1) Available at mstnr.me/RPIAlumni1

(2) Available at mstnr.me/RPIAlumni2

(3) Available at mstnr.me/RPIAlumni3

RPI's Spirit Day goal was to increase alumni engagement.

a page post from one of their friends.

O'Neill also used Storify[4] to communicate with alumni and keep them informed as the weekend progressed. He sent out Storify to alumni through social media and embedded it in the Spirit Day web page.

O'Neill stressed the importance of identifying the strengths of different social media and matching them with your audiences and campaign goals: "I think this kind of campaign is especially effective on Facebook, where one of the biggest points is to share photos. The photo sharing aspect made it really successful for Spirit Day."

The photo sharing benefits of Facebook were taken to the real world when O'Neill created a physical Facebook-like page on a movable blackboard. He took it to the hockey game and to the Heffner Alumni House, where people could "like" the photos in real life with thumbs-up stickers. O'Neill said this approach created buzz on and off campus that got people talking and excited about Spirit Day.

Engaging Alumni for Surprising Results

The results are proof that a multi-channel approach to engaging alumni works.

The three-day Spirit Day photo contest resulted in 54 photo submissions picturing 200 total alumni, including individuals, co-workers, families, babies, dogs, and even a Zamboni. There were nearly a dozen photos submitted by alumni who gathered other RPI graduates in their workplaces for a group photo, with some picturing as many as 60 alumni.

(4) Available at mstnr.me/RPIAlumni4

There were more than 120 tweets, and engagement on the Facebook page skyrocketed to almost 40 percent of followers talking about the posts. The Facebook page also gained 44 new followers, and the "real-world" Facebook photo wall got 196 "likes." Results on the web page were equally impressive, with just over 9,000 visits.

Following are just a few of the photos submitted for the contest. You can find more on the Facebook page:[5]

> » An alumnus and his niece, with this message: "I got my niece to help cheer. The horn is the infamous 1987 Brown horn, she is shaking the 1994 freakout rattle/pompom. Looking forward to the game—will be headed to Champs in Durham. Let's go red!"
> » An alumnus drinking coffee outside at a snow-covered table wearing RPI shorts and a sweatshirt while reading *Rensselaer Alumni Magazine*: "Typical morning in Colorado."
> » An alumna driving the New York Rangers' Zamboni wearing her red Rensselaer hockey jersey.
> » A couple showing that their RPI spirit runs in the family. Both alumni are wearing RPI gear, including their dog decked out in a red Rensselaer shirt complete with a red RPI toy bone.

The Spirit Day organizers selected two winners at the end of the campaign. The Most Spirited Photo went to Jessica Sweeney, '04, who submitted a photo of herself sitting on a red couch holding her baby, both clothed from head to toe in RPI gear. The Most People in a Photo with Spirit went to the alumni at GE Global Research. Forty-one of them stood together to form the letter "R" while holding signs with their class years.

Johnston attributed the campaign's success to the staff's ability to engage alumni. "Spirit Day was a great success, and the photo contest generated lots of excitement from our alumni. Using the different channels enabled us to connect with alumni, including young alumni, which is always a goal. It's hard to reach young alumni, and using social media helps us do that. Content shared through social media has a snowball effect, and it helped us reach even more people."

The Corporate Challenge

Another vital part of Spirit Day's success was the peer-to-peer engagement that took place among alumni as part of the corporate challenge. "Nothing we do in alumni relations is as successful as when we incorporate the peer-to-peer component. When we have this alumni engagement component in our events it always boosts

(5) Available at mstnr.me/RPIAlumni5

facebook   Search for people, places and things

You are posting, commenting, and liking as Rensselaer Alumni Association — Change to Michael O'Neill

Rensselaer Alumni Association · 1,366 like this
January 26 at 12:05pm

✓ Liked

RPI Spirit Day Photo Competition

Like · Comment · View

3,269 people saw this post   Promotion Unavailable

RPI used both traditional and
new media channels to encourage
Spirit Day participation.

involvement and numbers. Plus our alumni are naturally competitive.
If we turn it into a contest, they love it," explained Johnston.

As a recent alumna, Lenihan understood firsthand the
importance of this peer-to-peer engagement and staying involved
with her alma mater. As an RPI senior, she was president of Red &
White, a student organization whose members serve as Rensselaer
ambassadors. Now a design engineer at GE Aviation, Lenihan is
part of the GE recruitment team, where she plans events and looks
for new ways to get RPI alumni involved at GE.

"When I heard about Spirit Day I was trying to start an internal
RPI newsletter at GE," she said. "I thought a photo contest would
be an easy way to get content for the newsletter and get GE's RPI
alumni engaged. Mike liked the idea, and the corporate challenge
developed from there."

Lenihan said the corporate challenge at GE was such a success
that it grew to include other corporations nationwide. For the
corporate challenge at GE, Lenihan's approach was to target
specific RPI alumni at each GE site and ask them to organize an
event or participate in the photo contest by taking a picture of
all RPI alumni at the site. The most effective media channels for
communicating about the corporate challenge at GE were email,
followed by Facebook.

"For most alumni, communicating through email was the best.
But Facebook, Twitter, and Instagram were the best ways to reach
younger alumni," said Lenihan. "The photo contest was an easy way
to get RPI alumni engaged in the event and show their RPI spirit.
Almost everyone has a smartphone, at least from my generation,
and putting pictures online of your day-to-day life is common."

For the older alumni who might not be so savvy about social
media, Lenihan made sure to include her contact information.
"We wanted all alumni to participate. So, I made sure alumni could
contact me if they were having trouble submitting photos. I helped
someone set up a Facebook account, and an alumnus from the class
of 1939 emailed me a picture to post and submit for him. It was neat
to see their excitement and RPI spirit."

Making the Next Spirit Day Even Better

Both O'Neill and Johnston can attest that the impact and success of any new campaign is uncertain. "In the beginning we weren't sure how Spirit Day would be received. We got such a late start that I was worried it wouldn't go over well. From planning to implementation, we did it in four weeks. We started talking about it after we came back from Christmas break, around January 9. But once we saw the excitement from alumni and photos started flooding in, we got excited," said O'Neill.

Johnston agreed that they started the campaign a little late, and in the future will start planning and advertising earlier. "We definitely need to start promoting Spirit Day earlier next year. This will help us get more followers on our social media channels and engage more alumni. Going forward, I would also like to advertise our photo contest from the start, and expand our corporate challenge by involving our corporate and foundation relations department and our corporate match agents to promote Spirit Day and get more alumni in different companies to participate."

With the next Alumni Spirit Day scheduled for Feb. 1, 2013, O'Neill and Johnston have already started promoting the event. The 2013 Alumni Spirit Day is posted on the website so people will know about it well in advance. The 2013 event details will also be included in alumni chapter newsletters, and an article in *Rensselaer Alumni Magazine* is slated for the spring 2013 issue, which comes out in January 2013.

O'Neill said that for next year he also wants to expand RPI's social media network on Instagram and Google+, since both channels were just getting established at the end of the campaign. "Google+ is still slow, but where we've expanded the most is on Instagram. I am doing more Photo of the Day contests and even started a Follow Friday contest, where people can submit their best campus pictures. This has gotten our team in the habit of posting pictures at least once a day and gets our followers used to seeing our pictures more often. We hope this will get our alumni more engaged and willing to participate in Spirit Day."

Most important, O'Neill wants to involve more alumni in the planning and promotion of Spirit Day.

"Our goal at the office of alumni relations is to keep RPI alumni connected to their alma mater and help them feel great about where they graduated from. Spirit Day and the photo contest helped us do that," said O'Neill. "But it wasn't just what we did to promote the campaign on different channels that made it successful. It helped to have an alumna like Meg who was engaged and excited. She promoted Spirit Day to her friends and co-workers and helped create the buzz we needed with other alumni to make Spirit Day truly successful." **sw**

Crowdsourcing Content for #UWRightNow at the University of Wisconsin–Madison

By Melissa Soberanes

Melissa Soberanes is a writer and editor at mStoner. She has more than 15 years of experience helping nonprofit organizations and education institutions increase awareness and tell their stories through effective communications, media relations, and web strategies.

What does a day at the University of Wisconsin–Madison really look like? University Communications and Marketing wanted to find out. On April 18, 2012, the office launched #UWRightNow (UWRightNow.Wisc.edu) a first-ever multimedia project designed to capture the breadth, depth, and spirit of the university during a 24-hour period. The entire campus community plus alumni and friends from around the world were invited to share their thoughts about what makes UW-Madison such a special place.

This one-of-a-kind campaign expanded on the popular concept of the 24-hour photo project by opening up submissions to all kinds of content. It combined crowdsourced tweets, photos, and videos with staff-produced coverage, all posted on a website designed specifically for the campaign.

"We wanted to create a truly blended campaign that told the UW-Madison story through the university's perspective. We wanted to see the campus community self-reflected in this project," said John Lucas, a senior university relations specialist on the communications staff.

The campaign far exceeded expectations. A total of 1,018 stories, photos, videos, and tweets were posted to the site from as far away as India and the South Pole. Submissions came from all 50 states and 66 countries. They offered glimpses of everything from research in campus labs to students studying in Europe, to an alumnus checking in from Switzerland, to future Badgers sporting tiny red-and-white attire.

"What came through loud and clear was the unwavering connection people feel to this university," said Lucas. "Despite widely varied experiences and ties to UW-Madison, people conveyed loyalty, gratitude, and a strong feeling of community, even from thousands of miles away."

Capturing the Spirit of UW-Madison

The development, promotion, and implementation of #UWRightNow was no small task. It took a true team effort by dozens of people across campus to capture the spirit of UW-Madison in just 24 hours. Guiding the team were Lucas, Director of Web Services Nick Weaver, and Stacy Forster, who served as the lead writer and editor on the project.

"This was a big effort by UW-Madison staff, and it took a lot of hard work, planning, and promotion," said Lucas. "We brought together writers and communicators working across campus, and we really challenged our web team to do something different to contextualize this. The end result was very rewarding for our staff. It brought out the best of what we try to do on a daily basis."

This collaborative approach was key to the success of the campaign. At UW-Madison, University Communications and Marketing functions like a creative ad agency, with web services and editorial as part of the same department.

"Our web team is as much of a creative group as it is a technical group," said Weaver. "We work closely with the editorial team to come to the final product. This close collaboration helps to inform everything we do on a project, from the editorial content to the technical aspects of web design."

In addition to the collaborative team structure, four goals guided the campaign to ensure its broad reach, engagement, and success:

» Showcase the community's pride and excitement about its relationship to UW-Madison.
» Engage the broad UW community—give people a "voice" by offering the chance to submit content.
» Challenge university communications staff to explore new creative, technical, and content solutions.
» Connect with campus partners and encourage them to submit high-quality stories from their own programs.

Building the Right Kind of Website

The third goal, in particular, set the stage for the innovative website design done by the UW-Madison web team. Building the right kind of site was key to accommodating the diverse content that was going to be included.

"We wanted to capture the imagination and feel of our campus community. To do this we knew that we needed to create a unique experience, with content driving the project. Building a custom site seemed to be the best solution," said Weaver.

The web team used the WordPress platform with jQuery Masonry, a dynamic layout plugin, which offered the best adaptability for the type of content being collected and ultimately

#UWRightNow APRIL 18, 2012

On April 18, 2012, the University of Wisconsin-Madison highlighted 24 hours in the life of our campus.

See the tweets, pictures and stories students, alumni, staff, friends and the community shared in real time during the event to show the world what makes the university such a unique place every day.

Crew members take a patient into UW Hospital after Med Flight picked the patient up at a hospital in Dubuque, Iowa, Wednesday morning. Pilot Mike Kohrs and three other crew members made the flight.

Photo: John Maniaci, UW Hospital & Clinics.

12:18 pm

Start exploring »

The #UWRightNow campaign was built into a WordPress platform and used a dynamic layout plugin.

provided the right look and feel for the campaign. The custom design incorporated minimal styling and a subdued color palette, which ensured that there were no elements that would compete with the content. It also helped facilitate the fast-paced collective publishing that happened on the day of the event.

The website used a block design with windows for content. Weaver and his team drew their inspiration from the photo-sharing website Pinterest, which was getting lots of attention in early 2012. "We wanted to share chunks of content in a creative way. And from a web design standpoint, we liked Pinterest's unique content block approach," Weaver said.

Designing the website with mobile devices in mind was another key element of the campaign's success. The mobile version gave people a very different experience. Content was still front and center, but it was presented as a linear stream. Weaver explained that mobile optimization factors into any UW-Madison web project with a significant social aspect: "Social media is very much a mobile activity, and in pushing out a 24-hour project, we knew lots of people would participate through mobile. And they did; nearly 20 percent used mobile to access the website. This provided students, faculty, and staff with the ability to check in between classes and see what people were doing that day."

Content with a Shelf Life

The communications and marketing staff wanted content that they could repurpose—content with a long shelf life. They wanted stories that could be used in the future by admissions representatives, by staff who managed campus tours, and by advancement officers seeking to show donors the true spirit of UW-Madison.

This required significant editorial planning and a three-pronged approach to content development that included staff-generated content, content submitted by the university community, and content submitted through social media. This approach also required the team members to think about how they could tell the different stories at any given time during the 24-hour period and which medium—such as video or photography—would work best.

"This was such a wonderful way to tell UW-Madison's story. None of the approaches would have worked alone, but combined, they got everyone to participate and contribute to the project," said Forster. "It evolved organically and resulted in very natural, personal content that we didn't expect. Some of the best submissions were from people who talked about how their time at UW-Madison changed them and gave them a broader life experience. We often forget that everyone connected to UW-Madison has a personal experience and story to tell."

Lucas and Forster worked closely with university communications staff to think about both the submissions they would receive and the kinds of stories they wanted to showcase. They wanted to see the entire campus community reflected, so they sought out specific audiences and story ideas.

"We knew going in that we had alumni all over the world, and some famous alumni like Steven Levitan, the creator of 'Modern Family.' We also wanted to make sure that the many people working behind the scenes at UW-Madison were represented, like building maintenance," Lucas said. "The benefit to having 24 hours was that we could also reach out to departments and audiences that weren't being represented. We could go out and get them to participate."

The team also focused heavily on promoting the campaign through a wide variety of channels: Twitter, Facebook, other social media, the university's home page, print, advertising on campus news websites and Facebook, the faculty/staff e-newsletter, and email to campus partners and select international students. The site launched to the public on April 13, 2012, as a teaser. Its early unveiling allowed the planners to use it in promoting #UWRightNow and encourage genuine, not canned, submissions.

Early promotion to targeted audiences, in particular alumni overseas, also ensured that there would be submissions in the earliest hours of the project. "It was amazing to see how much great content we received prior to 7 a.m., when it really took off," said Forster. "It established a tone of community early on and showed a variety of stories that make up UW-Madison. People really responded to the campaign, and it was clear that they were putting a lot of thought into what they wanted to say about their experience at the university."

> **This was such a wonderful way to tell UW-Madison's story. None of the approaches would have worked alone, but combined, they got everyone to participate and contribute to the project.**

Grounds crew staff Aaron Hansen cleans up after "rolling the green" at the University Ridge Golf Course at dawn. Photo: Jeff Miller, University Communications

7:29 am   Share [+]

The first #UWRightNow photo was posted at 12:01 a.m. and the posts continued on through 11:59 p.m.

Overwhelming Response

"In the end, we were completely stunned by the reaction to the campaign. It was wildly successful, and really showed the amount of passion and the kinds of connections people have with the university," said Lucas.

Following are some of the impressive results:

» A total of 1,018 stories, photos, videos, and tweets were posted to the site in 24 hours.

» Submissions came from all 50 states and 66 countries.

» Nearly 14,000 unique visitors came to the site, spending an average of five minutes each.

» Twenty percent of visitors used mobile devices, such as smartphones, to access the site.

» The site was shared nearly 8,000 times via Facebook and Twitter.

» An article about the campaign[1] was included in the alumni magazine *On Wisconsin*.

Reactions from the higher education community were equally impressive. Following are just a few of the tweets captured on UW-Madison Storify:[2]

» Beautiful project by @UWMadison collecting 24 hrs of student social media + reporting bit.ly/HBHjKU

» Fun day-in-the-life project from @uwmadison, visualizing tweets,

(1) Available at mstnr.me/UWMadison1
(2) Available at mstnr.me/UWMadison2

From Thailand

To me, UW-Madison is no
other than the second home I
very much long to return. She
always gives me a driving
force to make a difference
especially in my [...more]

12:51 am

The photo variety on the
site ranged from personal
moments occurring in a student's
dorm or classroom to on-campus
events and activities.

stories and mmedia. Nice, easy grid display. uwrightnow.wisc.edu

» The best compliment you can get is: "I wish I would've thought
of that." Props to @UWMadison for #UWRightNow.

» Wisconsin really knows how to use social media in a higher
education environment. Cool idea: uwrightnow.wisc.edu
#UWRightNow @sportsgirlkat.

» #UWRightNow is the coolest thing i have seen in a while. Proud
to be a badger today and everyday. uwrightnow.wisc.edu.

» Reading through the #UWRightNow posts I am so proud to
be an alumna, and work at this amazing university—and how
wonderful to celebrate it!

With more than 1,000 submissions, there are too many to include
here, but they can be viewed in their entirety at #UWRightNow.[3]
Following are some of University Communications and
Marketing's favorites:

» a senior's submission of how she overcame adversity[4] during
study at UW-Madison, later referenced by the university
chancellor at the 2012 commencement

» pictures submitted by the staff[5] at UW's IceCube project
at the South Pole

» a photo[6] of UW Health's Med Flight program in action

(3) Link: uwrightnow.wisc.edu
(4) Available at mstnr.me/UWMadison4
(5) Available at mstnr.me/UWMadison5
(6) Available at mstnr.me/UWMadison6

- » a great diversity of posts[7] during the 4 a.m. hour
- » a story and photo[8] about the staff members who work overnight across campus collecting refuse and recyclable materials
- » a post by a junior[9] who claims that attending UW-Madison was one of the happiest accidents of her life
- » a photo and tweet[10] about the sunrise from College Library
- » a photo and tweet[11] from a Badger working at CNN
- » a photo[12] of a PE teacher at Woodstock School in Mussoorie, India.

Sound Advice

Upon evaluation of the campaign, Lucas said there was little that University Communications and Marketing would have done differently. "We kind of hit a sweet spot. But if we could do something different, it would be to better prepare for the kinds of responses we got. It was overwhelming at times. We planned on posting eight to 12 submissions per hour, but ended up posting more than 60 per hour," Lucas said.

For education institutions considering a crowdsourced campaign like #UWRightNow, Lucas stressed the importance of planning, promotion, and campuswide engagement. "Project planning is key to any campaign's success. You have to know what you want to get out of it and plan appropriately. Don't leave it up to whatever you get from crowdsourcing," he advised.

He also recommended that daily university engagement through various channels, including social media, already be commonplace. UW-Madison had already laid the groundwork for engaging audiences and communicating with them on a regular basis, especially through social media.

When it comes to telling engaging stories that best reflect an institution, Forster said, you should think as broadly as possible. "Turn over any rock. Think about all possible stories happening on campus. And, most important, make sure the stories come from the people who make up the institution, not just the communications office."

In addition, as Weaver pointed out, "Not every social media project needs to be elevated to this level or have a custom-designed website. You have to be honest about the time and effort required and continually evaluate what kind of involvement is needed. Consider whether your social media campaign complements a live

---

(7) Available at mstnr.me/UWMadison7
(8) Available at mstnr.me/UWMadison8
(9) Available at mstnr.me/UWMadison9
(10) Available at mstnr.me/UWMadison10
(11) Available at mstnr.me/UWMadison11
(12) Available at mstnr.me/UWMadison12

event like commencement, or if you are doing something that will stand on its own like #UWRightNow."

Moving in the Right Direction

Since the launch of the campaign, Lucas said there has been increased interest in replicating this process to engage and reach audiences through social media. Some departments are exploring ways to use this approach in a smaller capacity, like a "Day in the Life" for homecoming or a football game. Three offices in particular are using this approach with great success: Visitor and Information Programs, the University of Wisconsin Foundation, and the Office of Admissions and Recruitment.

"UWRightNow showed admissions the value of a crowdsourced campaign," said Lucas. "Admissions wanted to try something new to engage students and parents coming to UW-Madison for tours. It used the philosophy of crowdsourcing and social media to encourage visitors to tweet about their tour experience. Each new tour group can then see the posts and add to them."

Lucas said that even these smaller uses of social media and crowdsourcing are baby steps that will get everyone at the university to move in the right direction. "We are so proud of this campaign. It was a true 'lightning in a bottle' experience. We look forward to continue using this social media approach in new, fresh, and engaging ways," said Lucas.   **sw**

How Fictional Alumni Increased Engagement from Real Alumni at MIT and Cornell University

By Donna Talarico | @donnatalarico

Donna Talarico is the integrated marketing manager in the Office of Marketing and Communications at Elizabethtown College. She also runs *Hippocampus Magazine*, a monthly online literary magazine dedicated to creative nonfiction.

A shiny new state-of-the-art, cutting-edge research facility named for Tony Stark pops up on the MIT campus. Thousands of dollars worth of office paper stocks up every printer on Cornell University's campus for an entire academic year, thanks to Dunder Mifflin's Andy Bernard.

OK. So in reality, these prestigious institutions don't get that kind of mileage out of their fictional alumni. But the popularity of certain fictional characters helped their declared alma maters expand their social media fan base.

That was the idea behind the CASE Gold Award–winning MIT-Cornell Fictional Alumni Face-Off, where alumni who never actually walked the academic quads or graced the commencement stage at Cornell and MIT battled for the No. 1 spot. And although the cast of characters was imaginary, the results were not.

The Backstory

In the summer of 2011, Keith Hannon, then relatively new to his job as Cornell's assistant director for social media, was curious to see how the Facebook following of Cornell's alumni association compared to those of its peer institutions. He found that only one university, MIT, was keeping Cornell from having the most "liked" alumni association page. Hannon proposed to his followers a challenge: "Let's get more page likes than MIT."

Soon, MIT not only caught wind of Hannon's friendly trash talking, but also upped the ante. Amy Marcott, director of multimedia communications at MIT, posted about the rivalry on Slice of Life, the alumni association's blog, prompting members to take a look at what some Cornell alumni had been saying about them—and to take action to ensure they remained the most "liked"

Cornell/MIT
Fictional Alumni Tournament

Round One – Match Two

Sideshow Mel, *The Simpsons*

VS

Dilbert, *Comic Strip Legend*

Cornell University
Cornell Alumni Association

MIT ALUMNI ASSOCIATION

Sideshow Mel, of "The Simpsons," bested Dilbert in Round 1 of the Fictional Alumni Face-Off.

Ivy+ alumni association on Facebook.

"This actually accelerated their count, and they pulled away from us rather than allow us to catch up," said Hannon. "Then I started playing with the idea that competition could spark engagement. There must be a way to use social media to build competition between our schools."

Not long after Hannon began his casual quest for Facebook "like" supremacy, Cornell hosted the Ivy+ conference, a three-day "powwow" for the universities' alumni associations. There, Hannon met, in person, his peer institution counterparts, including MIT's Marcott. From there, the discussion of how to take the rivalry to the next level began.

The Heroic Challenge

Hannon and Marcott brainstormed ideas for a social media competition between the two institutions. Along the way, Hannon said, they started discussing the popularity of Andy Bernard, a character from NBC's hit comedy "The Office," who, according to the show's writers, graduated from Cornell. And then Tony Stark—a.k.a. the superhero Iron Man—came into the conversation; his comic book backstory includes an MIT degree.

"We thought a competition between fictional alumni would play nicely in the social space," said Hannon, particularly as it would build upon the friendly online competition that was already happening.

Making connections to fictional alumni is not a completely foreign idea, said Hannon. In fact, a 2008 issue of *Cornell Alumni Magazine* had featured a story about imaginary Cornellians. And Marcott knew from comments on past blog posts that her alumni association members enjoyed such pop-culture references.

The idea was not to give it all away, but rather unveil the new match-up each Monday. It definitely was a strategy to keep people engaged.

Hannon and Marcott, who was joined by her MIT colleague Jay London, researched literature, movies, and similar sources and came up with a list of fictional alumni, and from there the MIT-Cornell Fictional Alumni Face-Off began to take shape. Marcott even solicited the MIT alumni base for ideas on which characters should represent them.

While the two schools had been unofficially competing since August, the Face-Off was announced Sept. 19, 2011, and began on Sept. 26. The competition took the form of a bracket-style tournament. Each week, there would be a match-up between two fictitious alumni, until, after four rounds (consisting of a total of 15 pairings), a winner emerged from the final bracket.

The tools they used to carry out the competition covered a range of social media: a shared Wordpress blog, a shared Twitter hashtag, and individual Facebook pages and Twitter accounts. The common blog[1] provided a one-stop shop for information on each match-up contender, the bracket information, a list of weekly winners, and more. The blog also featured Twitter feeds of the hashtag #MITCU and links to each university's alumni association Facebook page.

Each Monday, the predetermined match-up was released via the blog (and subsequently shared through social media channels). The real alumni would then respond to a question such as "Which person, if real, has the potential to offer the greatest contribution(s) to society?" or "Which person, if real, would make the best professor or guest lecturer—and why?" Alumni could reply through any of three media: Facebook, Twitter, or the shared Face-Off blog.

"We each had our pawns for the first few match-ups and reserved the bigger names for later, so they weren't ousted right away," explained Hannon. "The idea was not to give it all away, but rather unveil the new match-up each Monday. It definitely was a strategy to keep people engaged."

Then, the trio of contest judges—Hannon, Marcott, and London—would pick a winner based on the quality of responses. They were looking for witty, clever, and even absurd posts. Each winning competitor would then move on to the next round. Most weeks, there was an obvious winner, said Marcott. For one round, MIT and Cornell invited judges from four other Ivy+ institutions (University of Pennsylvania, Princeton, Columbia, and Harvard). "That was a fun way to include our colleagues and to let the audience know it was unbiased judging," she said.

The Quest for Domination
The Fictional Alumni Face-Off relied on individual and collaborative efforts. Hannon, Marcott, and London took turns

---

(1) Link: mitcornellfaceoff.wordpress.com

writing the two weekly blog posts—one post set up the weekly competition, and the other declared the winner. Marcott created the website, while Hannon and Emily Muldoon Kathan, designer at MIT's Alumni Association, created graphics.

Although, between the two institutions, there were only three staff members managing the Face-Off, the nature of the contest meant it was not very time-consuming to run. The match-up was posted on Monday, and it was left on autopilot until the winner was announced on Friday.

"We let the community run with it," said Hannon. "It was not a huge time strain at all. I facilitated the discussion on social media, ruffled some feathers with the MIT alums, and left it alone until Friday; maybe I'd post a reminder."

While MIT expanded its campaign to additional channels—a widget on the Slice of Life blog, a news story on MIT's News Office website, and an article in an email newsletter that went to 90,000 alumni—Cornell relied solely on alumni association social media throughout the entire tournament. Hannon's reasoning for this approach was twofold: First, the contest was a pilot program, and he didn't want to draw on other resources. Second, and perhaps more important, he wanted to keep close control of the project—avoiding the problem of too many cooks in the kitchen.

The alumni responded to the questions via Twitter, Facebook, or the shared blog. And the comments kept things engaging; Marcott said the planners made it a point in the weekly wrap-up blog post to feature some of the responses for each competitor. "We'd often see people tweet or comment on Facebook expressing their excitement that their vote was quoted," she said. After some alumni expressed disappointment over the question for Round Two ("Which person, if real, would make the best housemate—and why?"), she asked for suggestions, which were used in a later round. "They appreciated knowing their opinions were heard," she said.

The Results

There was trash talk. There was debate. Some advocates wrote haiku on behalf of their chosen candidates, while others applied scientific knowledge to their arguments. "It was really fascinating to watch to see the degree to which people would argue for a specific character," Hannon said.

As the competition progressed, Hannon and Marcott saw an uptick in alumni engagement. Hannon added that the contest's colorful responses also appealed to the casual observers who were not directly participating.

Cornell had no specific quantitative goal; Hannon simply wanted to see more activity on Facebook. "We just wanted to see an increase in engagement through competition. Would more people

Fictitious Alumni Tournament

MIT ENGINEERS VS CORNELL BIG RED

The Madness Begins September 19th

Visit your Alumni Facebook page for details

Staff members from alumni associations at Princeton, Penn, Harvard, and Columbia served as guest judges in the Face-Off competition.

respond if we rallied together against a common 'enemy'?" he said.

Marcott agrees; because she had no idea of what to expect from the contest, she, too, did not set any quantitative goals. "The MIT Alumni Association is interested in increasing engagement, and I was looking for a way to get people to interact in a meaningful way—beyond liking a post or our Facebook page," she said. She also was able to verify names to determine which commenters were alumni and which were not.

Despite not having any magic numbers in mind, both schools saw an increase in Facebook page likes, comments, shares, and post likes. Facebook, in fact, proved to be the most active medium for both schools, but Hannon said that many Facebook readers would just click "like," whereas the heart of the contest was in actual written responses.

By comparison, Twitter proved less popular a means for participants to make their cases for competitors. "In general, I think people needed more than 140 characters, which is why Twitter didn't net us many responses—although we did get some lovely haiku," said Marcott. Still, Twitter had some advantages, Hannon said: It was useful for retweeting trash-talking tweets, particularly "dramatic tweets that played up MIT vs. Cornell." Plus, seeing what the other university's alumni were saying was a bit easier to do via the shared Twitter hashtag, compared with looking at both Facebook pages.

Hannon said the central Face-Off website was a valuable tool, and one that should be considered for any future collaborative efforts. It also received quite a bit of traffic: 31,557 lifetime visits, with the busiest day attracting 2,486 visitors (during Week Three). The most popular post, aside from "About the Face-Off," was the one announcing Week Three's match, Cornell's Andy Bernard vs. Tobias Funke (presented as a graduate of MIT on the sitcom "Arrested Development"). The most commented-on match, however, was Week Two: Sideshow Mel of "The Simpsons" (a Cornell grad) vs. cartoon character Dilbert (an MIT grad).

MIT's Slice of Life blog received a boost in traffic because of the contest—a 34 percent increase, in fact. And the Fictional Alumni Face-Off content proved to be some of the most visited pages; the post announcing the kickoff of the voting was the fifth most popular post in 2011 (out of 325 total posts).

But while the engagement level increased and Cornellians fought hard, Hannon acknowledged that Andy Bernard and the other fictional Cornell alumni were at a disadvantage. That disadvantage ultimately cost them the Social Media Cup, as MIT's Tony Stark came out on top.

The problem, Hannon said, was that Cornell doesn't have that many compelling fictional characters to talk about. "We had an office boob vs. an action hero who creates these incredible machines because of his MIT degree," he explained. "We had to scrape a little; Charles Foster Kane [of the classic movie "Citizen Kane"] is an unethical monster, and Andy Bernard, while a pop-culture icon, is generally regarded as a doofus who is a walking cliché of what it means to be an Ivy grad."

Regardless of who won the contest, Hannon said—as corny as it sounds—that both schools won. Engagement was up online and even off. For example, the MIT Club of Beijing decided to host an MIT-Cornell mixer the week the winner was announced. "This came as a nice surprise to all of us who worked on the contest. [The club] had been avidly following the contest and planned its own happy hour around the contest as a theme," Marcott said. Fifty guests showed up, roughly evenly divided among MIT alumni, Cornell alumni, and guests from other schools.

Lessons from the Superheroes

Hannon learned a few lessons from the Fictional Alumni Face-Off. First, he felt that the 15 weeks devoted to the competition (longer if you count the time off during winter break) was too long a time period to keep people engaged. He said that, at least from Cornell's side of the table, people fell off after the first round.

Second, he would have rethought how the match-ups were selected. "I would have looked more closely at the match-ups to balance the playing field—maybe only have one comic book hero, and more across the genres," he said. It was also a challenge to make the fictional alumni worth rooting for, he added.

The way the competition played out, the finalists were both fictional MIT alumni, with Ellie Arroway from the movie "Contact"

After the Fictional Alumni Face-Off between MIT and Cornell, the planners described their success in a presentation at the 2012 Ivy+ conference, held in June 2012 at Dartmouth College. (The Ivy+ group includes the Ivy League institutions Brown, Columbia, Cornell, Dartmouth, Harvard, Princeton, the University of Pennsylvania, and Yale, plus MIT and Stanford.) As Amy Marcott and Keith Hannon discussed the social media battle between their respective alumni associations—and a cast of characters that included superheroes and literary figures—Jonathan Horowitz, associate director for digital communications in the Office of the Alumni Association at Princeton University, began thinking. He had been following the Face-Off and had served as a guest judge.

"[The Face-Off] was presented in such a fun, different, and engaging way to alumni. I started to think, can we do something like this on an Ivy+-wide level?" said Horowitz. He brought up the idea during the session. "But it was a hot day in an un-air-conditioned room, so there were no ideas on the spot."

However, a few themes bubbled to the top. 2012 was an election year—perhaps something could be done with that. And Horowitz's peer, Steve Smith from Dartmouth College, mentioned the Olympics.

On the long ride home from New Hampshire to New Jersey, Horowitz couldn't stop thinking about the idea of a competition between all the Ivies. "Then the goofy word 'alumpics' popped into my mind—a fun little play-on-words with 'Olympics,'" he said. Then he realized "pics" was part of his new word, and he knew that many institutions have had success with using pictures in social media. He shared the idea with Smith and then the rest of his Ivy+ colleagues.

Cornell's Hannon was happy to find that people were intrigued and energized after learning more about the MIT/Cornell Fictional Alumni Face-Off, and he was eager to take part in sharing ideas for an Olympics-based challenge involving more institutions. One early idea, he said, was some type of fantasy-sport challenge where points would be based on real alumni competing in the London Games. That idea, while interesting, was quickly turned down because some universities might have an advantage over others.

After some collaboration, the group fleshed out the Alumpics concept. The winning idea was a 10-day competition, featuring 10 events centered on pictures that would show off different dimensions of the universities. Each day, a gold, a silver, and a bronze medal would be awarded; the awards would be based on the number of "likes" on photos posted to Facebook. Because the number of total page likes varied among the universities' Facebook pages, the Ivy+ group decided to level the playing field by using the ratio of photo likes to total page likes.

Although the Alumpics was only an inkling of an idea in June, turnaround was quick because of the time of year. "Summer, we're in project mode. It's easier to take on something more experimental then," said Horowitz.

Others agreed. Seven of the 10 Ivy+ alumni associations participated: Columbia University, Cornell University, Dartmouth College, MIT, University of Pennsylvania, Princeton University, and Stanford University.

Let the Games Begin

The Alumpics lit its virtual torch on July 30, 2012, and the games lasted through August 10. The event themes were reunion, history and tradition, mascot, academics, campus architecture, community service, commencement, athletics, campus nature, and alumni spirit. Each alumni association posted a photo on the theme to its Facebook page each day, and alumni were encouraged to vote by registering likes. Some photos were branded with Alumpics-themed imagery as well—each institution developed its own style.

To complement the Facebook aspect of the contest, a Twitter hashtag, #Alumpics, was used to promote the event—and encourage trash talk between the Alumpians. And, as with the MIT/Cornell Face-Off, a centralized website, Alumpics.Wordpress.com, was used to post the Alumpics schedule of events, medalists, and post-event blog entries.

Horowitz hoped that the Alumpics would bring in new alumni to Princeton's social media fray; more engagement was great, but just getting page likes was acceptable, too.

The Results

As in the Olympic Games, certain countries often seem to dominate in the medal count. The same can be said for the Alumpics. The same three institutions won medals each day:

- Cornell—10 bronze
- Dartmouth—8 gold, 2 silver
- Princeton—2 gold, 8 silver.

Over all, the participating institutions' 70 photos received 32,532 likes, and the alumni association Facebook pages gained a total of 3,428 new page likes.

Although only three universities took medals, all increased their engagement and following during the 10-day period. The Alumpics helped Princeton break a record: Its previous most-liked Facebook photo over the past two years had earned about 150 likes, but on the first day of the competition, Princeton's event entry received 1,140 likes.

"We grew our fan base remarkably. The level of action was incredible, beyond what we expected," said Horowitz. "People were sharing photos and retweeting left and right."

During the course of the Alumpics, six photos—four from Princeton, one from Dartmouth, and one from Cornell—received more than 1,000 likes.

"This blew our minds," said Hannon, explaining that Cornell's previous most-liked photo had earned about 400 clicks of the "thumbs-up" icon—and that was a photo of an alumnus with a Super Bowl trophy. "We just shattered that."

The institutions were also successful in gaining new followers. Princeton saw a 12.87 percent increase in Facebook page likes. But Dartmouth experienced the largest amount of growth; the college nearly doubled its following. Pre-Alumpics, Dartmouth was sitting at 1,512 fans; after only 10 days, the page hit 2,288. In fact, Hannon explains, Dartmouth's original following tally gave it quite an advantage in the competition—it was all in the math. "We soon found out that all Dartmouth had to do was get a few hundred likes [on a photo] and they would blow everyone out of the water," he said.

Education has deep roots in ancient Greece, where the Olympic Games were born. It seems fitting that Ivy+ institutions would combine an ancient tradition and rich history with new technology, all in the spirit of friendly academic rivalry. The Alumpics rallied school spirit by showcasing the people, places, and things notable across the respective Ivy+ campuses, while alumni associations experienced growth and activity in their online initiatives.

"It was a really fun contest," said Horowitz. "We engaged our alumni around a large world event. We knew—and this may be corny—that everyone would be a winner."

coming in second to Tony Stark after competing on the question "Which person, if real, would most successfully guide others to greatness—and why?"

For Cornell, this was a little bit of a letdown. "I think allowing the championship to be MIT vs. MIT was ethically the right thing to do based on engagement results, but in retrospect I would have lobbied harder for a Cornell representative in the championship match. It just felt very anti-climactic after a 15-plus-week tournament," said Hannon.

Marcott said that while there were a few passing comments and questions from administrators about how this contest would benefit MIT, she did not receive much pushback. In fact, the contest caught the ear of a big donor, which she said offered validation that the contest was meaningful. "After the tournament, in a high-level meeting regarding fundraising strategy, a million-dollar donor made an unsolicited point of mentioning his excitement that MIT and Tony Stark had won the tournament," said Marcott.

Hannon, too, considers the Face-Off a success, all things considered. "For a first run at something like this, I think we did well and learned much. Considering this cost us nothing but a little bit of our time each week, I think the number of alumni we engaged was pretty solid. I would have liked to see more commentary on the Cornell side, but the fact that we inspired our clubs overseas to form a mutual event in celebration of this tournament tells me we're on the right path. As these communities continue to grow and we learn more about what kind of content really hits home with our alumni, we'll generate more and more engagement, and ideally, involve more and more Ivy+ institutions," he said.   SW

Snail Mail + Social Media Engage Alumni at Nazareth College

By Fran Zablocki | @Zablocki

Fran Zablocki is a strategist at mStoner, where he leads multifaceted web projects that include communications strategy, design, development, and implementation. He formerly served as the web communications manager for Nazareth College.

You come home from a long day of work to find an unexpected package at your door. What is it? Who sent it? You take it inside, open it up, dig around the packing material, and lift out the cutest little plush bird! You recognize it right away as the mascot of your college, Nazareth. There's more—it has a nametag, identifying itself as Lucy, and a note attached to its foot, written to you by a former college classmate who just wanted to say hi and thought you'd like to have a surprise visitor. Lucy is so adorable and fuzzy; how could you resist taking a picture? And look, here are simple instructions on how you can share your photo online using a social mapping site created just for your reunion class!

This very experience has been shared by hundreds of alumni as part of the Flight of the Flyers program.[1] Produced by Nazareth College in Rochester, N.Y., Flight of the Flyers was created as an amusing, engaging way for the college to connect with its reunion alumni—and for them to connect with each other—tangibly and virtually at the same time.

Nazareth also hoped to reconnect with inactive alumni, increase attendance at reunion (yes, its *face-to-face* reunion!), and improve the information it had on alumni. A final goal was to build pride in Nazareth, which was surely furthered by the two awards the project won in 2009 from the Council for Advancement and Support of Education (CASE).

In the judges' report for the 2009 CASE Circle of Excellence Awards for websites, in which Flight of the Flyers won a Gold, one judge remarked, "This is the coolest thing I've seen in this

---

(1) The Flight of the Flyers campaign was removed from the web in late 2012.

judging. A smart use of the web that promotes engagement and prompts action in the real world." The site definitely helped engage alumni—47 percent of visitors came back for two or more visits, and preregistration for the 2009 reunion increased 22 percent.

Nevertheless, this entry generated a lot of discussion among the judges. Some argued that the website deserved an award because of the way it linked the real world with the virtual one; others noted that it seemed a bit childish, and its design was uninspiring. But, as one judge put it, "You can't argue with success. That's increased engagement in a time when perhaps people can't afford to travel to reunions, or perhaps older people can't travel to reunions, but this is a way they can engage."

Since launching in 2009, the Flight of the Flyers website has gone through four successful generations. According to Nazareth's former Director of Alumni Relations Kerry Gotham, the Flyers program began in 2007 as a way to encourage participation in the college's 2008 reunion—the second year in which the reunion was held in the spring rather than the fall.

"At that point, we wanted to grow our program," said Gotham. "We had 450 people at our 2007 reunion and wanted to do better in 2008. I was intrigued by the Travelocity commercials featuring the roaming gnome[2] and wanted to see if we could find a way to do something like that to build interest in our reunions. We wanted to go beyond the norm, do something different with the potential to have a peer-to-peer component."

Thus was born Flight of the Flyers. The college decided to send stuffed "Golden Flyer" mascots to alumni in reunion classes and invite them to forward the birds to other reunion alumni. A total of 3,000 potential alumni were registered members of reunion classes and could receive a mascot by mail. (Nazareth has more than 30,000 addressable alumni.) The college set up a simple forwarding system using the U.S. Postal Service's Click-N-Ship program.

Planning a Web-Enabled Golden Flyers Program

Alumni staff members believed that the campaign would be more engaging if it was web-enabled, so they began focusing on integrating the 2009 edition of Flight of the Flyers into a website.

The Flight of the Flyers website took the Golden Flyer Challenge to a new level. People who receive a Golden Flyer can take a photo of it on location, check in on the site's Google Map, and send the Golden Flyer to another reunion classmate. Members of reunion classes can request a bird through a form on the site, and alumni in other classes can participate by printing out a picture of a Golden Flyer and taking

> **The Flyers program began in 2007 as a way to encourage participation in the college's 2008 reunion—the second year in which the reunion was held in the spring rather than the fall.**

_____

(2) Available at mstnr.me/Nazareth2

The Find a Flyer section of the website allows alumni to document Flyer "sightings" and "migration" through photography and dynamic maps.

a photo of it, then checking it in on the Google map.

The site incorporates the following features, which encourage alumni to engage with each other and make data collection easier for the alumni office:

» Alumni can post their own updates and read what others have posted to the site.
» Alumni can invite less-active classmates to participate.
» "Lost" alumni can request a Flyer and reconnect with the college, sharing their contact information through a form on the site.
» The college collects the updates and data in a database, rather than hand-entering the information as in previous years.

All told, the site took about 310 hours of staff time to plan, build, and manage. Wall-to-Wall Studios provided strategy, design, and development for the project. Nazareth staff members planned to use the same basic site for five years, allowing them to amortize staff time and direct costs, resulting in a very cost-effective campaign. The Flight of the Flyers site was very much a team effort, Gotham said. "I have great partners here—it wouldn't have been possible to do this without everyone pitching in." In particular, he credited Mimi Wright, Kerry VanMalderghem, Colleen Brennan-Barry, and me.

Results

Nazareth is delighted with the results of the Flight of the Flyers—indeed, it's successful by any measure of engagement for a small college.

"Demographically, we have had a good range of participation through the years, with as many as 60 participants in one class; we had 10 to 15 participants in the classes with the lowest numbers," said Gotham. In 2009, he said, "We had more than 260 people participate in all. We had 600 people at reunion."

The broad response was a surprise to Brennan-Barry, who was the Nazareth website manager at the time. "We had some initial concerns that our older alumni might not be as comfortable and engage with the site as much as new alumni. That was happily proven incorrect when we realized that the classes that were placing in the top three for Flyer miles traveled included the classes of '59, '64 and '74!" That trend has continued, with the 2012 leaderboard showing the classes of '62 and '67 as the clear winners.

This is an important reminder, she pointed out, "that we can certainly reach different segments of our core population via different media, and that the preferred media of those segments is changing and evolving all the time."

Plus, Gotham added, "We've had a lot of great anecdotal and written comments about Flight of the Flyers. People said how much fun it was to take the picture of their Flyer—they enjoyed being creative with the photo and showcasing where they live or where they were traveling."

Also, the site helped people connect with each other. "People did make connections, they followed up, and we know that in addition to boosting attendance at our reunion, the site sparked informal reunions. People used a Flyer as a rallying point to get together in their area."

Brennan-Barry noted that visitors appreciated the absence of a direct "ask" on the Flight of the Flyers site. "I am glad that we made the decided choice not to use this site as a vehicle for direct fundraising, but more as a vehicle for connection. We did include a 'Donate to Nazareth' link on every page, but we listened to users when they told us that they have solicitation fatigue from 'constantly' getting asked for money from every organization to which they belong. Our choice to make this more of a place for us to connect with alumni and raise excitement for Reunion 2009 was, in retrospect, a good one."

As far as metrics are concerned, following are data from the website's first year, from June 1, 2008, to June 30, 2009:

» The site logged 3,127 visits.
» 1,867 visitors viewed, on average, 5.91 pages per visit and spent an average of about three and a half minutes on the site.
» 47 percent of visitors returned for two or more visits.

» 180 alumni checked in a Flyer via the site (only four Flyers per each of the 10 reunion classes have been circulating since June 2008).

» 123 alumni used the site form to request that a Flyer be sent to them.

And of course, the 2009 CASE awards don't hurt: The entire program won the Grand Gold in Alumni Relations, in addition to the Gold for the Flight of the Flyers site.

Lessons and Advice

When asked what surprised him about the Golden Flyers program, Gotham replied, "To be honest, I was surprised at how well it did take off. I thought it was kind of a harebrained idea. We wanted to have some fun—I had no idea how much people would like it."

One ancillary benefit of the Golden Flyers program is that it's brought the Golden Flyer mascot to the attention of people on and off campus, Gotham said. "We've only had an athletics program for about 30 years, and many people just didn't connect with our mascot. So this was a clever, visual, and direct way for them to make that connection. And they have."

Gotham noted that there were a few skeptics when the idea was originally floated. "But I did have the support of my boss, our vice president. Without that, it wouldn't have been possible." In the first two years of the program, the alumni office fielded only one complaint, which was about the cost of shipping the Flyer to the next recipient. (It costs each alumnus about $5, and it's easy to print the Click-N-Ship label from a computer.)

As far as the site production is concerned, Brennan-Barry noted, "We did some light usability testing about two-thirds of the way through the project, and I cannot stress how important and useful this was. I know that testing is almost always the first thing to be cut if a project is short on time or resources, but never discount the value of user feedback as you're creating this kind of interactive site. For a handful of $5 Starbucks gift cards, we received back a great deal of helpful information that saved us time and user confusion in the end."

Improving upon Success

In 2010, Brennan-Barry was focused on publicizing the program. "As we look at revising and reestablishing Flight of the Flyers for the reunion classes, we will be looking more closely at the communications by which we publicize the site and the program with the world," she said at that time. "In 2009, the site received strong traffic and interaction with minimal communication; I'm excited to think about how we might be able to connect with our alumni if our communications are stronger."

> We've only had an athletics program for about 30 years, and many people just didn't connect with our mascot. So this was a clever, visual, and direct way for them to make that connection.

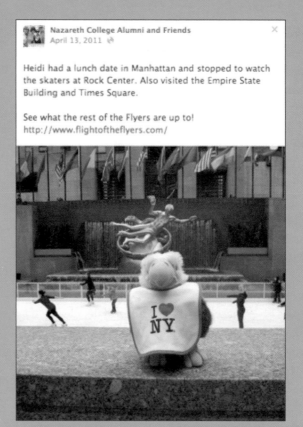

Nazareth College Alumni and Friends
April 13, 2011

Heidi had a lunch date in Manhattan and stopped to watch the skaters at Rock Center. Also visited the Empire State Building and Times Square.

See what the rest of the Flyers are up to!
http://www.flightoftheflyers.com/

The Flyer has been photographed around the globe and is most popular with older alumni.

And Nazareth did just that, promoting the Golden Flyer Challenge on its alumni and main college Facebook pages. The main event may be reunion each year, but alumni share pictures of the Flyers (and themselves with the Flyers) year-round and from an ever-growing list of fantastic locations. Over time, the Flyers have provided an indirect way for Nazareth to show how well-traveled its alumni are (and how many famous people they know!).

Gotham noted that originally the site worked too well, disappointing some alumni: Not everyone who requested a bird received one. To address this, more birds were released for each competing reunion year, and new birds were introduced even for years that hadn't had a reunion yet. The effect has been that alumni are now participating in the program and engaging with the college every year instead of just once every half-decade.

In 2011, the Golden Flyer Challenge Viewer's Choice Award was added to the program, providing an opportunity for alumni to vote via text message for their favorite Golden Flyer picture submission. The winner is then recognized at reunion and through social channels. Friendly competition is always a good motivator for engagement, and voting via text is another way to broaden the reach of the program beyond those who are physically attending reunion.

The program's success has led to spin-offs into areas beyond alumni. Since 2010, freshmen have received a Flyer chick at orientation with the following note: "Welcome to your new Nazareth nest. Keep me safe during your journey here, and when you are ready to take flight and graduate, remember to present this to someone in the Nazareth community who has made a difference in your life." This has been a great way to make new students feel like they are a part of the community right away, and when they graduate and see the Golden Flyer challenge, they already have a connection to Flight of the Flyers. It is also a great reminder to all those who receive the chicks that what they do is making a real difference for students—President Daan Braveman and many faculty have confirmed receiving these tokens of thanks at the end of the school year.   **sw**

Creating an Emotional Connection with Indiana University Alumni

By Erika Knudson | @Bullygrrl
& Rebecca Salerno | @resalern

Erika Knudson is associate director of marketing for Princeton University's Office of Development. Rebecca Salerno is the director of IU Communications' creative services team. When she was at IU, Knudson worked with Salerno and the IU Alumni Association to help improve online engagement with alumni.

A t Indiana University, we had a revelation about our online relationship with alumni—we thought they didn't care, especially young alumni. "You never visit," we sighed, dejectedly counting their virtual visits home. But what we realized as we set out to create a new IU Alumni Association website is that we needed to let them know how much *we* cared. Young alumni already loved us. We needed to demonstrate our love for *them*.

We started with a plan to redesign the IUAA website and ended up with a much more comprehensive and daunting task: We needed to virtually rewire our relationship with alumni.

With the new IUAA website and social media presence, we sought to transform the relationship between alumni and the institution, garnering committed and active participation from IU alumni in shaping the future of the institution, building strong networks of volunteers for both the IUAA and for alumni in their own local communities, and facilitating alumni support for each other in their professional and personal goals.

Call Your Folks

Yes, the IUAA had an outdated website. Our IUAA colleagues told us in our initial conversations and then in one-on-one stakeholder interviews that they knew the design was outdated, the pathways to information were convoluted, and the content wasn't connecting with alumni.

But there was more to the problem, and the website was just the digital surface—underneath that cluttered online presentation, the heart of the association was struggling. Membership numbers had been flat since the 1970s. The percentages of women and underrepresented minority groups were distressingly low. Despite the IUAA's efforts to appeal to new graduates by offering them a free one-year membership, those young alumni weren't opting in or else failed to re-up when the free year ran out.

Fewer alumni were finding membership relevant, and even fewer were signing up for the IU-branded credit cards or buying the license plate holders and other merchandise that had for many years helped ensure a strong balance sheet.

Visits to the IUAA website had flatlined, too. The IU institutional website sees over 100,000 unique visitors each month. But that energy wasn't translating to the institution's alumni association—the IUAA website had about 32,000 visits per month, and those visitors stayed an average of only 2.3 minutes.

The IUAA leaders didn't just want a better website. They wanted an online strategy that would help them galvanize the collective alumni imagination. They wanted the website to demonstrate value, to offer a meaningful experience, and to recapture the hearts and imaginations of alumni who'd treasured their IU experience ... but weren't seeing the connection between their halcyon college days and the alumni association.

When IU Communications entered the project, we realized we had a difficult case to make as a fee-for-service internal creative agency for the university. Doing this project right might be a significant investment for an alumni association that was looking for ways to make money, not spend it. And we thought the new executive director would want to see bottom-line results fast if he were going to make such an investment.

But he had a longer-term vision: He wanted greater engagement from the alumni, and he wanted the alumni association's online presence to be an important catalyst for that engagement. He had the foresight to understand that signing up for membership might be a fairly advanced stage of interaction and that we needed a strategy that would help rewire the alumni experience, progressively moving alumni to greater stages of engagement.

Wake Up the Sleeping Kids

The IUAA was very solid on who it already had in its camp: those 40-somethings and up who bled (cream and) crimson. They were predominantly Caucasian, more men than women. Geographically, those already-engaged alumni were from all over the world. But with half a million living alumni and only around 60,000 members, there was exponential potential for growth. In 2009, the year before the IUAA undertook its website project, the Recent Graduate survey of lapsed paid members who had received their first IU degree from 2004 to 2007 showed the following:

» About 60 percent were female.
» 76 percent were under 30 years old.

» 86 percent used Facebook.

» 59 percent used LinkedIn.

Remember, these were the *lapsed* members—they weren't inspired to continue their relationship with the alumni association. To revive flat membership numbers and build diversity among the ranks, we decided with our IUAA colleagues that we should segment our target audience to focus on current students and alumni who had graduated in the past decade. These were also the groups most likely to be heavily involved in social media and most reachable through those channels. Nearly half of IUAA Facebook fans were 18–34, and 27 percent were 35–44 years old.

An important part of the research for this project—in addition to internal stakeholder interviews, a review of recent research conducted by consultants, and an online survey of website visitors— was the equivalent of online Anthropology 101. We sought out the cool coffee shops of the internet—lingered in blogs and pored over image feeds and social media posts—to find out what the sleeping kids were up to. What mattered to them? If they weren't enthusiastic about their alumni association, what did they care about?

The answer, while gratifying, was very surprising. They cared about IU. They were having IU-themed weddings, dressing their babies in IU gear, talking enthusiastically about IU news, and even making IU-themed cakes. Famous young alumni were telling the world how much they loved their alma mater—alumni like Jessica Quirk, a prominent fashion blogger, who dressed in IU gear on her blog. Our target demographic was not engaged with the alumni association, but they were practically begging the institution to engage with *them* and recognize their devotion and achievements.

Planning the Family Reunion

In the earliest stages of the IUAA project, we determined that these tenets would guide our effort:

» In-depth research and thorough strategy would inform our approach.

» Collaboration between our IU communications team and the IUAA marketing teams would be essential—it would be all hands on the digital deck to transform the IUAA online presence.

» We had to create a *social* experience to gain greater measurable engagement with alumni.

» Compelling, relevant storytelling would attract our target audience, and we would use emotional and/or tangible incentives and fresh content to keep them coming back.

Initial research showed that alumni had a strong desire for the

Jessica Quirk, author of WhatIWore.Tumblr.com, frequently features IU gear on her site. (left)

Natalie Wise, BA '07, winner of the "Show us your IU style" contest. (right)

IUAA to demonstrate its relevance to them. In the online survey, they said that they wanted membership to get them special access, more tangible benefits. Many of the perks they asked for were already on the website, but they simply couldn't find them. When we asked them their top reasons for visiting the site, the most frequent answer was "to take the survey." Only 4.5 percent said they went there regularly to access the alumni directory, and 4.3 percent went to the site to update their alumni profile. Across the board, the IUAA content that had the highest awareness factor and most value as a service was *Indiana Alumni Magazine*. Alumni liked stories, in other words. More important, they liked seeing stories about other alumni ... or seeing themselves in the class notes section.

We knew we would have to approach this project with a strategic shift in voice, tone, and brand personality. We would have to work very closely as a combined team to provide more clarity on the alumni benefits and services the IUAA provides on its primary website.

Sarah Preuschl Anderson, director of alumni marketing, was the project lead from the IUAA and convened a working group that represented membership, events, career development, publications, the student alumni association, marketing, outreach, merchandising, and affinity relationships. This representation enabled us to think about our strategy holistically: How would it touch all aspects of the communications ecosystem? As Anderson later noted, "The website—words, design, photography structure, and strategy—is the product of many skilled minds and hands at IU and the IU Alumni Association, and I'm very proud of the work we did together. IU alumni can also be proud."

Two strategies charted the course of our project: online brand and content.

IU **8-word** Story Winner!
Rejected. Humbled. Re-focused. Accepted.
Discovered. Grew. Thrived. Remembered.

Nathan Sorrells, BA'04

Spirit of IU

Read the stories
from all the winners >>

The 8-word story contest was
judged by prominent IU alumni
Nancy and Michael Uslan.

Online Brand Strategy

The online brand strategy sets goals and objectives for the project, provides a target audience focus and detailed composite personas, analyzes the IUAA brand personality, and outlines how we can more effectively and consistently promote that brand promise through our creative approach to the website and other online marketing efforts.

The brand strategy and long-term plan sought to answer these questions about our online home for IU alumni:

- » What should the site feel like?
- » What does our family need?
- » Who are we talking to?
- » How do we want them to feel?
- » What is the brand-appropriate voice for the IUAA online?
- » How can we better promote the benefits that IUAA membership offers?
- » How can we leverage existing IUAA and IU content and online channels to build engagement with the IUAA, moving more alumni toward membership?

In addition, we collected information from our stakeholders, subject matter experts, and users about what they wanted to achieve or see on the website and what tasks they wanted to accomplish as they interacted with the specific areas of content. These are presented in our brand strategy as lists of IUAA goals, user needs, and user tasks.

These were the objectives we included in our brand strategy:

- » Create and implement a long-term online communications plan toward building membership in the IUAA.
- » Repurpose existing content and realign staff effort, shifting in some cases from print to online media, especially social media.
- » Examine research to target the most likely demographics for

membership and membership renewal.

» Assess best current assets, according to research, to attract and retain members through the online environment.

» Recommend ways to promote career assistance services more prominently on the website and in social media.

» Capitalize on currency of campus, school, and chapter and affiliate events through social media strategy.

» Leverage *Indiana Alumni Magazine*, a popular benefit, in social media and online, as well as in print.

Content Strategy

The content strategy is a tool for both the website redesign project team and content creators. It is the blueprint for a new way of thinking about web content.

The previous IUAA website contained an astounding number of web pages (nearly 4,000, including PDFs and archived publications). The voice and tone, presentation, and delivery needed to be refined to demonstrate the value of the organization to IU alumni and inspire them to get involved.

Users value content that is relevant to their lives, and they want to be able to find it quickly and easily. The content strategy outlines devices for website and social media managers to stay focused on the organization's goals and the users' needs as they prepare content for the various products, services, and experiences IUAA offers its audiences.

These devices include:

» Rally cry: This is the team motto, the call to the cause of creating content that is meaningful for alumni.

» Core purpose sentence diagrams: These sentences distill the core purpose of the content for each product, service, or experience.

» Call to action: What do we want the user to understand about the content after spending 1 second, 10 seconds, or 2 minutes interacting with it?

Invitation to the Engagement Party

To support both the brand and content strategies and to underscore the overall goal for mobilizing alumni to engage with IU, we outlined an engagement ladder inspired by the online engagement ladder described by Forrester Research. It explores online behaviors and interactions of the IUAA and audience members and aligns them with targets for increased involvement or advocacy. In this model, we show how we want to move tailgaters (those who visit us online but only passively) to ticketholders (people who opt in to the conversation and rate others' posts). Ideally, we said, we will create an experience that moves alumni progressively up the ladder to the status of fans (those who actively contribute content and rate and comment on others' posts) or ralliers (alumni and friends who create a significant body of content and rally others to engage with the IUAA).

Tell Us a Story ... Make It Social

Perhaps the biggest challenge of the project was developing a concept to make the IUAA and its online presence meaningful to alumni. We needed to develop a storytelling approach that would be uniquely IU, one that would inspire pride and capture that ineffable sense of deep emotional connection. So our research turned to its deep background, or soul-searching, phase. We knew what our alumni expected from the relationship. But we needed to find ourselves first.

Our quest for the story that would help us reach deep into the hearts of alumni and stoke their love for the institution turned to a trek through the university archives. In the writings of beloved former IU President and institutional icon Herman B. Wells, we found his description of the freshman induction ceremony from the 1930s. This was a ceremony that so touched Wells that he determined then and there to transfer from the University of Illinois to Indiana University. From 1933 to 1969, the first speaker at the freshman induction ceremony was "the Spirit of Indiana"—a young woman in a white flowing gown, embodying the spirit of the institution and representing the university's search for truth and knowledge. The following is an excerpt of the Spirit's traditional speech:

> The spirit that greets you here is the rich heritage of a glorious past made possible by students, who like yourselves entering the university, feel strangely far from home and intimate friends, but who soon adapted to their new environment. The university covets for each of you a like experience. ... Make the most of the opportunities while here, acquaint yourself with the best traditions of the university, leave them richer in tradition than when you entered it. Such is the Law of Progress. All that has been and all that is of the spirit of Indiana University welcomes you unreservedly.

We needed to develop a storytelling approach that would be uniquely IU, one that would inspire pride and capture that ineffable sense of deep emotional connection.

From this seed, the idea of a social media campaign to engage alumni grew into our idea for a "Spirit of IU" game and social media community. The Spirit of Indiana, a quaint but lovely figure in her flowing gown, has been transformed. She has a new life in social media. Spirit of IU[1] is a website that "welcomes unreservedly"

---

(1) Link: spirit.iu.edu

a community of IU friends. It is also a game that alumni and friends can play that celebrates alumni for how they express their individual loyalty to IU and gives them a chance to earn points and prizes, ultimately leading to a free membership in the alumni association. This game is promoted on the homepage of the IUAA website, refreshed regularly with new user-generated content. That content comes from the Spirit of IU website, as well as from the IUAA Facebook page.

The project team had no veteran game developers, so a great deal of research was involved in understanding how to conceive, develop, and program a game and how to structure a point system. One of the most compelling features of the Spirit of IU site is a series of contests hosted by famous IU alumni. These contests galvanize our target demographic and move them to greater engagement with the IUAA.

Our inaugural contest had a fashion theme, inviting alumni to submit photos of themselves wearing IU colors. Alumna and well-known fashion blogger Jessica Quirk of WhatIWore.Tumblr.com hosted the contest. We were pleased by the variety and creativity of the entries, and because the contest was timed simultaneously with the release of Jessica's book, *Four Seasons, One Closet: Endless Recipes for Personal Style*, we were able to give each of our 10 winners a signed copy of her book in addition to IU apparel donated by IU Licensing & Trademarks. The grand prize winner of the contest, Natalie Wise, BA '07, is also a blogger, and she wrote several blog entries about the experience and even showcased the IU apparel she won on her blog. When we contacted Natalie to tell her she won the contest, she wrote back:

> Indiana holds a special place in my heart. It's where I grew up, and I graduated IU High School and IU for my undergraduate degree, so I feel I have a special history with IU. I'm so excited to be chosen because this outfit gave me so much confidence. What girl doesn't like wearing IU red? I keep my IU hat and tassel on a shelf in my living room; as soon as I heard of the contest, I knew I wanted to incorporate them. Midwesterners and IU alums are just like my outfit: bright, creative, inspired, and happy. We want to make the world a better place. And where else to start than with a fabulous outfit?

In our second contest, we asked power duo Nancy and Michael Uslan, IU alumni who have made significant contributions to literacy and cinematic history, to host and judge an eight-word IU story contest. Nancy is the driving force behind the Books & Beyond Project, a collaborative literacy project that partners

IU students with charter school students in Newark, N.J., who write books and send them to students in post-genocide Rwanda. Michael is executive producer of the *Batman* movies and *Where on Earth Is Carmen Sandiego?*, among many other major productions. While a student at IU, he also developed the first for-credit college course on comic books.

All of the winners were able to personally connect with our alumni celebrities and feel celebrated for their own part in supporting the Spirit of IU. Here are the eight-word stories from our winners:

> » Nathan Sorrels, BA '04: "Rejected. Humbled. Re-Focused. Accepted. Discovered. Grew. Thrived. Remembered."
> » Nicole Calandra, BA '96: "Learned how to learn, I want to return!"
> » Katherine Lewis Albers, BA '01: "Third generation IU student. Family knows best."
> » Laura Bliss, current student: "Hopelessly in love with all things Hoosier."
> » Adam VanOsdol, BA '05: "Teter to Ernie Pyle: Earned degree my style."
> » John Blue, BS '85, MS '92: "Life friends, Met wife, Stayed connected, Always returning."
> » Colleen Law, BA '93: "Huge campus got smaller every day. Thanks friends!"
> » Eric Knabel, BS '93: "Good times. Good friends. Great education. Lifelong memories."
> » Jim Keplinger, current student: "I enrolled a boy and graduated a man."
> » Nicole Green, BA '04: "First friend at orientation: decade later, best friend."

Let the Social Games Begin

One of the challenges of this project was finding an application that could support all the aspects of our vision for a renewed alumni connection. We knew it had to be cool and fun and offer something beyond a connection via Facebook or Twitter. It had to feel like the online equivalent of going back to college, to a place they loved as much as their favorite hangout in Bloomington.

The application we were seeking needed to support features such as member profiles, photo uploads, location-based services, contests, a point system for the game, and Facebook and Twitter integration. Building an application from scratch was not an option— our timeline would not permit it. We had been consulting with our developers throughout the concept development process about the feasibility of implementing our ideas, and after we received

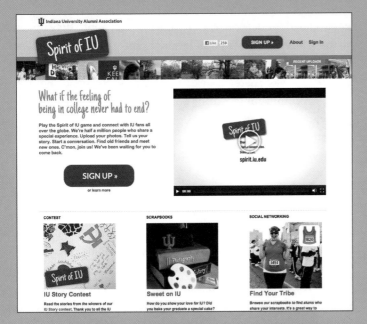

The Spirit of IU website employs gamification to encourage engagement.

IUAA's sign-off on the concept, our team went to work researching applications that could support the features we outlined in the concept. We identified six applications that met some or all of the criteria: BuddyPress, SocialEngine, Ning, SocialGo, Big Tent, and KickApps. After our team evaluated the costs, features, and pros and cons of each social network builder, we determined SocialEngine was the best match for our Spirit of IU site.

We had seven months from the time we selected SocialEngine until the launch date of both the IUAA and the Spirit of IU websites. Our information architect, interaction/visual designer, content specialist, and two developers worked together to set up and customize SocialEngine. During this process, we had to make some concessions. For example, SocialEngine did not have a GPS feature for photo uploads, so the idea of a map with images from IU alumni around the world had to be scrapped. We also could not customize SocialEngine as much as we initially thought. For example, we wanted the Spirit of IU homepage to feature a video description of the game, along with some benefits that alumni would enjoy by joining the community. Our developers told us we could not customize the layout of the SocialEngine homepage like this—it is set up to go to each member's individual page at login. Our solution was to build a custom page outside of SocialEngine so we could educate alumni about the community before they signed up.

As we worked matching each aspect of our concept to the software, we problem-solved on the fly, determining whether some of the SocialEngine plug-ins were adequate as-is and which ones we needed to customize more. The point system we devised for our game called for users to earn points for each photo they uploaded to the site, with higher point levels for specific types of photos. However, we quickly realized that it wasn't possible to award points this way. Instead, we decided to go with SocialEngine's built-in options for awarding points to users based on their actions—uploading any photo, getting a friend to sign up, or joining a photo community such as IU Pets, IU Babies, or Sweet on IU for those who loved to whip up IU-themed treats.

Lessons Learned

The big lesson from this project is the importance of researching technical options during the storytelling development process. We started with the storytelling, thinking the technology to support our stories would be easy to find because we found so many great examples on the web. However, when we started to look at the technology options available to us, we had to make several compromises because of our timeline, budget, and software limitations.

The upside is that we did allow ourselves to dream big with the initial concept, focusing on what our alumni would want to do. Working the opposite way—starting with the software and then trying to find a way to use it creatively to tell a story—might have worked, but we believe it would have limited our final product.

Iain Tait, executive creative director at Google Creative Lab and former global interactive executive creative director at Wieden + Kennedy, the agency behind Old Spice's "Man Your Man Could Smell Like" social media campaign, explained the importance of stories and software at the Creativity and Technology conference in London in November 2010: "The modern agency has two products: stories and software. You're in denial if you think gaming is a niche world. This is the kind of storytelling and level of experience that consumers expect from us. The bar is set incredibly high."

During this project, we have learned how high that bar is. We weren't experts in gaming, and although our contests were successful, the core game still hasn't taken off the way we envisioned. Part of the reason is the user experience. The sign-up process takes several minutes, the application itself is sometimes sluggish, and shortly after our second contest ended, major technical issues with the server sidelined the site for nearly a month.

In recent months we've been working on streamlining the sign-up process, optimizing the server setup, and improving integration with Twitter and Facebook. We are also examining the game prizes and working with campus partners to improve the offerings so alumni will be more motivated to participate. While it might have been easier to scrap the game site once we started encountering technical problems or issues with participation, we recognize the long-term benefits. We've created a foundation that we know will continue to be important in building relationships with alumni, and we need to continue to observe their behavior and enhance the experience we offer accordingly.

As IUAA Executive Director J.T. Forbes said, "I have the remarkable opportunity to meet IU graduates from all over the world with vastly different backgrounds and very different ways of expressing their IU spirit. Though social media has its roots in academia, and nearly every university has a Facebook page or Twitter account, Spirit of IU is intended to be more user-driven, playful, and even competitive. We hope the game will grow in popularity over time and in true social media fashion become whatever our alumni want it to be."

The Spirit of IU Coalesces

The Spirit of IU story continues to unfold. The individual expressions of alumni love of IU are coalescing into a story on all of IU's social media channels, including Twitter, Facebook, YouTube, and the Spirit of IU site.

Since the launch of the new IUAA and Spirit of IU websites, we have seen increases in the time spent on the sites and number of pages visited. The number of unique monthly visitors has increased from 32,000 per month before the launch to more than 60,000 in March 2012, during the NCAA basketball tournament, and 49,000 in April 2012. More than 45 percent of site traffic has been generated by referrals, which speaks to the power of social media. The number of active users on the IUAA Facebook page has more than doubled, and the total number of Facebook "likes" is now 11,416, a 40 percent increase since the launch of the sites. The number of Twitter followers has more than tripled, from 1,500 before the launch to 4,769. And the Spirit of IU community continues to grow. In August 2011, we had 456 members. After we marketed the community at alumni events and via social media, the community grew to 800 members.

We're excited about all the personal connections we've been able to make with alumni online, and in June 2012, a new IU Alumni Attitude study revealed that alumni profess a strong loyalty to IU, but they want the IUAA to tell them how to express that loyalty more publicly. The Spirit of IU community will help alumni do this and show the world their generosity in helping others, their commitment to the university, and their determination to do good in the world. As one of our contest winners, Julie Otis, BA '11, told us, "It feels awesome to be considered as part of the Spirit of IU." **SW**

Embracing Rivalry to Increase Annual Fund Participation: Elizabethtown College and Messiah College

By Melissa Soberanes

Melissa Soberanes is a writer and editor at mStoner. She has more than 15 years of experience helping nonprofit organizations and education institutions increase awareness and tell their stories through effective communications, media relations, and web strategies.

A little friendly competition never hurt anyone, especially long-time soccer-field rivals Elizabethtown College and Messiah College. Capitalizing on the well-established, spirited competition between the two colleges, Elizabethtown and Messiah created the Battle of the Blues campaign (Elizabethtown's school colors are blue and gray; Messiah's, navy blue and white).

Battle of the Blues put a unique spin on the college annual fundraising campaign by pitting young alumni of both colleges against each other in a competition for the highest number of donors, not dollars raised. In hopes of increasing young alumni giving, Battle of the Blues targeted alumni who had graduated within the last 10 years. The winner was determined by the rate of participation since Elizabethtown and Messiah had different alumni bases. The campaign launched in July 2011 and ran through the end of October, closing with a soccer game between the rival colleges. It's a big game for both colleges, and it now had the added competition for donations.

The idea was inspired by similar competitions between Lafayette College and Lehigh University and between Colorado College and the University of Denver. Ashley Martin, the assistant director of annual giving at Messiah College, had been looking for an innovative way to increase participation among recent alumni. Recognizing the competitive spirit between Messiah and Elizabethtown, Martin approached Elizabethtown.

"I think it was successful for many reasons, but central to this was the partnership with Messiah College, which allowed us both to capitalize on our existing rivalry," said Melody Bitkoff, director of the annual fund for Elizabethtown College.

Promotion of the giving challenge and participation centered on the Battle of the Blues website,[1] created specifically for the campaign, and the Twitter hashtags created for each school (#GoEtownBlue and #GoMessiahBlue). Both schools used the website to post information about the challenge, link to donation forms, provide updates on standings, and incorporate the Twitter feeds. It was these Twitter hashtags that really generated buzz and encouraged the friendly competition between the two colleges. The website pulled and displayed related tweets to encourage participation and allow visitors to follow the "trash talk" taking place.

While both colleges shared the overall campaign goal to engage young alumni, and both used social media, each approached the challenge differently, developing different logos and print materials and achieving different results.

Elizabethtown College's Approach

Elizabethtown College's development office and marketing and communications office worked together on an integrated approach to promote the Battle of the Blues campaign. Communication channels included print, direct mail, email, advertising, YouTube, Facebook, a student phonathon, and word of mouth through team captains.

"We wanted to reach our alumni in different ways, particularly the methods that young alumni respond to the most," said Bitkoff. "And we wanted to make it fun and interactive." She added that it was essential to have volunteers in place to help send out messages on all channels.

Elizabethtown used social media extensively, creating a Battle of the Blues Facebook page and promoting the campaign on the college's Facebook page and regional alumni club pages. The staff also created videos to post on YouTube and include in the email solicitations. While these efforts were helpful, Bitkoff noted that email and direct mail proved to be the most successful ways to secure gifts from Elizabethtown's young alumni.

"Facebook and Twitter were recently added to our fundraising and marketing campaigns. During the campaign, about 20 alumni tweeted and we had 100 Facebook fans, but we had an initial open rate of 38 percent for email," Bitkoff said. "By campaign's end, donations from direct mail made up the majority of contributions received, at 45.2 percent."

Even so, the staff found that incorporating the social media channels allowed for greater immediacy and urgency. "The social media tools available today help us do things on the fly if we need to," said Donna Talarico, integrated marketing manager for the office of marketing and communications. "We can communicate more quickly and with less lead time then print. It also provides an instant feedback and donation mechanism, and an immediate call

---

(1) Link: BluevBlue.com

to action. People can click, link, and donate right away."

Another communication channel that worked well for the Elizabethtown team was traditional word of mouth, via team captains selected from each class of the target audience. The chosen captains were already donors, had a high level of participation as alumni, and were well known in their classes. Bitkoff explained that it was crucial to have volunteers in place to help send out messages on all channels, and that the use of team captains enabled Elizabethtown to capitalize on the "friend-raising" that comes naturally to social media.

"Our team captains acted as cheerleaders and champions to help promote the challenge and secure participation," Bitkoff said. "If I could motivate my volunteers to tweet then it would cause a snowball effect, extending the reach of the campaign."

Messiah College's Approach

Messiah College also developed an integrated communications plan to promote Battle of the Blues and encourage young alumni participation. The college employed email, print, direct mail, a phonathon, video, Twitter, and Facebook.

Messiah created two Facebook ad campaigns. The first one targeted alumni who had graduated within the previous 10 years to push them to "like" Messiah's Battle of the Blues Facebook page. The second one targeted alumni who already liked the page, thanked them, and encouraged them to make a gift. It proved quite successful, with 38 percent of recent alumni Facebook fans making a gift during the campaign.

Martin acknowledged that while using social media was helpful, Messiah had a relatively small following on social channels. Like Bitkoff, Martin also found that print and email were still the most successful ways to reach Messiah's young alumni.

"We really threw everything at the wall. We made sure to use print, letters, email, and social media. Social channels were particularly helpful in communicating the different giving options and live stats. We had an artist rendering of the new building for Messiah's capital campaign, which we posted on Facebook," said Martin. "But the key to using social media is to have a clear strategy in place. Know what you want to post and when, and be prepared to monitor activity on your social channels so you can respond quickly."

Another effective channel for Messiah was the phonathon, which provided a valuable opportunity to tell alumni why their gifts were important and to get them excited to participate. "It was all about educating our young alumni so they would be more likely to give in the future. It helped us get our alumni riled up and want to give at that exact moment. We had callers who were very passionate about giving, and the Battle of the Blues campaign really spoke to our

> We really threw everything at the wall. We made sure to use print, letters, email, and social media. Social channels were particularly helpful in communicating the different giving options and live stats.

The participation-based competition targeted young alumni, encouraging them to donate and connect.

alumni's competitive streak," said Martin.

Messiah also relied on a hardworking group of alumni volunteers who played various roles in supporting the campaign and encouraging participation. Anthony Thomas, '06, a member of the Messiah College Alumni Council, reached out to young alumni through phone, email, and Facebook. He said that most alumni he communicated with thought Battle of the Blues was a fun way to get involved.

"This is a big rivalry for us. Battle of the Blues was a great way to talk about alumni engagement from a different perspective of rivalry and athletic competition. The emphasis was not about the donation amount, but was about alumni giving what they could and supporting Messiah," said Thomas. "Battle of the Blues brought alumni back to a time when they were at Messiah and when it was a fun, positive experience."

Todd Holtzman, '08, also a member of the Alumni Council, played more of an advisory role, coming up with ways to promote Battle of the Blues. He agreed that the event offered an easy way to reach out to alumni and talk about giving back to Messiah. He said it was fun to talk about the contest and rivalry first, then talk about the importance of financial support.

Winning Results

The final score of the Battle of the Blues campaign was close. Elizabethtown won the donor competition with a participation rate of 7.85 percent, over Messiah's rate of 7.72 percent. Kelly and Carl Marrara, graduates of Elizabethtown, accepted the trophy on the college's behalf. Still, Messiah maintained its pride on the soccer field, winning the men's soccer game 2–0 and the women's soccer game 3-0 over its rival.

The Battle of the Blues allowed the colleges to engage in a rivalry away from the athletic fields.

But staff at both colleges agreed that they came out ahead as fundraising winners. By using this competitive campaign approach, both Elizabethtown and Messiah increased giving and participation by young alumni and jump-started their social media efforts. "We're hopeful this will promote continued giving in the future," said Talarico.

Elizabethtown reported securing 56 new, or first-time, donors, and the donations from Battle of the Blues represented more than 75 percent of the total young alumni participation secured for the entire year in FY2011. Even better, in FY2012 its young alumni participation was 12.23 percent, compared with 9.72 percent in FY2011. The campaign also encouraged more gift amounts under $100, with an average gift size of $28.

Messiah reported receiving gifts totaling more than $22,000 from 469 young alumni. Of these donors, 123 were lapsed and 54 were new donors. Most important, Messiah's young alumni participation has continued to increase and is currently more than 13 percent.

Battle of the Blues: Take II

Battle of the Blues was such a success that Elizabethtown and Messiah did it all over again in the fall of 2012, but with a few adjustments. For starters, staff at both colleges agreed that the 2011 campaign was too long, and in 2012 they ran it for only five weeks, from September 4 to October 6.

The website saw a facelift with new messaging: "They say the

More thoughts on the topic...
The LL Challenge: The Inspiration Behind Battle of the Blues

In May 2010, development staff from both Lehigh University and Lafayette College were looking for a new way to increase giving from young alumni. Capitalizing on their longstanding rivalry both on and off the field, they explored the idea of a giving challenge among young alumni 10 years out. The result: the Lehigh-Lafayette Challenge.

Little did staff know that the LL Challenge would grow in popularity and size over the next three years and serve as inspiration for other campaigns, such as the Battle of the Blues (Elizabethtown College vs. Messiah College). Elizabeth Anderson, assistant director of the Lafayette Annual Fund, said that sometimes all it takes is a crazy idea, especially in development.

"We thought outside the box and looked for a new way to engage our young alumni. We had to find that one thing that both schools could rally around. This is one of the biggest rivalries for college football in the area," Anderson said.

The LL Challenge launched with the fall 2010 game and targeted only current seniors and graduates from within the previous 10 years. The challenge took place in the five days leading up to the big game and was strictly a participation challenge. The winner was the school with the highest number of gifts from young alumni, with Lafayette receiving two points per gift because of its smaller size. On game day there was also the option to text $10 gifts. That first year, Lafayette won, beating Lehigh by just 14 points for a final score of 777 to 763.

The LL Challenge has grown and changed since it first launched. In year two, the LL Challenge was 18 days long (Nov. 1-18, 2011) and was open to all alumni. Alumni could also text gifts throughout the challenge, not just on game day. This subtle change had a big impact on the final numbers. Lehigh won with 2,529 points; 899 represented text gifts received from 723 individuals. Lafayette came in a close second with 2,074 points. As the program heads into year three in November 2012, the biggest change is who can participate. The LL Challenge is now open to everyone in the community, not just alumni.

Chad Davis, director of the Lehigh Fund, said the idea was to make giving to the LL Challenge easy and fun, and that the multichannel approach helped both institutions do just that. Channels used included print, email, phone, social media, and an LL Challenge website. Promotion also took place during the more than 60 telecasts of the game.

Facebook and Twitter were the most popular avenues of communication. While Lehigh had a separate LL Challenge Facebook page, Lafayette primarily used its alumni relations Facebook page. Friendly trash talk was prevalent on Twitter. During the 2011 LL Challenge, both competitors used the hashtag #Rivalry147, referring to the 147th game between Lehigh and Lafayette. In 2012, the tag will be #Rivalry148.

"Making it easy to get people engaged was critical. Social media provide a tremendous opportunity for people to hear from their peers rather than just the institution. Social media make the experience real and provide an easy way for people to share and engage with each other," said Davis.

Both Anderson and Davis said the challenge was successful in many ways, from increasing young alumni giving to engaging and exciting an entire community. It gave people a platform to talk about giving in a fun, nonthreatening way. And best of all, the LL Challenge opened the doors to educating young alumni about the importance of giving.

---

second time is a charm. It's the same game, the same rules, the same players, but it's the second year and the stakes are higher."

For the 2012 Battle of the Blues, Elizabethtown created a new Facebook page[2] and started promoting the event earlier. Facebook ads were more effective with click-throughs linking directly to the online donation page. The ads received 288,392 impressions, with 71 click-throughs. Communication also got an overhaul. A postcard was mailed out the first week of the competition, and all communication came from team captains, with increased emails and letters. Bitkoff said the college also reached out to alumni who gave last year and asked them to renew their gifts for 2012. Elizabethtown's strategy: defense. Its message: "Messiah challenged our young alumni ('03–'12) to defend our coveted trophy in the Battle of the Blues: Take II!"

Messiah also created a new Facebook page[3] for the rematch. The message: "Last year, E-town defeated Messiah College by a

---

(2) Link: facebook.com/goetownblue
(3) Link: facebook.com/GoMCBlue

Woo! Battle of the Blue challenge! Shout out to my boyfriend's alma mater (he donated cuz of that - I just asked him) #casesmc

4 minutes ago via HootSuite

Home   Connect   Discover   Me

Although the colleges utilized social media heavily, they also relied on email, phone, and print communications.

slim margin in the first ever Battle of the Blues. Now is the time to claim the trophy and bring it to Grantham where it belongs." New for 2012 was a Battle of the Blues donor website[4] for easier online giving that offered donors five designated areas for support. Messiah also planned ahead in 2012 and created several videos to help promote the challenge. Martin said that Messiah's "underdog" strategy really excited people, particularly students. Even though students are not the target audience, Martin said they were very engaged and helped promote the 2012 competition.

For the second year in a row, Elizabethtown won the Battle of the Blues campaign, with a donor participation rate of 4.82 percent, over Messiah's rate of 4.60 percent. Messiah maintained its victory on the field, however, with a final men's soccer score of 4-0 and a women's soccer score of 3-0.

Despite their respective victories, both colleges again came out winners in their fundraising efforts. Elizabethtown reported that it raised a total of $8,590.48, with an average gift size of $38.52. And of the 221 alumni donors, Elizabethtown had 20 first-time donors and 57 lapsed donors. Messiah reported that it raised $11,434.90, with an average gift size of $41.43. Out of the 276 Messiah alumni donors, 24 were first-time donors and 57 were lapsed.

Martin and Bitkoff offered some advice for other institutions considering a campaign like the Battle of the Blues. First, prepare to be surprised. In the case of the first Battle of the Blues, the big

(4) Link: messiah.edu/gomessiahblue

surprise was weather: A freak snowstorm on Oct. 29, 2011, forced the colleges to postpone the big soccer game to Oct. 31, extending their giving battle for a few more days.

Second, ongoing communication between the teams running the competition at the rival colleges is vital, so make sure to set clear collaboration guidelines and detail the expectations beforehand.

Some final advice came from Holtzman, the alumni volunteer from Messiah: "Be willing to try out new ideas to engage alumni. Think outside the box. In many cases alumni are eager to be involved in ways beyond just helping to promote a campaign. Alumni can provide valuable ideas, insight, and feedback on what resonates best with their fellow alumni." **sw**

The Great Give Online Giving Campaign Goes Viral: Florida State University

By Justin Ware | @JustinJWare

Justin Ware is director of interactive communication at Bentz Whaley Flesser. Ware and BWF worked with FSU's annual giving team during the planning of the Great Give.

I n 36 hours, Florida State University's annual giving team led an online-only campaign to raise $161,000. During those 36 hours, the Great Give campaign surpassed that goal, raising more than $186,000 and introducing hundreds of new donors to philanthropy at FSU. They did it thanks to solid planning and understanding the nuances of communicating online and via social media.

Planning the Great Give

Three months is an awfully short period of time for planning a first-of-its-kind online giving campaign with a six-figure goal. In fact, when then–Director of Annual Giving Chad Warren announced the idea, I was concerned enough to kindly suggest moving the date back a few months to better establish an online and social media community for FSU's fundraising efforts. After all, it had only been a month since the FSU team had participated in an online and social media training workshop. They were, essentially, starting from scratch, and already they wanted to put the ideas in motion with the goal of producing real fundraising results.

"We didn't know. There was just a lot of uncertainty," said Warren in an interview shortly after the Great Give. "From the fundraising side, could we raise $161,000 in 36 hours with what we felt was little promotion?"

Warren and his small staff of two fundraisers had been hearing a lot about what online giving can mean to an annual giving program. Warren had attended enough conferences that evangelized about the ability of social media to boost fundraising programs that he and his team decided it was time to put modern tools to work for FSU. In fall 2011, they got the wheels rolling on a plan not only to increase the online giving dollar amount, but also—perhaps even more important—boost the number of new donors to the university.

The FSU Foundation received tens of thousands of gifts in 2011, but, Warren said, "only about 1 percent of them came in online. So we knew we had a great opportunity to secure gifts online and start to promote that as an accessible way for a donor to give."

This desire to build a stronger online giving program for FSU was more than just faith in a new communication fad. In the months since the Great Give, data from multiple studies have demonstrated the need for connecting with donors online. According to donorCentrics' *2011 Internet and Multichannel Giving Benchmarking Report*, gifts from online donors, on average, tend to be nearly twice the size of gifts made through other direct-response means, such as direct mail or phone, and online donors have higher average household incomes and apparently greater lifetime giving potential as well. In addition to those staggering numbers, the *2012 Nonprofit Social Network Benchmarking Report* says the value of a Facebook fan is more than $214. That means every time someone "likes" your Facebook page, it's worth $214. Given the wide disparity between the number of well-run Facebook pages and those that appear to have been neglected, I would guess that the online-savvy organizations that participated in the study raise far more than $214 per fan. Of course, a lot of nonprofits with a Facebook page earn far less.

With a strong sense that significant online giving numbers were possible, Warren and his team started planning the Great Give in late fall 2011. They kept things simple and announced a significant but obtainable goal: Raise $161,000 to celebrate the school's 161st anniversary.

The Great Give was set for Jan. 23 and 24, 2012, just a few short months from when the campaign was first discussed. And the three-person annual giving department had not yet developed any electronic resources for this campaign. Warren wasn't sure how successful the campaign would be, so the decision was made to build the media—online giving sites and social network communities—entirely in-house with FSU staff.

"We wanted to keep this low-key; we didn't want to spend any money," said Warren. A small amount—less than $10,000—was used for advertising and promotion, primarily through direct mail. Other than that, the online giving forms would be built by the FSU information technology staff. Creating, monitoring, and managing the online chatter would have to be done by the annual giving team members with the assistance of any volunteers they could tap.

In the weeks leading up to the campaign, Warren and team produced YouTube videos and used social media to engage supporters and build excitement. They also did a little old-fashioned fundraising, meeting with supporters in person and over

> This desire to build a stronger online giving program for FSU was more than just faith in a new communication fad. In the months since the Great Give, data from multiple studies have demonstrated the need for connecting with donors online.

The Great Give campaign website as it appeared in January 2012.

the phone to ask for their help in securing not just donations, but also the support of their friends during the Great Give. Some call them "influencers," but a more forceful term that gives a better sense of this group's importance and clout is "online ambassadors."

Online Ambassadors

Going viral, something most online campaigns hope will happen in some form, is dependent on an organization's relationship with its online ambassadors. The ambassadors are the internet users who have built strong followings on the web. They tend to use multiple social networks, maintain blogs, and create their own videos or photography. More important, ambassadors can influence the online behavior of other internet users. In many cases, it's something as simple as convincing someone to watch a popular video. But it may also be convincing their followers to give to their favorite organizations and causes online.

The FSU annual giving team worked with volunteers and university staff to identify the online ambassadors and inform them of the Great Give and the role they might play in making the campaign a success. They also made a strong effort to engage students in the campaign. "The student volunteers, they are always looking for a way to get involved," said Daniel Krueger, assistant director of annual giving. "We just said, 'We have this event and we want it to be great. And the only way it's going to be great is if we get student involvement,' and that's where they came in."

Krueger and his team identified student leaders who could enlist a larger group of students to help spread the word about the campaign. Working with individuals like the student body president, the FSU annual giving team provided students with the resources to start a guerrilla marketing campaign. "We actually gave them little cards with QR codes so that other students could scan them, and it would take them right to the site," said Krueger.

Students were also given brief training to teach them how to talk to potential donors about the impact of their gifts. Krueger said, "I think the most important thing is to tell them why they're making a gift. You know, not just make a $10 gift to something, but tell them that they could do it to the college that they belong to, that we had specialized funds to meet the need of whoever was making that gift."

Heavily involved students are an annual fund director's dream. Not only do they enlist the support of other student donors, but they are being introduced to philanthropic support of the university before they even collect their diplomas. Plus, they can be influential in getting less-connected groups of donors—parents, for example— involved in fundraising. For those reasons and more, Krueger says the students they engaged and developed into online and offline ambassadors were a big reason the Great Give surpassed its goals.

"Without them driving student traffic there, this would have been just a normal alumni campaign," he said.

Campaign Kickoff

With a fresh round of emails and social updates, the Great Give was off to a strong start. In just the first few hours, the campaign raised $25,000. The early fundraising boost was a perfect excuse for a quick email update to the various groups of online ambassadors.

Warren's team had prepared prepackaged updates for each social media network and delivered them to their online ambassadors via email. For example, for Twitter, each update was less than 140 characters, including any links. The team also prepared messages for online ambassadors to share on Facebook.

Warren said they would put these prepackaged social network updates in an email with text that read, for example, "If you are at your Facebook page in the next five to 10 minutes, here's a suggested Facebook message to put on your wall."

At first, Warren said, there was concern about the enthusiasm of their supporters. "Would they feel we're inundating them with emails, and would they not want to be engaged?" wondered Warren. "And it was actually the opposite. After about the second or third update, they were asking us, before we got to them, 'What's the next update?' 'Where are we at?' Everyone got really excited, and by the second day, it was not *if* we were going to hit our goal, it was *when*, and that got everybody really excited."

The prepackaged emails and the momentum they added to the campaign are another example of the role online ambassadors play in determining the success of an online campaign. In addition to connecting with students, Warren and the annual giving team met, in person and electronically, with FSU staff, alumni, and other supporters of the university's mission. The ambassadors were told to expect emails from the annual giving team and were encouraged to help them spread the word online via any of the various social networks where the ambassadors were active.

"In order for this to be successful, we needed the support of everybody. And so I said, 'If you can give us 10 minutes of your time, we will be successful.' And I think we did that."

Online ambassadors are the people who will get behind any well-planned effort and throw their full support behind that effort. They are also influential members of alumni groups, professional associations, church groups, and any number of other communities. When ambassadors ask members of their community to support something, they often will. For this reason, connecting with online ambassadors and enlisting their help in driving messages about a campaign will be an increasingly important component of all future online giving efforts.

Changing the Meaning of Word of Mouth

One of the more fascinating aspects of the Great Give might have been what the campaign illuminated about a shift in the meaning of a common phrase: word of mouth.

"What is word of mouth?" asked Warren. "Because we think of word of mouth as having a candid conversation, a personal conversation. A lot of times now, more than half the communication we have is electronic—Facebook, texting, that type of thing—so are we perceiving that now as word of mouth?"

During this campaign, the FSU annual giving team conducted a survey alongside the online giving process. After the gift was secured, they asked the donor, "How did you hear about the Great Give?" The largest response was word of mouth, with 57 percent of all donors saying that was how they learned about the Great Give. Second was email, with a 31 percent response. Considerably further down the list was Facebook and FSU websites, at just 2 percent each. That's roughly equal to the response rate of direct mail. But Warren doesn't see social media as ineffective; his hunch is that those numbers reflect a change in the definition of word of mouth.

"You're communicating and promoting it, but is it through a chat or through a text message or through an email?" Warren thinks a large number of those who reported "word of mouth" were actually thinking about conversations they had via text message or a post they saw on a friend's or family member's Facebook wall. Again, online ambassadors were a big factor in the success of the Great Give, and they weren't sharing their updates by going door-to-door to everyone they knew. They were sharing news of the campaign through social network status updates provided by the FSU annual giving team.

Final Results

At midnight on January 25, just 36 hours after the Great Give kicked off (and about three months after the idea was first introduced), the campaign had raised more than $186,000 and introduced nearly 300 new donors to the university.

"From the successful completion of the Great Give campaign even until now, months later, it is a regularly heard conversation [at FSU]," said Perry Fulkerson, vice president for central development at the Florida State University Foundation.

The Great Give online-only campaign was a huge success for a small investment. FSU spent just under $20,000 on direct mail promotion and fundraising counsel before the event, for a $186,000 return. It worked so well because the fundraisers identified their influential online ambassadors, and then asked those ambassadors to spread awareness about the campaign. FSU's annual giving team manufactured a viral giving campaign.

"The best thing we could do was reach out to members where they were and how they were communicating," said Krueger. "That's really, I think, the difference-maker. If we only did direct mail, this would have been a failure. But we found out where people were and where they were communicating and how they wanted to be heard, and that's how we reached out to them."

Thanks to today's virtually unlimited entertainment and media options, we live and work in a highly segmented communications world. Some people are primarily Facebook users. Some rely on email as their main form of online communication. Others focus solely on Twitter, while a growing number have taken to the newer social networks like Pinterest and Instagram. Some don't use any social media but are heavy text message communicators. As a modern media specialist, you can't afford to ignore any of those communities and the users who converse in them—at least not those in the half dozen or so most highly trafficked sites. The best online and social media strategies include an integrated approach that involves not only multiple social networks but also traditional websites, plus offline tools like direct mail and earned media placement on TV and radio.

FSU's annual giving team understood this, and for that reason the Great Give was a tremendous fundraising success that is now being emulated by other leading higher education institutions.

Next Steps

There is little doubt FSU will be conducting another online campaign in the very near future. "Planning began almost immediately to do it again and to improve our marketing efforts on the front end to gain wider exposure," said Fulkerson.

Given the low response rate to the direct mail component of the Great Give, it would be tempting for anyone considering something similar to drop the snail mail approach. Warren said eliminating direct mail was part of the post-campaign discussion. "We have learned that we can do this on a shoestring budget and not have it cost us anything," said Warren. "So if we choose not to do any direct mail appeals, we can literally do this for zero dollars."

However, a 2012 Convio and CARE USA study shows that donors who give the most give both online and off—they are dual-channel donors. Are those donors giving in both places because that's how they want to give? Or, would they give even more if efforts were increased to steward online donors where they chose to give—online?

With the online gift comes a mailing address along with the credit card information. Sending new donors a piece of mail is a decades-old, proven practice in the fundraising world, but the fundraising world is drastically different today than it was even five years ago. It is a risk, but reallocating direct mail resources to an online-only approach for donors who gave their first gifts online might reduce waste and result in more efficient overall fundraising. It's possible that approach is already working for some forward-thinking organizations. We just don't know yet, because the practice of going online-only for online-acquired donors hasn't been around long enough to be studied extensively.

Of course, organizations—especially those as large as FSU— have a diverse pool of donors with very diverse communications preferences. For that reason, Fulkerson says FSU will continue a broad approach with an array of communication tools.

"Our approach to fundraising has always been multifaceted, with the emphasis on relationship-oriented major gift fundraising," said Fulkerson. "The success of the Great Give validated for us the strength of online giving. We have a significant number of new donors who will continue to be solicited through our various channels, including online efforts, direct mail, and our call center. The biggest success for us is broadening our base of support, which is good for the present and great for the future."

One thing is for certain: FSU leaders will continue to put more focus and effort into developing their social media strategy for fundraising. "We have made a conscious decision even before the Great Give that we would invest in a social media strategy," said Fulkerson. "The success of the Great Give confirmed our thinking that social media is important as part of our multichannel approach to fundraising."

An email sent to supporters immediately following the Great Give campaign.

Online and social media communication is an emerging field. For any academic communications program to consider itself cutting-edge, it's important to have a new media component to its course offerings. Krueger says FSU's annual giving team is hoping to leverage that educational need to help development staff accomplish their fundraising communication goals.

"What if we made a project out of this to help us further break through that shell around our student body?" wondered Kruger. "We had success [with the Great Give], but I think there's still far more that we can do. So why don't we use [student coursework] to figure out what we can do to better market to other students? That's exciting to know that we'll have some people working with us to reach out to a body that's untapped."

"Exciting" is an excellent word to describe online fundraising's potential. It can work for any organization—large, medium, or small. The key is to provide a valuable online experience for your most influential supporters—your online ambassadors. Identify them, build a strategy around giving them what they want in the way they want it, and then work with them to build viral support for your campaigns. **SW**

Social Media and its Role in a Crisis at Missouri University of Science and Technology

By Andrew Careaga | @andrewcareaga

Andrew Careaga is director of communications for Missouri University of Science and Technology (Missouri S&T) in Rolla, Mo.

During a campus emergency, social media can be a communicator's best resource for getting the word out quickly and efficiently. But when so many others have the same tools at their disposal, managing an institution's message on social media during a crisis can become a challenge, as we at Missouri University of Science and Technology (Missouri S&T) learned one spring morning in 2011.

Moments after a man armed with an assault rifle drove onto the Missouri S&T campus in Rolla, Mo., with police in pursuit, the university's communications staff sprang into action. First, the team dispatched simultaneous text, phone, and email alerts to all students, faculty, and staff signed up to receive emergency notifications from the university. On the heels of that mass notification, the communications team posted similar notices on the university's official Twitter and Facebook accounts and switched the campus home page to a fast-loading, text-only site reserved for such emergencies. Throughout the morning, we used the web and social media as our primary means of communicating to students, faculty, staff, family members, the news media, and the public from first word of the gunman's appearance on campus through his capture four hours later.

Even while university communicators swiftly and effectively used these channels to get the word out, we weren't the first to inform some members of campus about the incident. As the campus police chief was informing me of the rapidly unfolding situation, another communications staff member was already learning about the incident via Facebook.

As Missouri S&T's situation from May 2011 illustrates, social media can turn anyone with an internet connection into a real-time reporter and broadcaster of unfolding crisis situations. Colleges and universities must come to terms with this new reality of instantaneous—and sometimes inaccurate—reporting of news as it breaks on our campuses. University communicators also need to understand how best to use social media tools to get their messages out during a crisis. Just as individuals are empowered to share information online with no oversight, communications professionals in higher education must be empowered to use social media to share their institution's messages during a crisis. But if communicators wait until a crisis hits before they become familiar with Facebook, Twitter, and similar platforms, it will be too late.

From Hot Pursuit to Campus Lockdown

At about 8:40 a.m. on May 12, 2011, Missouri S&T Police Chief Christine Laughlin called to notify me of the in-progress car chase. The campus of 7,600 students is primarily an engineering and science university located in a community of about 20,000 in south-central Missouri. At the time of Laughlin's phone call, the campus was not yet the focal point of the crisis. A man armed with an assault rifle was speeding through town, pursued by police, but heading toward Missouri S&T. Laughlin anticipated that the driver would enter campus, and she was right. The driver, later identified as Cody Wilcoxson, crashed his car on a pedestrian walkway on campus, jumped out, and ran into a nearby building, McNutt Hall.

As I was still composing the mass notification, I received a second phone call—this time from another S&T police officer, who informed me that the suspect had entered McNutt Hall. The building was being locked down, and officers from campus, the Rolla Police Department, and other agencies were preparing to enter.

I altered the message to notify the campus of the latest developments. The first mass notification was terse and to the point:

> ALERT! McNutt Hall is on lockdown. Active shooter on campus.

It was pushed out as a text message, email, and voice notification.

Minutes later, other communications staffers posted the same message on the university's Twitter feed (@MissouriSandT) and Facebook site. Both sites are managed by the communications staff, and several staff members have administrative rights to post messages. The first alert was posted to Twitter at 8:53 a.m. and to Facebook at 8:55 a.m. (Minutes earlier, a local Facebook user who was tuned in to a police scanner already had the scoop and had posted information about the car chase on a Facebook page called "Hometown Rolla.")

Meanwhile, other staff members worked with the university's IT department to quickly replace the university's website, MST.

edu, with the university's "In Case of Emergency" website,[1] a fast-loading, image-free hub designed to quickly communicate university messages during a crisis. The redirected website also became the outlet for official university news about the crisis situation as events unfolded.

As police learned that the suspect had left the campus building, S&T Police Chief Laughlin placed the campus on lockdown and asked that all students, faculty, and staff on campus remain in place. The communications team shared that information and also advised off-campus students, faculty, staff, and the public to remain off-campus. The communications staff continued to post updates on the website, Twitter, and Facebook to keep the campus and public informed.

Using a more conventional crisis communications approach, an institution might say nothing publicly until an official press release could be drafted, approved by top-level administrators, and prepared for distribution, or until a press conference could be called. In this rapidly changing crisis, however, the S&T communications team flipped that conventional approach, sharing information publicly via social media more than 90 minutes before issuing its first news release and more than two hours before local law enforcement held its first press conference on the issue.

The Missouri S&T communications team consists of 15 staff members trained in graphic design, public relations, media relations, video production, web design, and web production, as well as two administrative staffers. But on May 12, 2011, the entire team entered crisis communications mode. I composed the mass notification, and other team members pushed the message out via social media and the S&T website. Still others fielded phone calls but were soon overwhelmed by the volume.

By default, the university's online presence—a combination of website and social media—became the hub for all of Missouri S&T's crisis communications that day. There simply was not enough time, staff members, or phone lines to respond to all of the phone calls from journalists and families. The website also became the outlet for official news as events unfolded. Area news media covering the situation reported on how they relied on S&T's social media channels and website to get information about the four-hour campus lockdown. The *St. Louis Post-Dispatch* even prepared a Storify account[2] of S&T's web and social media communications efforts, titled "How a university covered its own lockdown."

Lessons from the Lockdown

While we may not have handled the situation perfectly, our use of

> **In this rapidly changing crisis, however, the S&T communications team flipped that conventional approach, sharing information publicly via social media more than 90 minutes before issuing its first news release and more than two hours before local law enforcement held its first press conference on the issue.**

(1) Link: alert.mst.edu
(2) Available at mstnr.me/MSandT2

During the crisis, Missouri S&T replaced its website with its "In Case of Emergency" site to share updates as the event unfolded.

social media during a tense and protracted situation offers some valuable insight into the value of social media as a communications tool during a crisis. Thanks to social media, the Missouri S&T team was able to provide information immediately, establish a presence that served as a source of information for off-campus constituents and the news media, and feed all constituencies periodic updates in the minutes and hours following the initial announcements.

The success of our efforts during this episode was based on three things:

» planning to ensure that communication was handled by the right department
» understanding of the roles and responsibilities of specific departments during a crisis
» understanding of the impact of social media and the ownership of and access to the institution's primary social media accounts.

The best crisis communications strategies begin with sound planning. As former U.S. President Dwight D. Eisenhower, who commanded the Allied Forces in Europe during World War II, said: "Plans are nothing; planning is everything." No plan can ever provide the solution to every possible crisis. But the process of planning—of understanding processes, roles, and the need to come together as a team—is very valuable.

While the planning process trumps the document that results

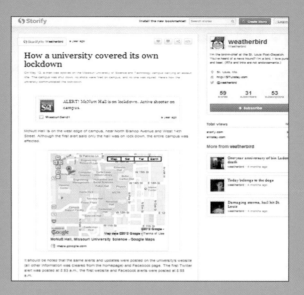

The *St. Louis Post-Dispatch* used social media to tell the story about how S&T covered its own crisis with this Storify article, "How a university covered its own lockdown."

from the effort, a written crisis communications plan is crucial because it provides high-level guidance and documents the roles and responsibilities of various campus units during a crisis. That plan should include a statement acknowledging the impact of social media in spreading official and unofficial messages. College and university communicators should commit to developing a crisis communications plan that takes into account the use of online and social media.

Even more important: An institution's central communications team should direct all crisis communications planning and execution. (This is not the same thing as leading an institution's emergency response; that role is typically assigned to a first responder, such as the campus police department.) With social media's ascent as a news- and information-sharing tool, it is imperative that campus communicators understand the power of social media and learn how to use these tools to communicate during a crisis.

At Missouri S&T, for example, the crisis communications plan focuses primarily on spelling out the roles of various campus departments involved in responding to emergencies. The plan places the responsibility for communicating during a crisis squarely upon the communications department's shoulders. But it also states up front that social media's widespread use will factor in to how information is shared during any crisis—whether that information comes from official institutional channels or from individual users of social media.

"Social media cannot be ignored," S&T's crisis communications plan states. "With the widespread use of online communications systems, rumors can spread quickly via social media and online forums. Therefore, it is critical that responses be issued as quickly as possible via various channels of online communication, including social media networks like Facebook and Twitter, as well as the university website."

During the gunman incident on the Missouri S&T campus, the communications team maintained constant communication with the outside world via social media and the website. While the team members worked with campus and city police to gather more information for a news release, we continued to post updates to Twitter and Facebook in hopes of keeping the campus as informed as possible, even though information was limited.

Here are a few of the early posts to the S&T Twitter account, @MissouriSandT. Each post provided a bit more detail, even though information about the situation and the suspect's whereabouts remained sketchy. After the first few tweets, the S&T communications staff decided to add the campus url to each tweet to direct people to the website, where more information would be posted later.

> Suspect has left campus. Those on campus continue to secure buildings and stay indoors. If you are not on campus avoid campus.
>
> Shooter no longer on campus but Missouri S&T remains on lockdown. Check www.mst.edu for updates.
>
> No shots were fired on campus. No injuries reported.
>
> Campus is still on lockdown and operating under emergency conditions. mst.edu/
>
> Suspect was last seen near White Columns Dr. wearing a blue and white t-shirt and possibly khaki cargo shorts. mst.edu/
>
> Suspect is a caucasian male with sandy blonde hair and is considered dangerous. mst.edu/
>
> Suspect is possibly bleeding from hand. mst.edu/
>
> If you have information regarding the suspect please call the Rolla Police Dept. 573-308-1213. mst.edu/

We added similar posts to the university's Facebook site, which was abuzz with chatter from fans ("Is everybody all right at MST?" "Everyone OK in McNutt?" "Please keep us updated"). Two staff members monitored Facebook and Twitter while others worked on the website, fielded media calls, and coordinated with me to prepare a news release. By that time, I was at the incident command post, coordinating communications with campus and local law enforcement and working with journalists onsite.

Another staff member, who was off campus when the incident occurred, later joined me to assist with the media. I did not direct the social media efforts; communications staff members, many of them trained in social media usage and crisis communications, were coordinating among themselves with the department's assistant director providing oversight (while also attempting to field media calls).

Meanwhile, news organizations followed Missouri S&T's Twitter feed to glean the latest on the unfolding crisis. "The first description we got of the suspect was from their [S&T's] Twitter page," said KSDK assignment editor Jennifer Feldman during a report on that St. Louis TV station's noon newscast. Feldman added that local law enforcement didn't have time to provide information to the media, so reporters turned to Twitter as a primary source for updates.

By 10:26 a.m., more than 90 minutes after the incident began and several social media posts later, the S&T communications staff issued its first news release. It began:

> The campus of Missouri University of Science and Technology remains in lockdown mode after a man who fired shots near campus entered a Missouri S&T building around 8:45 a.m. CDT today.

A link to the release was immediately posted to the university's Twitter and Facebook sites and on the university's website. Follow-up releases throughout the morning were handled the same way.

By early afternoon, the suspect had been captured, and Chief Laughlin ordered the lockdown lifted. S&T communicators informed campus through the mass notification system (text, voice, and email alert) and told the rest of the world through social media.

In the aftermath of the event, grateful parents, students, and employees expressed their appreciation to the university and law enforcement for their handling of the situation. Again, social media played a prominent role. Here are a few comments from S&T's Facebook page:

> Our son was on campus—we're so glad that it is over.
>
> We are so glad the campus emergency system is working well. Good job on the alert. Our son is staying put & they're listening to the police scanner.
>
> The school did an amazing job with the lock-down & alert system. Job well done & we're relieved it is over.
>
> Glad my daughter was home, but I really appreciated the steady communication and conservative approach to keeping the campus safe. Hopefully this will be the last

News outlets, such as NBC affiliate KSDK in St. Louis, relied on Missouri S&T's Twitter feed as their source for information during the crisis.

time there is ever anything besides nerf guns on campus!!!!

Good that everyone is safe... The school did a good job to keep all its students notified.

So glad everyone is ok. Thank you for your swift actions and notifications to the students. Mom of current student

And thank you Missouri S&T for being so quick to take action and protect the students!

It is very reassuring as a parent of a student that goes to S&T to see the action that is taken to keep the students safe. My son is currently home for the summer but at least I know that if he had been at school his safety would have been high priority.

Beyond Social Media

Missouri S&T's successful use of social media during this crisis was part of an integrated strategy that incorporates as many communications platforms as possible to share messages during a crisis. It all begins with planning.

Creating a solid crisis communications plan involves buy-in from across the campus. An institution's chief communications officer should create a crisis communications team that includes representatives from many campus departments, as well as from student, faculty, and staff organizations. It's essential to include representatives from campus units that would have responsibility for carrying out specific duties during a crisis, such as communications, IT, police or security, environmental health and safety, and student affairs. In addition, because every crisis is different, and a crisis can affect a variety of constituents, it's important to include representation from alumni relations; development; admissions or enrollment management; human resources; and governing bodies, such as a faculty senate, student council, and staff council.

This team should not be the creators of a crisis communications document. That is best left to the campus communications staff. Rather, the role of the larger team is to review the plan, endorse it, and provide periodic reviews of the document, perhaps annually.

But having a plan is not enough. To ensure they are as prepared for a crisis as they can be, campus communicators should take these additional steps.

Conduct tabletop exercises. Working with the university's first responders, communications staff should spend time "working the plan." It's a good idea to routinely conduct tabletop exercises in which teams simulate a crisis situation to practice managing a crisis before it occurs. At S&T, the campus police and communications staff come together at least once a year to conduct a tabletop exercise. These are led by Chief Laughlin and focus not only on crisis communications but also on emergency response.

Test your systems. It's important for communicators to test their institution's mass-notification system regularly to ensure that the system works. At S&T, the communications department tests its system once a semester. The communications staff notifies campus in advance of the test—again, using social media, as well as internal email and other communications tools—to prepare students, faculty, and staff for what's planned.

Have a backup website. The institution should be prepared to switch out its regular website with a quick-loading, text-only version. This could be one similar to Missouri S&T's "In Case of Emergency" site (Alert.MST.edu), which functions as an informational resource during noncrisis times. During a crisis, traffic to your main website will increase dramatically—at S&T, traffic increased nearly tenfold from the previous day—so you want to make sure your site loads as quickly as possible. Besides, the usual imagery and messages of a higher ed website may be inappropriate during a crisis or emergency.

It's also a good idea to have a mirror site hosted off-campus to ensure that your website works during a natural disaster, power outage, or other emergency that could take your site offline.

Monitor social media conversations. It's a good reputation-management practice to always monitor online conversations about your institution. During times of crisis, it's even more important to do so. Set up Google Alerts (Alerts.Google.com) for your institution's name, nickname, and other keywords (such as the name of your sports team or mascot) to receive updates via email or RSS feed whenever these keywords are mentioned in news reports or on blogs. In addition, monitor Twitter, Facebook, YouTube, and other social media avenues for mentions of your institution during and after a crisis.

Debrief and learn afterward. Immediately following any crisis situation, an institution's communications team should meet with others on campus to conduct a debriefing of the event and how it was handled. At S&T, the communications staff convenes the crisis communications team for a one-hour debriefing and invites campus leadership to sit in as well. During these meetings, the communications staff reviews the timeline of a crisis; discusses response; and shares results, including data on website visits, social media interactions, and traditional media coverage. These debriefings can be learning experiences for the individuals responsible for managing crisis communications, as well as the other institutional leaders responsible for setting policy.

Prior to that broader debriefing with others on campus, the communications staff should hold a similar meeting of its own to discuss lessons learned from the experience. Following the May 2011 crisis at S&T, the communications staff tweaked its internal processes to improve communication to the campus and outside world, response to media inquiries, and monitoring of online chatter about a crisis as it unfolds. **SW**

Socializing the News at Tufts University

By Georgy Cohen | @radiofreegeorgy

Georgy Cohen is director of online content at Suffolk University in Boston. She is also co-founder of Meet Content, a content strategy blog and resource for the higher education community. After seven years at Tufts University, she left in November 2011 to run her own independent higher education consultancy, Crosstown Digital Communications.

In the past few years, the communications landscape in higher education has changed significantly. Social media have emerged as a major way not only to communicate with key audiences and share content widely, but also to discover information through listening and conversation. Content platforms such as YouTube enable people to publish and share video content more easily than ever before. Audience expectations around photo and other multimedia content have risen, too, thanks to the continued innovations of online publications such as those of CNN, *The New York Times*, and Salon, as well as the rise of blogs.

The big question that these changes pose, which many of us are still trying to answer, is this: How do we reconcile top-down communications with this new bottom-up flow?

In 2009, we at Tufts University set out to resolve our own issue—having two distinct top-level university news websites, Tufts E-News and Tufts Journal, operating out of the same division, a problem that was a consequence of legacy organizational structure. As you might imagine, having two publications churning out original, high-quality content on a regular basis was confusing for audiences and an inefficient use of editorial resources. The project took a high priority.

But given this new and shifting landscape, solving this problem wasn't just a matter of merging two sites together. We needed to create something entirely new.

Introducing Tufts Now

The new news site, named Tufts Now,[1] launched in February 2011. Running in a Drupal content management system, the project was a collaboration between the offices of Web Communications,

(1) Link: now.tufts.edu

Publications, Public Relations, and University Photography, in partnership with a vendor to aid with design and development. The co-leads on the project were Taylor McNeil, news editor in Publications, and myself, then the manager of web content and strategy in Web Communications.

From the beginning, the goal we identified for the project was to create a news and events hub for the university. Beyond the central-level news operations, we knew the university had several other news sources with valuable content worth featuring. We also saw great value in incorporating content from the university events calendar. [2]

But the biggest opportunity was with social media. We knew we wanted to make our stories hyper-shareable, so it was essential to provide the standard array of social media sharing icons (displaying total shares for each, of course) on both news stories and news releases. Most-emailed and most-read stories were collected in a small tabbed widget on the Tufts Now homepage. Once we relaunched our university events calendar later in 2011, event listings were also shareable via social media.

But icons and sharing functionality alone do not make a news site "social." In addition to our standard news coverage, we sought opportunities to highlight content informed by and created via social media and to find smart opportunities to bring the voice of the university community into our coverage.

The way I have come to think of this is acknowledging our community as the co-author of our brand story. Obviously, our priority as a web communications office was to create content that talks about what is important to the university and how it is relevant to our community—to tell our story. But as we found when we began digging into content created by members of the university community, they were saying many of the same things we were. Why not take advantage of that?

Somewhere in the midst of all of these efforts, the Web Communications department changed its mission statement: "to use the web and emerging technologies to engage our audiences with the Tufts story."

With that mission in mind, the tricky part was realizing that we are no longer the sole owners or tellers of that story, and part of our charge was now to use technology to bring the whole of that story under one roof.

Collecting Social Content

In the summer of 2009, well before the launch of Tufts Now, I started a university blog called Jumble.[3] The goal of this blog was

---

(2) Link: events.tufts.edu
(3) Link: sites.tufts.edu/jumble

The Tufts event calendar allows viewers to segment audiences and events quickly and easily.

simply to give a home to an unexpected bounty of user-generated content uncovered via my daily social media monitoring.

My listening dashboard—the humble workhorse that is Google Reader—plumbed YouTube, Twitter, Flickr, blogs, and beyond for Tufts-related content, with the unintended consequence of finding amazing material, created mainly by students and alumni but also by faculty and staff. By and large, this content highlighted cool and unique aspects of the Tufts experience. Some examples:

» former President Lawrence S. Bacow, his wife, and several faculty and staff performing a routine in the 2010 Tufts Dance Collective spring show[4]

» the Tufts Culinary Society's custom recipes for tasty entrées and desserts created from ingredients found in the dining hall[5]

» the Tufts Hillel bloggers' accounts from service trips to Rwanda, Morocco, and elsewhere[6]

» fun responses to hashtags such as #sillyreasonstoattendtufts and questions by prospective students about why Tufts is so awesome, collected via Storify[7]

» a Tufts alumni hip-hop duo briefly breaking the Top 10[8] on the iTunes pop chart, hot on the trail of Jay-Z and Coldplay

» promotional trailers for dozens of student clubs and events, as well as gags and skits recorded on video by roommates, classmates, lab mates, and even faculty—including one renowned researcher

(4) Available at mstnr.me/Tufts4

(5) Available at mstnr.me/Tufts5

(6) Available at mstnr.me/Tufts6

(7) Available at mstnr.me/Tufts7

(8) Available at mstnr.me/Tufts8

performing an original rap about stem cells.[9]

Much of this content aligned organically not only with the university's brand messages but also with the overall vibrancy of the Tufts experience—a vibrancy we would later seek to communicate via the new news site.

As Jumble grew, it quickly became a team effort rather than a solo endeavor. In essence, we were curating content before we knew what "content curation" was.

Besides Jumble, there was a growing ecosystem of blogs from other offices across the university—Undergraduate Admissions, Career Services, Digital Collections—and various student groups. We eventually created a dedicated space on the Tufts Now homepage to highlight this content, as well as a section within the regular Tufts Now newsletter.

In October 2010, Web Communications launched a Social Media Hub,[10] which integrated social media accounts from across the university into a central website, in order to facilitate an at-a-glance look at what the Tufts community was saying and doing. The news site project team discussed whether to fully integrate the Hub into Tufts Now, but eventually decided to feature links to specific pages on the Hub within the main center well of the Tufts Now homepage.

The main center well proved to be our best opportunity at the time to bring news and social content together within the same space. While the primary tab featured the four most recent news stories, the other wells highlighted a variety of social content:

Photos. Past photos from the "Spotlight" photo feature were archived here, as well as links to the Flickr tab on the Social Media Hub and the University Photography blog.

Videos. This space featured a rotating embed of particularly compelling pieces of video content created by members of the university community. The featured video could be a short student film, a trailer for an upcoming event, or a skit video created by a class. Also placed here were links to the YouTube tab of the Hub and links to YouTube favorites and playlists.

Facebook. This is where the default Facebook "like" box lived, as well as a link to the Facebook tab of our Social Media Hub.

Twitter. The main university Twitter feed (plus a follow button) occupied this space, as well as a link to the Twitter tab of our Hub, where we called out Twitter accounts of note and pulled tweets from lists of student groups and official school accounts.

While this tabbed widget was the best solution at the time for showcasing a blend of content, time and data have shown it may not

---

(9) Available at mstnr.me/Tufts9

(10) Link: socialmedia.tufts.edu

have been the best in the long run. This fall, based on analytics and usability findings, Tufts plans to make changes to the Tufts Now homepage that will feature more diverse content up front.

So, we had shareable stories and social content featured on the homepage. But what about the news content itself? How do social media bleed across what has historically been a hard and fast line?

How To Make News Social

We had created Jumble to give a home to a lot of the amazing content we uncovered by monitoring social media—cool videos, blog posts, images, and a host of powerful stories. While posting some of it on Jumble was great, some items called for more. In fact, Web Communications was already finding opportunities to use the information and content discovered through social media monitoring to inform E-News and website content.

Back in February 2009, Web Communications published a story in E-News that was based on a Flickr gallery discovered through regular social media monitoring. The photos captured a marriage proposal between two Tufts graduates that took place under Bowen Gate. (According to Tufts lore, couples who kiss under the gate will eventually marry.) The prospective bridegroom enlisted his friend to hide in the bushes and take photos of the proposal, aware that most proposals lack photographs recording the moment. It was a great opportunity to showcase a bit of university tradition come to life, with photos that no university photographer could have hoped to capture.[11]

E-News also featured an undergraduate who created webcomics about Tufts,[12] students and alumni who created popular iPhone apps,[13] a student theater troupe that performed two plays at the legendary Edinburgh Fringe Festival,[14] and a graduate student and undergraduate student who collaborated to create an agriculture course[15]—all of which came from leads sourced in whole or part via social media.

The advent of Tufts Now presented an opportunity to ramp up this approach even further. One of the first stories published on Tufts Now was a profile of a young alumnus who co-founded Warby Parker, a hip mail-order eyeglass company. Not only does the company sell stylish, affordable frames, but for every pair purchased, it donates a pair to someone in need around the world. Entrepreneurship, international influence, active citizenship—it hit all the right brand notes.

As Jumble grew, it quickly became a team effort rather than a solo endeavor. In essence, we were curating content before we knew what "content curation" was.

(11) Available at mstnr.me/Tufts11
(12) Available at mstnr.me/Tufts12
(13) Available at mstnr.me/Tufts13
(14) Available at mstnr.me/Tufts14
(15) Available at mstnr.me/Tufts15

Chase Gregory received local attention for her Tufts-based comics while in school there.

How did we learn about this alumnus? He had delivered a talk at TEDxUPenn about his work with Warby Parker, and the bio included in the YouTube video of his talk mentioned that he'd graduated from Tufts. After confirming the affiliation in the alumni database (as well as confirming that he was not already on the alumni relations radar), Web Communications immediately posted the video,[16] with some additional context, on Jumble.

But that was just phase one. Next, I interviewed him for a feature story, and a staff photographer went down to New York to take portraits of him at the Warby Parker offices. The story[17] led the Tufts Now homepage for a week.

Posting about this alumnus on both Jumble and Tufts Now was not a duplication of effort. We rode the short-form, real-time wave with Jumble and then dove deeper for background and story with the Tufts Now feature.

Another example: For four weeks before 2011 freshman move-in, we posed a series of questions on Facebook. For instance:

» What do you wish you knew as a freshman?
» What songs are on your back-to-school playlist?
» What are your favorite local hangouts?
» What are your Tufts secrets?

The questions resulted in awesome Facebook threads packed with tips, jokes, and friendly rivalries between dining halls. This alone would have been great, but we went further, taking a representative sample of the responses to each question and bundling them into a Tufts Now story,[18] linking to the Facebook

(16) Available at mstnr.me/Tufts16
(17) Available at mstnr.me/Tufts17
(18) Available at mstnr.me/Tufts18

The Tufts Beelzebubs performed with President Barack Obama and First Lady Michelle Obama in December 2010.

thread for the full discussion—and, in the case of the playlist question, linking to playlists created on Grooveshark and Spotify. Here, not only did social media discussion inform news content, but the news content drove readers back to the social media discussion to continue the dialogue.

Another highlight of the 2010–11 academic year was Tufts' oldest male *a cappella* group, the Beelzebubs (known as the Bubs), being featured as the voices of the Warblers on Fox's "Glee." Throughout the season, Jumble noted when the Warblers debuted a new song (such as their rendition of Katy Perry's "Teenage Dream") on the show, linking to video the day after.[19] This came in addition to posts about other highlights for the Bubs that year, including performing at the White House,[20] singing "Take Me Out to the Ballgame"[21] at a spring training baseball game, and presenting their annual spring concert.[22]

In May 2011, a feature story for Tufts Now about the Bubs' banner year[23] contextually linked back to all of the relevant Jumble posts from those milestones. While Jumble captured those milestones in real time, Tufts Now was the ideal platform to wrap up the year and reflect on the Bubs' accomplishments.

More examples:

> » Our annual feature about the Tufts team running the Boston Marathon included stellar race pictures by Tufts' photographers and a collection of tweets by supporters, spectators, and even the runners, sharing our @TuftsLive live coverage Twitter account.

(19) Available at mstnr.me/Tufts19
(20) Available at mstnr.me/Tufts20
(21) Available at mstnr.me/Tufts21
(22) Available at mstnr.me/Tufts22
(23) Available at mstnr.me/Tufts23

» Our profile of an English Ph.D. student who studied the connection between serial narratives (be they by Charles Dickens or Joss Whedon) and fan communities was prompted by a podcast interview that fell into our RSS bucket.

Making the Magic Happen

To bring stories like these together, the Tufts Now team hosted biweekly editorial meetings with communicators from across the university. In addition to story ideas drawn from communications staff, calendar milestones, emails, news stories, and similar sources, many of the ideas shared at the meeting came from social media. Sometimes, they turned out to be more relevant for a school- or department-based publication than for Tufts Now. But more often than not, they were viable. In these meetings, we also discussed opportunities to generate stories from social media conversations, as was done with the move-in and marathon coverage, or to use social media to amplify a more traditional written news story.

This approach tended to yield a multitude of stories focused on students and young alumni—two essential yet challenging audiences to reach. It also helped diversify the substance of Tufts Now news stories, as Storify collections and user-generated YouTube videos shared real estate with the in-depth written feature stories for which Tufts has been winning awards for years.

I like to call this a multidirectional news flow. The ideas and stories weren't just coming from the top down; they were being sourced from the ground up. We were weaving social media content and news content together in ways such that the line between the two was indistinguishable.

Does it weaken the brand of the university to present user-generated content alongside university-authored content? I don't think so. If nothing else, it strengthens the brand—finding stories that otherwise would have gone untold and letting the brand-compatible parts of the community's conversation and content represent it.

Hindsight Is 20/20

While this approach yielded many editorial successes and contributed to the overall success and growth of the Tufts Now platform, it was not a perfect process. It was a new approach to communicating the news of the university, and it was not fully integrated into the editorial process and workflow.

In an ideal world, there would have been more education, training, and subsequently understanding surrounding the new modes of information discovery and content development for all contributors and staff members. The domain of a few would have become the practice of all, and it would have been improved and enriched by the added perspective.

That said, this may not have been possible. After all, the whole publishing industry is going through a phase of figuring out how to publish in this hypersocial, *uber*-digital world. How do we wedge historically print-based publications, staff, and processes into a pixelated space, alongside the black box of user-generated content? For some, it's a crisis. For others, it's a reawakening.

The unavoidable truth about grappling with these changes is that it's going to be messy. It's going to come in fits and starts. It's going to take a lopsided shape, especially in the early stages. Things start happening and bubble up and suddenly become *de rigeur*, without ever having been the subject of a meeting, much less having been incorporated into a communications strategy. We might look around and suddenly realize, "Oh, hey, we're publishing like *this* now."

The Need for Iteration

So, what's the best way to handle this messy and unpredictable yet incredibly promising future?

We must be open to new ideas for conducting old business. We have to be forthcoming with our reactions to them but willing to give them a measurable chance. We need to be attentive to how they perform, have the courage to toss the bad and keep the good, and be honest about how new practices might change our organizations.

The bottom line is that communicators need to be willing to iterate, adjust, and evolve—yes, in order to survive, but more important, to both serve the needs and meet the expectations of our audiences.

Tufts Now broke new ground and altered the university's communications landscape in permanent ways, forming the right kind of foundation for further evolution. The changes in the publishing world aren't going to stop. All we can do is figure out how we are going to handle them as they come. **sw**

A Summer Ticket Giveaway Increases Virtual Traffic at Webster University

By Melissa Soberanes

Melissa Soberanes is a writer and editor at mStoner. She has more than 15 years of experience helping nonprofit organizations and education institutions increase awareness and tell their stories through effective communications, media relations, and web strategies.

Summer is typically a slow time for traffic to college websites, blogs, and social media. But in 2011, facing the usual summer online doldrums, Webster University wanted something that would shake up its audiences and create more traffic to its website. So the Global Marketing and Communications staff devised a campaign to boost traffic to Webster's online properties.

That campaign was an expanded Summer Ticket Giveaway that would increase both brand awareness and engagement with prospective and current students. And the way to make it happen was by using social media.

For several years, Webster University had partnered with the Verizon Wireless Amphitheater in St. Louis in an effort to market Webster to a younger audience during the summer months. The university distributed free tickets to concerts at the amphitheater to student groups and the University Center in hopes that people would pick them up. While the ticket giveaways generated some increased awareness among the younger demographic, it didn't produce the brand recognition or audience engagement that Webster wanted.

In 2011, Patrick Powers, director of digital marketing and communications, and Kathy DeBord, graphic designer, turned the Webster Summer Ticket Giveaway into a multi-channel social media campaign. Webster's Global Marketing and Communications team secured 200 tickets to seven different concerts through its partnership with Verizon. And Powers developed a comprehensive plan to distribute these tickets through various social platforms.

"Social media is where people are. The statistics are mind-boggling about the number of users on these platforms. If we don't

Powers attributed the campaign's success, in part, to meeting individuals in spaces that made sense to them—using the right tools to talk with the right people.

take advantage of these channels, then we're missing out on a great opportunity," said Powers.

His campaign used Foursquare, Twitter, and YouTube, with each channel providing a different way for participants to win concert tickets. The target audience was prospective and current students (generally between 16 and 35 years old), living within 90 miles of the St. Louis campus, who used social media. All efforts were coordinated through a central blog.[1]

The campaign's objective: "to build brand awareness and increase engagement while driving traffic to the Webster University website during the summer months, a time when activity on the site is usually low." And the results were impressive. Powers measured traffic coming from social channels to the blog server in June and July 2011, with 2,476 visits (up from 230 in 2010); 1,384 unique visitors (as opposed to 125 in 2010); and 4,628 page views (up from 747 in 2010).

Powers attributes success to the integrated approach taken to combine social media channels in a way that allowed them to work together. "It's no longer enough simply to be on social platforms broadcasting institutional messages to students. It takes an integrated approach to engage them where they are while still driving them to meet your institutional goals," said Powers. "We find that specific social media platforms resonate better with different audiences. Tailoring your messages for that audience on the right platform helps to build more meaningful engagements and stronger connections."

Finding the Right Combination

Powers knew that to develop a successful campaign, he had to select the right combination of social platforms. Facebook is the most popular channel at Webster, but Powers didn't want to find

(1) Link: blogs.webster.edu/summerticketgiveaway

ways to navigate around the Facebook terms of service. (Facebook prohibits giving away items in exchange for content.) So, he settled on using Foursquare, Twitter, and YouTube.

But he noticed that activity spread from one channel to another. "While we did not purposely use Facebook, we found that people who won tickets on Twitter would announce their winnings on Facebook. We saw how these channels worked together and how people used these channels differently, all in the effort to connect socially."

Each channel offered a distinct way for the target audience to win tickets.

Follow us on Twitter. Once a week, Webster sent a tweet encouraging people to re-tweet a message. The message included links to Webster's Twitter account (@WebsterU) and blog. For example: "2 tix courtesy of @WebsterU to the first 5 ppl to tweet: '@WebsterU is hooking me up with Styx/Foreigner tickets!'"—plus the blog link and the hashtag #STL.

Check in to Webster University on Foursquare. Powers built a check-in special on Foursquare that people could unlock when they checked in to specific locations on campus. For this campaign, the special was unlocked for people who checked in to Webster Hall, the Welcome Center (located within Webster Hall), and Webster University. Tickets were redeemed at the Welcome Center front desk. He created all the campaigns so that people who had already used Foursquare to check in to these locations could not unlock the special. The goal was to increase foot traffic among prospective students and those who had not previously engaged with the university on this platform.

Post a video to YouTube. Each week on the blog, people were encouraged to submit videos to YouTube that answered the question "Why Webster?" The first five people to email a link of their video won tickets. The winning videos were posted to the blog.

Impressive Results

Twitter proved to be the most effective channel for communicating about the Summer Ticket Giveaway, generating an impressive 822 mentions, 263 new followers, and 871 website clickthroughs (a 204% increase from 2010). Powers also pointed out the additional benefit from the word of mouth taking place on campus from faculty, staff, and students. Although this is hard to measure, it seemed as though everyone following @WebsterU was talking about the campaign, even though they may not have retweeted the messages.

Following are a few sample tweets:

@pattysenft: Thanks @websteru!!! You are awesome! Thanks for hooking me up!

> While we did not purposely use Facebook, we found that people who won tickets on Twitter would announce their winnings on Facebook. We saw how these channels worked together and how people used these channels differently, all in the effort to connect socially.

@StephPhillips13: Enjoying @billycurrington courtesy of @websteru! @kennychesney up next! Turned out to be a nice nite too!! twitpic.com/5xeuuh

@ryansechrest: Just picked up a shirt from the @websteru bookstore to wear to my free concert on Wed

While Twitter was very active, Foursquare was the fastest-growing social platform for Webster during the campaign. The Summer Ticket Giveaway campaign earned Webster 308 people who viewed the various check-in specials and 213 people who unlocked the specials.

YouTube was the least successful of the three channels, resulting in only one user-generated video.[2] Still, the four-minute video submitted by student Andrea Pepper provided an authentic testimonial that has been viewed more than 250 times on YouTube.

In addition to tracking web traffic and the number of tweets, videos, and check-ins, Powers set up a unique url for each set of tickets so he could determine the type of artists that generated the greatest buzz among the target audience. For example, tweets mentioning the band 311 drew twice as many people (153) to the website as did Motley Crue and Poison (75).

"Tracking and tagging messages around the bands we had tickets for will help us select the most attractive concert partnerships in the future. Knowing which bands are the most popular helps us make better decisions and find better points of connection with our audiences," said Powers.

Putting a Plan in Place

Powers is absolutely certain that developing a plan with a goal and clear objectives before the launch was key to the success of the campaign. "To really be successful in social media takes thought, planning, and preparation," he said. "From day one, we set a clear goal and clear objectives. We could refer to the plan and stay focused on accomplishing the goals."

Global Marketing and Communications set the goal of the Summer Ticket Giveaway to align specifically with goal five of the Webster University strategic plan: "Enhance our reputation." In order to meet this goal, the planners set three clear objectives for the campaign:

» Build brand awareness using social media.
» Increase engagement among the university community.
» Drive traffic to the Webster University website.

---

(2) Available at mstnr.me/Webster3

The Power of a Check-in

One if the fastest growing platforms last year on the Webster University campus was Foursquare. In an effort to capitalize on this growth, we built a check-in special that people could unlock when they checked-in to specific locations.

The Foursquare check-in targeted prospective students and aimed to get them on campus. (top)

Although the contest lived on Foursquare, Twitter, and YouTube, Powers found that winners took to Facebook to inform family and friends when they won tickets. (bottom)

Setting goals and objectives that aligned with the university's strategic plan also provided a means to measure the progress of the campaign. Powers explained that at the end of the campaign the staff could go back, platform by platform, to measure the progress toward the objectives.

Lessons Learned

The 2011 Summer Ticket Giveaway was a huge success for the Global Marketing and Communications staff members. They developed an integrated social media campaign that reached and engaged a broader audience then ever before, drove traffic to the Webster website at one of the slowest times of the year, and built brand awareness that enhanced Webster's reputation. They also learned some valuable lessons along the way that will inform and guide future campaigns.

One of the most unexpected lessons was about demographics. Powers explained that with Webster's more traditional campus, he expected the audience would comprise mainly traditional-age undergraduates. "The demographics ended up being skewed from what we thought and weren't limited to just 18- to 25-year-olds. We had participants who were 17 and 40 years old tweeting that they won tickets and checking in," said Powers. "It opened our eyes to how these platforms are evolving. Social media is not just for young people anymore." This twist showed just how far-reaching an effective social media campaign can be.

Powers said his team also gained valuable insight into how people use social media and just how far they are willing to go on an institution's behalf: "People were willing to tweet on our behalf, but less willing to create a video. People will only go so far; you can't force their behavior."

Powers also said that moving forward, he will get more people involved in managing the campaign. He planned, executed, and measured the 2011 campaign by himself, with support from DeBord, who managed the tickets.

"It's challenging to do this kind of campaign as a one-man shop," he said. "Just because you're running a social media campaign doesn't mean there isn't a lot to do on the back end. It's not just tweeting. We had to secure tickets, give them out, and keep track of everything, including results."

But he remains convinced that the most vital component of the campaign's success was the planning. "At the end of the campaign, we could say that we were successful because we met all of our objectives, and we had the data to show our success," Powers explained. "Without goals and objectives, you have nothing to measure against. You can't go back in time and create a plan. You have to have the plan to begin with."   **sw**

Growing Brand Reach Through a Real-World/Digital-World Game: Trinity International University

By Joel G Goodman | @joelgoodman

Joel G Goodman is a jack-of-all-trades marketer, designer, and front-end developer. He spent six years in higher education web marketing and holds a master of arts degree in Media Studies from The New School for Public Engagement.

In Fall 2011, the newly created Marketing and Creative Services office at Trinity International University (TIU) needed a winning campaign that would bolster brand visibility while improving yield for the coming academic year. Completely reorganized in structure, staffing, and mission, we felt compelled to prove our merit to university administration. But at the core, we simply wanted to do something cool.

Rooted in Research

The concept for a massive game grew organically out of conversations in our studio. Fueled by the latest studies in admissions and recruitment, we knew that a strategy that facilitated strong engagement with the university could improve yield, increase campus morale, and unify the community—both on campus and during a new student's transition into college.

"We knew that we had ground to gain in trying to influence more of our accepted students to make deposits and actually enroll," said Rachel Yantis, director of marketing for the university. "The campus community at TIU is such that playing on the relationships and connections on campus seemed like lower-hanging fruit than creating new inquiries at the top of the funnel."

Through on-campus interviews and discussions, and external research,[1] we could see that the ability of new students to make connections to the TIU community before they stepped on campus was important to keeping them at our institution. It was apparent what outcomes new students expected; the work came in discovering ways a small team could produce those outcomes effectively, and then in making the sale to university decision-makers.

---

(1) Available at mstnr.me/TrinityIU1

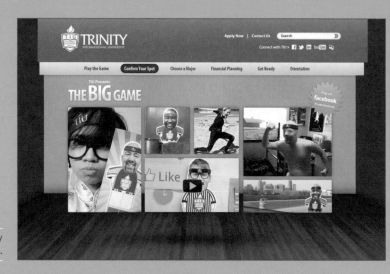

The campaign sought to visually appeal to high school students.

Crucially, Yantis fed the idea for the new campaign through the admissions staff first, looking for their feedback. "Their experience working with prospective students, specifically in the context of TIU, was very helpful in helping me avoid missteps as I made further presentations," she said. "Part of the success of our pitch was that our idea showed something radically different from past campaigns, which affirmed our direction. We also believed that our current students not only would be interested in the idea but would help execute The Big Game."

Having data on hand to back up our plan made all the difference. Without reasoned data to validate what seemed to be a radical approach to boosting enrollment compared with the tried-and-true methods, our excitement would have come across as conjecture. And when it comes to doing cool and radical new things, conjecture is the same thing as risk to those who need convincing.

For us, defining the results we wanted to see—better yield, increased campus morale, and stronger community unification— piqued the interest of the university's decision-makers, leaving them open to trying something new.

The Student Viewpoint

Armed with energy and backing, our team quickly fleshed out our idea. We started with the concept from the classic "Flat Stanley" game, which involves creating a paper cutout of a person and then asking participants to snap photos of themselves with that cutout at various exotic locales. We agreed that the cutouts should include images of popular faculty and staff members—representatives of the community whose presence would contribute to continuity as accepted students became enrolled students—and the university's president.

Visually, the concept would need to be accessible to high school seniors without seeming too immature. At this point our staff recognized a possible challenge. We were well aware that we might not be the most high school–savvy bunch. We thought the game was a cool idea, but we recognized the age gap between our staff and the average high school senior. The youngest member of our team was 23 years old, and while she was closer than most of us to our target demographic, there was still a bit of a disconnect.

We needed a reality check on our own ideas, and the best way to get that was to consult with current students. Yantis created an internship position and brought on Matt Allen, a senior studying marketing and graphic design. Several student worker positions were also created, and freshman graphic design major Alex Johnson joined us in crafting the game. "Feeding off the energy of our students was inspiring and life-giving," said Yantis. "Students like being together and are willing to work hard to execute cool ideas."

These two students not only validated the idea of the game, but also contributed to creating a more robust and exciting version that would be rolled out to newly accepted students and the current student community. "We felt confident that The Big Game would be a success because once we laid the groundwork, the students took the driver's seat and made it happen," said Linzy Westman, creative media producer.

As the strategy took shape, Wayne Kijanowski, the university's design director, crafted a visual style that was quirky and competitive. For each representative whose image was to be used in the game, a photo of the head was enlarged, given a TIU-branded sweatband, and placed on a color-coded, cartoon-like football uniformed body.

As web marketing manager for the university, I played off the idea of a diorama in which these cutout characters lived. Then I redesigned the section of the university's website that focused on accepted undergraduate students, knowing that the online component of this project would provide exciting website content and create an opportunity to engage students beyond the fun factor of the game.

The aim of the game was to create a welcoming atmosphere and energy that TIU was lacking. The university's official Facebook community was dead, only a few undergraduate students used Twitter, and general community existed on campus and almost nowhere else. This game needed to jump-start community involvement online, especially as Facebook would be the primary place accepted students would gather before showing up to new student orientation.

The Big Game

Out of multiple planning meetings with our student staff, The Big Game was given life. The game went something like this:

Visually, the concept would need to be accessible to high school seniors without seeming too immature.

Chosen faculty and staff members would become the captains of color-coded teams. Their likenesses would be turned into "Flat Captains" and handed out to our students. Each Flat Captain would be assisted by hand-picked students who were already heavily involved in shaping the campus community. These included resident assistants, student ambassadors from the admissions office, and students in the Emerging Leaders program. Current undergraduate students would be distributed among those teams. Then, each newly accepted student would receive a mailing with a Flat Captain cutout and a team assignment.

We created a Facebook group for each team and launched a new Facebook page for the undergraduate college. We built a simple Facebook app, matching the visual style of the accepted student website, to usher participants onto their teams. The goal was simple: to have enough content flowing through the Facebook groups and page to present a feeling of activity.

To accomplish this goal, we created challenges and put them to the campus community. These primarily involved asking people to take their Flat Captain on different missions and posting photos or videos to their team groups. Each group would vote to choose the best entry, and the one that got the most team "likes" was launched to the weekly finals. The Gamemaster (Matt Allen) would repost the favorite from each group to the main undergraduate Facebook page. These would again be voted on, this time by anyone who visited the page. The one that got the most likes won, and that team received points. As points were tallied, prizes would be handed out, with a grand prize outing during the fall semester up for grabs.

Most of the challenges were developed in advance, leaving wildcard challenges throughout The Big Game up to the discretion of the Gamemaster (and the marketing team). The campus community joined in February 2012, three weeks before the general acceptance mailing went out, and by the time newly accepted students received their team assignments, there were a lot of fun posts and hundreds of student-produced images and videos lighting up the Facebook groups and page.

Videos relaying personal greetings from each team captain were produced several weeks before launch with nothing more than an iPhone and some video editing software. These videos welcomed students to their teams and invited newly accepted students to join the TIU community.

For newly accepted students—and their parents—who came to the TIU website first, we provided easy ways to get connected to the action on Facebook without distracting from the "get stuff done" mentality of the accepted student site. Pulling in video and photos from the Facebook groups, we were able to show visitors what was going on rather than simply pleading for them to come and play.

We built a simple Facebook app, matching the visual style of the accepted student website, to usher participants onto their teams. The goal was simple: to have enough content flowing through the Facebook groups and page to present a feeling of activity.

The Big Game concept built on a popular game, known as "Flat Stanley."

President
Craig Williford
Blue Team Captain

Campus Visibility

Launching The Big Game to our campus community first proved to be the most important tactical decision in the whole campaign. Visibility is key to growing this kind of community; it gives your campus something to rally around.

We had a student body that was hungry for something fun like this. They loved the rivalry—especially with their professors and student affairs staff serving as the talking heads of the game. One happy side effect of trying to create a welcoming experience for incoming students was that we created a stronger campus community that was mobilized to talk about and share campus happenings online and in person.

To launch The Big Game, we organized a rally on campus with help from our interns. As a Christian institution, we used one of the chapel gatherings during the week to pass out team assignments and university-branded sweatbands and to kick the whole thing off with a promotional video. The kickoff video[2] was written, staged, and designed by our student staff with some conceptual input provided by Marketing and Creative Services staff. The students recorded the footage on an iPhone, and Matt and Alex edited it themselves, including embedded music, sound effects, and voiceovers.

(2) Available at mstnr.me/TrinityIU2

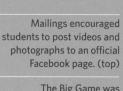

Mailings encouraged students to post videos and photographs to an official Facebook page. (top)

The Big Game was positively received by both incoming and prospective students. (bottom)

The reaction was even more positive than we'd hoped. "I was shocked when students seemed excited to join a team and get a TIU sweatband, which honestly seemed preposterous when we ordered them," said Yantis. "Later, students were wearing their sweatbands with their paper captain sticking out of them, and I remember thinking that The Big Game would actually work."

Once the game had launched on campus, our student workers put up posters and began hosting weekly socials—on their own. "I think one of my biggest surprises was when our marketing intern, Matt Allen, began playing music on Fridays outside the dining hall. I think that was a big indication that this wasn't just something the marketing team had created, but something that had become part of the actual culture," said Yantis.

Our office had giant foam cutouts of the captains made and let them loose to the students. In expected fashion, the large Flat Captains would show up in random places around campus, captain-stealing pranks ensued, and hilarious photos and videos began appearing in the Facebook groups. "Students wore their team colors to different events," said Westman. "We even saw other departments on campus utilizing the teams for their own activities."

The momentum for the game continued to grow because of the dedication of the students running it. Matt, the Gamemaster, and Alex, who was quickly deputized, administered the Facebook groups as part of their assigned work. They surveyed all of the content coming in, assigned points, prompted participants on wildcard challenges, and introduced twists throughout the weeks. They also reported the team standings both on Facebook and on campus each week.

Meanwhile, the student leaders we had recruited encouraged discussion in the groups, rallied the teams, and worked with the team captains to make sure their visibility remained high in the groups and on the pages. These students also played a vital role in welcoming the accepted students who began joining teams. Yantis met with the student leaders during the planning period to give them training and perspective. The simple act of spending an hour with the students over Jimmy John's sandwiches instilled an ownership and excitement in them that fueled active participation in the game.

A Different Sort of Success

Our team set goals at the beginning. We knew we wanted the game to improve yield, campus morale, and community unification. But we originally conceived of the game having a huge impact on enrollment and that, come fall semester, we would be welcoming a larger group of new students into the community.

We were expecting strongest results with admitted students, but the results of our game went in a completely different direction. We saw the largest increase in social media participation from current students. There was also a higher level of campus engagement in general. With unexpected results like this, it would have been easy to consider our goals unmet.

Yet, there was a rather large upside in the experience. Through launching the game so intensely within our campus community first, we saw increases in community unification and morale. The surprise to us was the effect the game had on current student retention efforts. Internal datasets from exit interviews and ongoing student surveying indicated The Big Game made it easier for those who had always felt out of place to join a team and participate. Community and campus unity increased through the game, and this decreased the risk of student attrition.

Keeping a flexible mind toward the results allowed our office to still sell our win, even if it was one we weren't expecting. Great traction in student retention is certainly not a bad thing, but this campaign produced a number of other benefits to TIU's brand reach and volume:

» By doing the groundwork of giving our students a platform within Facebook to talk, we encouraged our community members to voice their opinions about TIU. And by giving them a great experience with the game, we saw an increase of engagement with our brand. This culminated in more likes to TIU-posted content, more sharing of university-sponsored activities and content, and cross-media engagement on networks like Instagram and Twitter.

» Our students continued to invest in the life of the university. "One of the most rewarding moments for me was when the incoming Student Government Association asked to meet with me to discuss their ideas for school spirit. I hadn't had a direct relationship with them, and I attribute their desire to talk with me to the energy The Big Game created," said Yantis. The energy the students put into developing their own community on campus continues to manifest itself in online content.

» Most importantly, conversations continue to happen across media. To our team, that's the biggest win. Students, parents, alumni, and friends continue to talk about TIU face-to-face, in blog posts, across social networks, and through other media like text messages and phone calls. These conversations are what fuel a better institutional reputation.

All in the Game

The Big Game proved a valuable and challenging project for the Marketing and Creative Services team at TIU. But by playing the game right—creating a strategy not only for executing the campaign, but also for gaining campus buy-in—we generated more content than we knew what to do with, gave our students something to latch onto and enjoy, better unified our campus community, and made connections beyond our institutional walls.

Rachel Yantis noted the effects of The Big Game at new student orientation: "We had a table for The Big Game to connect with incoming students. Each of these students would have received a mailing and team assignment, since the game was designed for them. But I was interested to see how many students—and parents—recognized the game. The majority of students who stopped were familiar with The Big Game. Many were able to say 'I am on the purple team' or 'I am on Dr. Washington's team,' which was very promising. Interestingly, in the cases where the student wasn't all that familiar with The Big Game, the parents would say that they remembered the mailings."

Yantis recognizes that these observations aren't scientific proof that The Big Game increased the number of students who enrolled at TIU. But, she adds, "I do think it was very encouraging that the majority of students and parents were familiar with the game and, I believe, experienced a bit of 'feeling like an insider'— which is a great start for feeling part of the community!" **sw**

Promoting Faculty Experts: The University of Nottingham and the Election of 2010

By Michael Stoner, mStoner | @mstonerblog

Michael Stoner is the president and a co-founder of mStoner, Inc. In more than 30 years as a communicator and consultant, he has provided strategic advice on institution-wide web strategies, led countless web development projects in higher education, and earned an international reputation as an authority on integrating marketing, communications, and technology.

When citizens across the United Kingdom went to the polls on May 6, 2010, to elect a prime minister and members of Parliament, they were participating in a historic election, no matter its outcome.

The campaign was a hard-fought contest between three contenders. Gordon Brown, the sitting prime minister, was facing his first election as prime minister; his victory would mean an unprecedented fourth term in office for the Labour Party. If David Cameron were elected, he'd head the first Conservative Party government in 13 years. And if Nick Clegg won, his Liberal Democrats would assume a much higher profile in a coalition government.

There was no clear favorite among these three candidates, and the campaign featured an unprecedented three live, prime-time TV debates. Significant issues faced the country, including a lagging economy.

In this closely watched contest, the University of Nottingham's communications and marketing team recognized an opportunity to strengthen the profile of its School of Politics and International Relations. The school, one of the largest in the United Kingdom, was already ranked in the country's top 10. University leaders believed they could use the run-up to the election to position the school's faculty members as definitive sources of election information to the media, academic colleagues, and the public at large, thereby raising the profile of the university as a whole.

And so communications and marketing staff members began their planning. They might have relied primarily on old-fashioned PR techniques. But, by combining standard PR methods with a blog, YouTube, email, and Twitter, they created a much more effective campaign, one that far exceeded the goals they set.

"From the outset," observed Emma Leech, the University of Nottingham's director of communications, "we were able to link traditional media relations and press releases with Twitter lists to target journalists better, working out who our priorities were and anticipating their needs. This enabled us to introduce new, fresh academic perspectives to the world of political commentary. The work has also had great legacy value, strengthening academics' relationships with influential journalists for the long haul."

The Election 2010 campaign marked the first significant effort to develop communications linked to the university's strategic plan, which was released as the runup national election campaign was beginning. The Election 2010 campaign plan focused on integration, alignment, and innovation—guiding principles in Nottingham's strategic plan.

Campaign Strategy and Goal Setting

Accordingly, the communications and marketing team developed campaign objectives that focused on bolstering the university's and department's reputation and impact, student recruitment, and capacity building. The objectives included:

» involving at least four new politics academics in media activity by the end of the campaign and developing their media expertise
» positioning Nottingham academics as key political commentators
» generating at least 20 pieces of national and international coverage, with an estimated advertising value of £1 million (a return on investment of 66,567 percent)
» expanding the media networks for the school and wider university and, in the process, establishing links with five major new media outlets
» supporting student recruitment and increasing applications by at least 5 percent
» trying out (and succeeding with) a new PR approach that incorporated online channels and that could demonstrate impact for the U.K. Research Assessment Framework, a new tool that will be used to assess the quality of research in U.K. universities beginning in 2014.

> **The Election 2010 campaign marked the first significant effort to develop communications linked to the university's strategic plan, which was released as the runup national election campaign was beginning.**

Organizing a campaign like this wasn't a straightforward undertaking, though. One of the risks was that everyone was new to some of the technologies and concepts behind social media. "This was a new approach both for the communications team and our academics," Leech emphasized. "In general, the academic community had been slow to adopt social media, and some expressed concerns about it. Some were concerned about the practicalities of

The hub for the Election 2010 Campaign consisted of a blog, podcasts, and an experts list featuring six Nottingham faculty members.

creating dialogue and interaction and policing feedback. We had to persuade them to trust the relevance of their research."

Quick responses and rapid turnaround of new blog posts were crucial; academics needed to maintain a frequent flow of content and be opportunistic 24/7 to take advantage of the internet news cycle. They also needed to learn to write in a succinct and direct way.

The communications and marketing team knew that engaging champions among the faculty was an essential step in making the campaign work. Leech and Andrew Burden, digital communications manager and the lead staff member on the campaign, reached out to Philip Cowley and Steven Fielding, two key professors in the school. Cowley, professor of parliamentary government, blogs about factors that influence parliamentary votes at Revolts.Co.UK. Fielding, professor of political history and director of the Centre for British Politics, has served as an expert source for many in the media. He is a specialist on the British Labour Party and on popular perceptions of politics. Once they agreed to work on the Election 2010 campaign, they helped to overcome some of the concerns and resistance among the faculty, including a perception that some of the research was too "niche" for this campaign.

However, there were still concerns. "Some thought that they wouldn't be able to write in an accessible, but still academically sound, way," said Burden. Even Fielding admitted to some skepticism: "I was not sure we would be able to attract much interest, that we could write in an attractive way and be able to adapt our academic expertise to make it sufficiently interesting to journalists and others." But both he and other faculty members soon found that it was easier than they first thought.

Gaining initial faculty enthusiasm and support for the campaign

The website for the School of Politics and International Relations featured updates and content from the Election 2010 blog during the campaign. (left)

Faculty member Steven Fielding also shared his views about topics in the election on *The Guardian* newspaper's website. (right)

was only part of the challenge. Burden and his colleagues wanted to identify as many faculty members as possible who could participate in the effort, which meant that they had to research academics and their specialties and persuade them to sign on as bloggers and media sources. And once they signed on, some of these promising academics needed media training so they could respond appropriately to media queries.

Of course, the communications and marketing team members had to identify members of the media whom they would target in their outreach. The communications team sought to engage intelligent, informed traditional media outlets in major print and broadcast media in the United Kingdom and abroad in addition to important bloggers and online media with an interest in U.K. politics. To develop a master media list, the communications team members worked with faculty members to identify sources with whom they already had connections. They also researched media using media databases, online Twitter journalist lists, and online forums and associations with a focus on politics.

Another important audience was prospective doctoral students and researchers and those who influenced them. To increase the visibility of the politics department among this audience, Nottingham used a different strategy: publicizing the Election 2010 blog. The team ensured that the blog and initiative were on the home and school pages on Nottingham's website and that School of Politics staff and recruiters included the blog in their presentation talking points. The team also displayed clippings from prominent articles in public areas of the school so visitors—and current students and staff—were kept up to date on developments.

In addition, marketing staff members kept their school and

college contacts informed about the campaign and launched a series of YouTube videos, which they dubbed "Politics in 60 Seconds,"[1] that explained key political concepts in one minute.

The planning, research, and faculty outreach were the hard parts. "Implementation was relatively easy, after we identified our key audiences and those journalists whose attention we were trying to attract," Burden said.

The Campaign Under Way

Having laid the groundwork, Burden, the academics, and others in communications and marketing were ready for Election 2010 to begin.

The centerpiece of the campaign was a blog, Election 2010, built on Google's Blogger platform and sporting a simple, clean, straightforward design: posts in the left-hand column, an index of topics on the right.

Nottingham's blogging effort officially began on Feb. 4, 2010, with a short post by Fielding, titled "Why AV, why now," a comment on an alternative voting scheme proposed by sitting Prime Minister Gordon Brown, an idea that Brown had once opposed.

Once the blog launched, marketing team members pushed out notifications about it to the journalists they'd identified, promising that the blog would present "perspectives on the election you won't find anywhere else, by political experts, based in the School of Politics and International Relations at The University of Nottingham."

As faculty began posting in response to developments in the political campaign, Nottingham staff alerted reporters, positioning the faculty blog writers as experts with whom the reporters could follow up directly. As the election heated up, and faculty began posting more frequently in response to developments in the news, the communications staff reached out to relevant media using press releases, email, and especially Twitter, backed up by social bookmarking.

"We knew journalists would be looking for stories throughout the election," Burden observed, "but we wanted to give them something different, providing stories based on research already undertaken or ongoing." The plan worked. "I was really surprised at how quickly it caught on."

Of course, a political campaign occurs over the course of several months and, in the internet age, in a 24/7 time frame. Being responsive to current news is essential. During the months leading up to the election, Burden and the faculty members worked together, often at odd hours, to respond to media queries and post to the blog and to Twitter. Burden's iPhone was his constant companion as he and Cowley traded messages, edited posts and tweets, and collaborated on outreach to Nottingham faculty and to the media.

We wanted to give them something different, providing stories based on research already undertaken or ongoing.

_____

(1) Available at mstnr.me/Nottingham1a

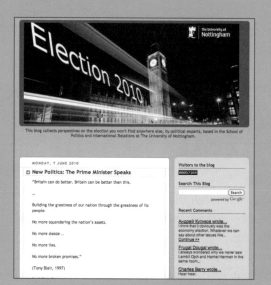

This blog collects perspectives on the election you won't find anywhere else, by political experts, based in the School of Politics and International Relations at The University of Nottingham.

The Election blog did the heavy lifting for the campaign, allowing the academic experts to share their views in response to breaking news about the election.

Following up with the media—by email or even by phone—after something was posted on the blog turned out to be incredibly valuable. Journalists, both national and international, picked up leads and began paying attention to what faculty members were posting on the blog. "It demonstrated to us that if you get the right placement for a story early on, it acts as a catalyst for further international coverage," said Leech. "We didn't realize we might dominate election coverage to the extent we did. This campaign definitely exceeded expectations."

The faculty champions proved their value again during the heat of the campaign. "Our greatest challenge was to maintain a steady, high-quality flow of topical blog contributions from the School of Politics and International Relations faculty," Burden said. Both Cowley and Fielding targeted willing colleagues and edited their blog posts. "We did have to edit some a bit, to begin with," Cowley remarked, "but the costs of editing soon diminish as people get used to it. And most don't object to being edited."

And success bred success, Burden noted. "As media placements increased—showing that reporters were paying attention to what was posted—so did faculty enthusiasm, which in turn generated more insightful and compelling blog activity."

By mid-April, the blog was clocking about 1,000 visitors a day. During the campaign, there were 104 blog posts by academics, delivering 50,362 visits and 90,000-plus page views, with 81 percent of traffic from the United Kingdom, 5 percent from the United States, and the remainder from the Philippines, Canada, Australia, and Ireland.

Twitter was a particularly powerful tool, Burden reported. One tweet alone resulted in 825 click-throughs to the blog. In total, 123 tweets generated 7,779 click-throughs.

With a national election looming, the media and PR team at the University of Melbourne decided to see if Nottingham's initiative could take root successfully in Australian soil, creating the university's own 2010 Federal Election blog.

Melbourne adapted the Nottingham model in some interesting ways. For one, Melbourne's campaign involved many people from across campus—in fact, one of its main goals was to create widespread engagement. "We used academics from across the university—not just from politics—as expert commentators and bloggers. And we used the site as a vehicle to get to traditional media, as well as a vehicle

to engage with the general public," said Diane Squires, media and PR director in University Marketing and Communications. "We also encouraged our students to engage and asked academics to identify students from within their courses who might blog for us. As a result, we had a number of students who regularly blogged."

Like their colleagues at Nottingham, the Melbourne staff promoted their site through Twitter. They also ran newspaper advertisements, sent news alerts about the site to the media, and ran a banner on the university website's home page to promote the blog. And on election night, they

had a student tweeting regular updates from the @UniMelb Twitter account.

Though she acknowledged that Melbourne was late in getting the campaign launched, Squires said that it was still successful. "We didn't set specific target numbers, but looking back, I would have liked to have seen more people visit the site. We had 6,553 visitors throughout the four-week campaign. While most of those visitors came from Australia, we also had visitors from the United States, the United Kingdom, Indonesia, Singapore, Hong Kong, and New Zealand. The international visitors were a bonus for us."

Assessing the Outcomes

Those numbers are interesting and impressive, but Nottingham's Election 2010 campaign had truly significant results, some of them unanticipated.

» Eight academics were involved in the Election 2010 campaign—twice as many as Burden and his colleagues had hoped for initially.

» Nottingham achieved 466 items of coverage, and more than 75 percent of them were in significant national or international media such as The London Times, The Wall Street Journal, and others (compared with the original target of 20). Eighty-four percent of the coverage about the live television debates featured University of Nottingham spokespeople. And, best of all, the majority of mentions were in the main body of an article, primarily in the top half.

» Burden noted that every item of national media coverage in the United Kingdom on Election Day featured a University of Nottingham spokesperson. Furthermore, the campaign reached well beyond U.K. borders. Leech remarked, "One of the really significant results for us was the chance to break into American news: University of Nottingham politics academics were cited several times on U.S. news channels such as Bloomberg, *The Wall Street Journal*, and *The New York Times*. And the effects are lasting: We continue to gain better press coverage in the United States, and it's easier to place other stories."

» The campaign's effect on recruiting for the School of Politics and International Relations was remarkable. Burden said that applications rose 15 percent after the campaign. "It's difficult to attribute this 100 percent to the Election 2010 campaign, but the spike in applications for the school was far in excess of the national average," he said. "And, aside from the blog and the YouTube series 'Politics in 60 Seconds,' the school wasn't doing anything different." Leech also believes the increase in applications can be attributed to the campaign. "From verbal feedback and written mentions of the campaign during visit days at the university in the summer and fall of 2010, when prospective students came to visit the university, there was a clear sense that it has contributed to the increase in student numbers in 2011. Teachers, career advisers, and opinion leaders became aware of the school because of the campaign and recommended it to students as they sought information on politics courses."

There are other substantial, lingering effects as well. The development and implementation of this successful campaign provided valuable experience for Burden and his colleagues. Their success was honored by a number of different organizations, including the Council for Advancement and Support of Education, which awarded this campaign a Gold Circle of Excellence Award for Best Use of Social Media in 2011.

Those honors boosted the confidence of the communications and marketing staff members and, moreover, increased their credibility internally. Paul Heywood, head of the School of Politics, noted the positive internal buzz about the Election 2010 campaign in an email to Leech: "The blog was a terrific success. It was very pleasing to see it generate such interest in terms of numbers of hits, but it was even nicer to hear positive comments from people across the university: lots of colleagues from academic and central." Finally, the academic focus of the initiative enhanced the communications and marketing team's credibility with their academic colleagues.

The politics faculty who participated in the Election 2010 campaign also learned something. "I think it has helped me become a better writer and communicator," Fielding remarked. "I did more than just the blog during the election but, partly because of the blog, I appeared on TV a few times. I am more aware of the needs of an audience now—be they reader or student."

At Nottingham, one more enduring effect of the 2010 Election campaign was the launch of NottsPolitics.org,[2] a blog for the School of Politics and International Affairs. "Certainly the success of the election blog gave us the confidence to do the other, more general blog," Cowley said.

And a further indication of its impact was seen on the other side of the world: The University of Melbourne replicated the format and concept to do its own campaign for Australia's federal election in August 2010. **sw**

_____

(2) Link: nottspolitics.org

Appendix: The Emergence of the Social Web

To understand how social media became significant to those who wanted to engage with their constituencies in a powerful and compelling way online, it helps to know about the communications landscape of the 1990s and the first decade of this century—the context in which social media emerged and became influential.

The beginning of the 21st century saw a confluence of conditions in what came to be widely called "Web 2.0" after O'Reilly Media and MediaLive hosted the first Web 2.0 conference in 2004. Web 2.0 set the stage for an era of "social computing," which differed greatly from the previous era of computing in several significant ways.

Using the internet became simple and increasingly necessary because you could do more—and more important—things there. By 2005, there were substantial changes in how people used the internet. The internet had always been used by people to communicate with each other, but the web provided a new way to share information, in an environment that permitted video and images of all kinds to supplement or supplant plain text. The world discovered the web, which largely had been a network that enabled researchers to share information and data, in 1994—though science fiction readers recognize it in novels like William Gibson's *Neuromancer*, published in 1984, and Neal Stephenson's *Snow Crash*, published in 1992. The big breakthrough was the creation of Netscape, the first widely available web browser, released publicly in December 1994.

The late 1990s saw the mass adoption and commercialization of the web. By 2005, millions of people all over the world used it to search for information, to shop, and to conduct their business. Because online tools had become easy to use and offered great utility, many people began to feel at home online. It wasn't like the early 1990s, when you had to master the arcana of modems and logins to use the internet: By 2000, surfing was fairly simple. And you could accomplish a great deal online: researching products and services and then purchasing them, managing your money, scheduling activities, playing games, gathering news.

Creating content to share online became simpler and more democratic. The first widely used drawing and painting programs—MacDraw and MacPaint—were released in the 1980s and allowed Mac users to create something besides text documents and spreadsheets. By 2005, individuals were empowered as creators in ways never before possible. Many people had computers and easy-to-use software such as drawing tools, word processing software, and video-editing tools, or at least could gain access to them. And hardware such as digital cameras and video cameras were increasingly common and cheap. People began using these tools and developing myriad forms of personal expression.

Sharing became easy and common. They also began sharing the content they were creating. By 2000, there were simple ways of creating a website and using it to share your thoughts or other creations: Usually, the most recent entry appeared at the top, followed by other "posts" in reverse chronological order. Websites like this had existed for years, but they were increasingly called "blogs" (from "weblogs") and became more much common. Other platforms, which enabled people to share photos and images, became increasingly common as well. For example, Flickr was released in 2004 and YouTube in 2005.

And various technologies enabled further sharing. RSS, for example, enabled bloggers to import content from other blogs or share their own content easily. Social bookmarking sites encouraged people to bookmark their favorite websites, articles, and other resources—and share them with their friends.

Participation grew to be not only valued, but encouraged. As blogs became more common, their creators enabled commenting systems that allowed visitors to share their thoughts. This kind of audience participation was encouraged as other platforms emerged.

Social Media Changes How We Think About Marketing

Web 2.0 set the scene for the era of social media, which began in the early 2000s. People began using this term to refer to all the online content created and shared using the new 2.0 technologies like blogs, image-sharing platforms, etc. The emerging paradigm for communication became the crowd—many people communicating to many others—rather than broadcasting, in which an individual entity (like a corporation) controlled the means of communication. This meant more dialogues rather than monologues, and the beginning of an era where online conversation became an important goal, rather than one-way communication.

It also became possible to imagine a world in which people generated content to share with others and helped to create a destination site in and of itself. This is called "crowdsourcing," and it is the operative principle behind sites like YouTube and Flickr, where much of the content is created and shared by individuals, rather than institutions.

Social content began to be shared through social networks. The first important social network of the Web 2.0 era was MySpace, launched in 2003. It was not the first online social network—that was The Well, which inspired Howard Rheingold's classic *The Virtual Community*, published in 1993. But MySpace enabled millions to share their writing, images, podcasts, comments, and other content in a social environment that presaged Facebook. Facebook, launched at Harvard in 2004 by Mark Zuckerberg and friends, spread virally to other colleges and universities in Boston, then to the rest of the Ivy League and Stanford, then to other .edus, and was then unleashed to the world at large.

Facebook was different because it achieved a massive scale so quickly and because it enabled every user to share and share alike across a broad social network. And colleges and universities, which had struggled in adopting various social approaches to marketing and engagement, began to understand that with Facebook, they had an opportunity to "fish where the fish are."

As Facebook spread, public awareness of social media increased. The news media paid attention, and the hype grew. And so did the number of channels that one could consider "social" channels.

Social Media Arrives on Campus

As businesses began incorporating social media in their marketing and engagement strategies, universities followed. The goals for these initiatives varied.

Staff in alumni relations began experimenting with alumni community tools developed by a number of vendors such as Harris Publishing (now Harris Connect). These offered aspects of later social tools like Facebook: Alumni could develop and store a personal profile, which was searchable within the community's directory. A variety of tools enabled alumni to connect with one another, including email, threaded discussions, events calendars, alumni news, and others. Universities reported various levels of success with these communities. One problem that many alumni reported is that the communities were clumsy to use and often didn't have enough users to warrant frequent returns. The ease-of-use challenges and lack of reach contrast significantly to social networks like Facebook and LinkedIn, where alumni can easily connect to one another—and to many other friends and associates.

Admissions staff were also very active exploring how social media could assist their institutions in student recruitment. By the end of 2005, dozens of universities had launched blogs focused on student recruitment,[1] and many had significant results to report. For example, officials from Ball State University, which had launched an extensive blogging program that encouraged comments from students, reported in a presentation at the 2006

---

(1) Available at mstnr.me/apdx1

Symposium for the Marketing of Higher Education that 70 percent of parents of prospective students visited the university's blogs.[2]

Other institutions began experimenting with MySpace, Flickr, podcasting, and numerous other social channels. Many of these experiments were initiated by junior staff members who were themselves active on social networks and realized how powerful they could be in reaching important audience segments. As some of the implications of this new style of communicating became evident, some senior staff were skeptical or even hostile to the use of social media.

One major concern among institutional leaders was that the free-flowing nature of conversation on social networks enabled those with a grudge against the institution to hijack the conversation, diverting it from a discussion that was more productive—and, quite frankly, reflected positively on the institution. There were well-publicized incidents of so-called trolling in the commercial world that could be cited to support this viewpoint.

More broadly, leaders in PR and marketing often failed to recognize that online discourse had shifted from the familiar broadcast model to the conversational model of social media. One-way messaging is rarely effective in the new social channels, so simply posting a news release on a blog or sharing it on Facebook is not effective. People who use social networks want to engage—and they expect engagement in return.

Today, social media and social networks are much more deeply embedded in our lives and culture, and senior leaders understand the value of supporting social initiatives—and even in participating in them themselves. In fact, a growing number of presidents are active on social channels, using them to connect with their many constituents.[3] And some colleges and universities have learned how to manage these social channels effectively, creating opportunities to integrate them into campaigns focused on achieving specific goals.

---

(2) Available at mstnr.me/apdx2
(3) Available at mstnr.me/apdx3

Index

A

achievement strategies, 100–103
adaptability
  importance of, during execution, 21
  MSU rap video, 109
  Powered by Orange campaign, 30, 32–33
  Tufts Now news website, 200
  VU hiring campaign, 117
admissions applications
  increases in, 44, 47–48, 216, 222
  used as measurements, 10, 20
admissions marketing strategies
  Ampersandbox campaign, 84–90
  Election 2010 campaign, 215–222
  Loyola University Chicago, 69–76
  SMC's student ambassadors, 91–97
  TIU Big Game campaign, 207–214
admitted students
  Golden Flyer program, 153
  Loyola University Chicago, 69–76
  SMC's student ambassadors and, 94
  TIU Big Game campaign, 207–214
  use of social media with, 5
advertising strategies, 16, 17, 73, 167–168
advocacy, 5, 26, 54, 56
alert systems, 182, 190
Alexander, Evelyn Jerome, 121
Allen, Matt, 209–214
alumni associations
  Cornell University, 139–146
  Indiana University, 154–165
  Madison College, 60
  MIT, 139–146
  updating contact information, 64, 120
  (see also inactive alumni; older alumni; young alumni)
alumni engagement strategies
  Flight of the Flyers campaign, 147–153
  Indiana University campaign, 154–165
  JHU Fantasy Reunion campaign, 118–124
  MIT-Cornell Fictional Alumni Face-Off, 139–146
  RPI photo contest, 125–130

alumni support and advocacy, 5, 14, 24–25
Alumpics competition, 145
ambassadors, 21–22, 39, 176–178
  (see also student ambassadors)
American University, 35–44
Ampersandbox campaign, 14, 84–90
Anderson, Sarah Preuschl, 157
anecdotal stories, 20, 150
  (see also storytelling approaches)
Anthem video, 105, 106–107
application features, 162–164
Arroway, Ellie, 144
assessments (see measurements; results and outcomes)
Attention Matrix, 100
audiences
  educating, 36, 37–39
  follow-on engagement, 15
  importance of authenticity and, 29
  knowledge of, 5, 10, 11–12, 15–17
  multi-channel campaigns and, 9
  segmenting, 11, 71, 75, 150, 156
  tailoring messages to, 71, 116, 126, 202
  (see also specific audiences)
authenticity, 12
  Madison College referendum, 58
  MSU rap video, 110
  NMMU's flash mob, 51
  Powered by Orange campaign, 29, 30, 32
  RIT recruitment campaign, 80
  SMC's student ambassadors, 92, 94
  #UWRightNow campaign, 134, 137

B

Baker, Cindy, 89
Baker, David, 26–34
Bales, Jon, 52, 60
Barhorst, Bettsey, 52, 60
Battle of the Blues campaign, 11, 166–173
Beeler, Nate, 35–36, 37, 41
Beelzebubs, 198
behind-the-scenes videos, 105
benchmarks (see measurements; results and outcomes)
Benny (OSU mascot), 27
Berklee College of Music, 103
Bernard, Andy, 140, 144
Bitkoff, Melody, 166–173

Blogger platform, 91, 219
blogs and blogging
  Election 2010 campaign, 217–222
  Jumble blog, 193–200
  Loyola University Chicago, 71, 72–73, 74
  Madison College referendum, 56, 58
  as marketing tool, 16
  mascot search, 64–65
  measurement of traffic, 19
  MIT Alumni Association, 139
  MIT-Cornell Fictional Alumni Face-Off, 141
  MSU rap video, 106
  Powered by Orange campaign, 26–27
  RIT recruitment campaign, 77–78, 82
  SMC's student ambassadors, 91–97, 92–93
  Spirit of IU campaign, 161
  strengths and weaknesses of, 13–14
  ticket giveaway campaign, 202–204
  use of, in institutional advancement, 6
brand awareness strategies
  consistency in, 99
  Election 2010 campaign, 215–222
  frequency of use of social media in, 5
  IU alumni engagement campaign, 157–159
  Powered by Orange campaign, 24–34
  ticket giveaway campaign, 201–206
  TIU Big Game campaign, 207–214
  UWRF student achievement campaign, 98–103
  WONK campaign, 35–44
Brei, Linda, 52, 56
Brennan-Barry, Colleen, 149–151
Broaddus, Henry, 84
budgets and cost factors
  Ampersandbox campaign, 89
  campaign planning and, 17–18
  Flight of the Flyers campaign, 149, 151
  Great Give campaign, 175, 179